BENT

NOT

BROKEN

Lauren Roche

ZYMURGY PUBLISHING

GREAT BRITAIN
2001

© Lauren Roche 2000

First published by Steele Roberts Ltd,
Wellington, New Zealand

Photo of Lauren by Vlad Petrovic *Images by Woolf*

The excerpt in Chapter 19 is from
The Lord of the Rings,
The Fellowship of the Ring (Book 1) by JRR Tolkien,
quoted with kind permission of
HarperCollins Publishers Ltd.

Brain Damage
Words and Music by George Roger Waters
© 2000 Roger Waters Music Overseas Ltd, USA
Warner/Chappell Artemis Music Ltd,
London W6 8BS
Reproduced by permission of
International Music Publications Ltd
All Rights Reserved.

Cover design: Nick Ridley

Published by

ZYMURGY PUBLISHING
Newcastle upon Tyne

© Great Britain & Ireland 2001

isbn 1-903506-02-6

All rights reserved. No part of this publication may be reproduced, transmitted
or stored in a retrieval system, in any form or by any means, without permission in
writing from Zymurgy Publishing.

Printed by
Omnia Books Limited, Glasgow

To

Miramar Grandma,
a hero in anyone's book;

Geck, a much-loved friend,
and father to the incomparable Paulie.

Arohanui

Lauren

•

"I have been bent and broken, but – I hope –
into a better shape."
ESTELLA IN *GREAT EXPECTATIONS* BY CHARLES DICKENS

"The bent reed he will not break
The smouldering wick he will not snuff out."
MATTHEW 12:20

Prologue

1980

No gardens border the state flat where I live with my baby son. There is a three-storey drop from my bedroom window to the hard surface of the carpark below.

I am eighteen, a prostitute and the mother of a ten-month-old boy.

Exhausted and depressed, I stand at my window mentally measuring the drop. I want to be sure that when I throw my baby out and jump after him, we'll both die.

Christopher sleeps in my arms, his eyes flicking back and forth under his thin, veined eyelids. I adore him and don't want to leave him behind when I die. I am sure death will be best for him too. I want it to be quick.

I stroke his downy hair, tears washing down my cheeks. He continues to sleep as they splash on his face, an occasional twitch showing he can feel them.

I close the window and sit on my bed, sobbing.

I am too scared to jump …

1999

I lost my own mother through a drug overdose twenty-two years ago. Pam Roche was a complex and tragic person — addicted to drugs, alcohol, and trouble. Her life was short but she packed a lot of living into it. She finally ended it all, aged thirty-two, in 1976. I am now five years older than she will ever be.

When sober and calm Pam was as good a mother as many. When drunk or upset her rages were terrifying. There was no pattern to her behaviour — no clue as to how she would act from one day to the next. She had as many phases as the moon, but lacked its cyclical predictability. Over the years I've come to see her as a lunar being — for many years I've looked for her at night. Sometimes there's less of her to see as she floats in the sky wrapped in the soft shadow of the earth. During this phase she casts less light, but on these darker nights she is no less real to me — my sleeping mother, my Mother Moon.

I miss her still.

1

I wake. My heart is racing, my body bathed in sweat. I am wreathed in the dream again, the one that haunted my childhood — my prophetic dream. The sheets tangle around my body, my pillow drops to the floor, I cry out.

In the dream I am six years old, visiting a museum with my mother and her friend. They are oblivious of me as they wander around and talk, uninterested in my favourite exhibits. I return again to the Maori whare with the tukutuku panels on each wall. I listen to the recorded commentary describing the meanings behind its intricate carvings and panels and imagine myself living in such times. What was it like to live in a carved house like this, with no electricity or plumbing, to dodge other tribes' warriors, to live off the land?

The massive ocean-going waka is on this floor too. I love the stories of the early Polynesian migrations — huge canoes filled with pioneers, treasures and small children. Their bravery enthralled me. Dwarfed by the long, narrow bulk of the canoe, I imagine it voyaging, wave-tossed, star-led across the Pacific.

Up a set of wide steps, covered with cold grey lino, is the Egyptian exhibit. Here I always find myself drawn to the mummy case — is there really a dead person in there? I look for my Mum, but she's deep in conversation with her mate — I think they've forgotten me.

There's a crash behind me. A man is lying on the floor. Mum tells me to check and see if he's okay. As I bend over him he leaps to his feet, grabs me and runs off through the museum with me under his arm. The light dims all around us as he takes me from the main passage, his feet slapping loudly on the tiled floor. I can smell the sweat on his dirty

1

body and a mix of tobacco and booze — familiar smells, which should be reassuring, but they're not. My head flops against his shoulder; I try to cry out, but my mouth is dry with fear. I look back at my Mum — far away in the distance, still talking to her friend — she hasn't even noticed I've gone.

Then I wake, heart thumping, the feeling of abandonment as fresh as ever.

Who am I? And why do I dream that dream? I am Lauren Kim Roche, a Scorpio baby, born in the year of the Ox. I arrived on the Sabbath on Guy Fawkes Day, 1961.

Pam Roche, my mother, was eighteen when she had me and had only been married for five months to my father. He was twenty-one. All my grandparents opposed the marriage from the start, despite the pregnancy. Mum's parents were horrified. "He's just got out of borstal!" Dad's family thought he could do better too. My parents were determined to be together though, and married. Dad felt like Pygmalion — he thought he could improve his new wife. Mum was looking forward to setting up her own home. She had a handsome husband and high hopes for their life together with their new baby.

The photos of the event aren't terribly Bride & Groom. Mum wore a light brown suit, Dad a darker one. They both looked young and nervous, but happy and optimistic. I was an unseen and unspoken presence at the nuptials. All the grandparents-to-be, despite their misgivings, attended the ceremony.

Although I wasn't planned, Mum and Dad loved me very much. The first months of my life were spent in a sleepout at the back of Mum's parents' home in Miramar. It had power but no plumbing, so all cooking, washing, bathing and toilet facilities were in the house at the front. Mum had to trudge, arms full of nappies, to the main house several times a day. Dad had to run the gauntlet of the in-laws whenever he left the property. No matter how supportive Mum's parents were, it must have been a difficult start to their married life — trapped in a tiny room with no privacy. To compound it all, Dad soon found out that he didn't like babies and would shout at me to shut me up.

In 1963 my sister Tracey was born and we became eligible for housing assistance. We moved to Taiaroa Street, Strathmore; into a semi-detached state house typical of the early sixties. The street was shabby; identical houses in rows and in need of paint and repairs. Clothing hung airing out of upstairs windows, broken toys nestled with remnants of beer bottles in the gutters. The occasional swing or slide set rusted in back yards. Most people seemed to have a skinny dog and three or four children.

Life in Taiaroa Street was less protected than it had been in Miramar. A neater, more affluent suburb, Miramar had wide tree-lined streets. Strathmore clung to a windswept hill overlooking the airport. It was the place the poor people lived. There were far more brown-skinned people in Strathmore and hordes more children. I loved it.

Our house became a party house where money was spent on flagons of beer and cartons of smokes. Guitars played late into the night, people sang, laughed, cried.

One night Mum found a tin of red paint and she and her friends changed Taiaroa Street's sign to read 'Coronation Street.' They painted their feet and ran up and down the road leaving trails of crimson footprints. For weeks we could see where they'd been. That party became a legend. Even Dad thought it was funny.

We would wake in the mornings to a house stinking of smoke and beer. Brown bottles were piled on the benches and tables; some skittled on the floor. I often got up before my parents and would drain the dregs from all the beer bottles. I tipped them as far as I could, throwing my head back like a grown-up and feeling the warm, flat liquid drip down my throat. I could have developed a pre-school drinking problem, until the day I swallowed a sodden cigarette butt and was promptly sick. I never drank the dregs again.

Dad's job took him across the Cook Strait to the South Island, where he captured deer for farming, netting them from helicopters. I missed him when he was gone, which was often a couple of weeks at a time. He also liked to hunt and spent most weekends shooting deer and goats in the bush-clad hills north of Wellington. He had a large network of friends and preferred their company to ours, so we didn't see much of him.

Mum missed him too and often told me how much she loved him. She tried hard to make a go of their marriage, but found things too quiet with Dad gone. Soon she began to have parties while he was away. She always held them at home so Tracey and I could be close to her.

When Mum expected Dad home from one of his trips south she'd arm herself with a pair of binoculars at a window that overlooked the airport to see if he disembarked from any of the planes. If she saw him and he didn't arrive home within half an hour she'd start to phone his mates, then the pubs. He was usually unavailable or abusive and would get himself home when it suited.

Mum spent a lot of time at the kitchen table silently weeping, a beer in one hand, a cigarette in the other. She wanted desperately for her marriage to work, but it wasn't the happy refuge she'd hoped for. Perhaps another baby would help.

In late 1965 my youngest sister Shelley was born. Dad wasn't impressed — "Not another fucking girl!"

Until Mum and Shelley were discharged from hospital I stayed with Mum's parents. I loved it at their place. Things were calm and quiet. There were no parties, no fights, no alcohol.

When Mum got home the crying got worse. Dad was absent more often than not and she was stuck with three demanding kids under the age of four. The parties gave her adult company. My sisters and I spent many hours half-awake in our pyjamas at the top of the stairs, listening to what it was like to be a grown-up. Two little blonde girls and a dark-haired one, growing up fast.

The day we got a black-and-white TV was a highlight. It gave Mum something else to distract her when Dad was away. I was allowed to watch Lost in Space so long as Tracey was asleep. I even tried conning her to pretend to be sleeping if she wasn't yet, but she would have none of it.

After one hunting trip just before Christmas 1964 Dad arrived home with two baby goats for Mum to look after — he had shot their mother and felt sorry for them. One of the goats climbed onto the mantelpiece and ate our Christmas cards. Mum got to clean up the turds on the carpet and mop up the smelly piss. We loved watching her feed them with a bottle, their tails wagging as they bleated and slurped. I can't imagine what the housing people would have said if they found out we were keeping wild animals in the living room. Mum was resigned to caring for them. She would have been heartbroken to lose her castle, but still put up with Dad's mad ideas.

What happened to our card-eating goats I have no idea; it didn't pay to wonder too much about things that disappeared in the night. I got used to people and things being there one day, gone the next.

Taiaroa Street was full of barefoot, rowdy children, most with runny noses. We would play together on the footpath or street; all of us with mums who couldn't be bothered with ankle-biters. The street curved round the hill and was great for screaming down on trikes and other ride-on toys. One of the girls rode into the path of a reversing car and was run over. We all grouped silently to watch the fire engine wash her blood away. She didn't die, but spent a long time in hospital. Her accident made no difference to the way we played — the street was the only place we could all play together.

Near the end of the street was a patch of manuka and toetoe scrub. Us older kids would cut down toetoe to make kites, using the stems, string and brown paper. Although these creations never flew, we didn't stop trying.

When I was three I caught the measles and was hot, headachy and miserable. Mum cleaned up my bedroom and me for the doctor's visit. She looked up to doctors and was horribly embarrassed when he arrived to find Rangi, one of the little neighbourhood boys, in bed with me, still wearing his muddy gumboots. He had sneaked up the fire escape — we thought he could hide under the sheets. Mum was sweetness and light about it in front of the GP, but I could see I'd be for it when he left. Sick or not, she walloped me when he'd gone.

Another time Rangi shared a meal of berries with me. The black berries were on a pretty white-flowered plant that grew next to the swings in our back yard. We decided they were a new kind of medicine that we should share with my Mum because she always seemed so tired. We ate a few handfuls each, then woke Mum and offered her some. She recognised them as deadly nightshade and hauled herself out of bed to call an ambulance. Rangi and I had our stomachs pumped and were admitted to hospital overnight.

We survived. The bush didn't.

Before I started school, Mum took me there on a visit. She let me wander off with a couple of older girls, who pulled down my knickers and took turns looking at and touching me between the legs. It wouldn't have lasted for more than a few seconds, but it frightened and confused me. Why would someone want to do that?

Despite my initial fears of meeting these girls again, I loved school. It was the best part of my life. Everything was set up for children — it felt right and I loved to learn. Things became easier for Mum, too, having only two kids at home for most of the day. Although she loved us, and at times lavished care and kisses upon us, she had more interesting things to do with her life and found alcohol and drugs were the best way to reach to her preferred world. Besides, two kids are much easier to care for than three are when you're miserable more often than not.

To give Mum a break, Grandma and Grandad often looked after me. I was their eldest granddaughter and they indulged me, taking me on holidays all over New Zealand. Tracey didn't seem to mind and Shelley was too little to notice. I also spent time with Mum's sister Jenny. Aunty Jenny's idea of a punishment was to tickle me until I apologised and begged for mercy. It seemed to work more effectively than smacking — I'm sure I was better behaved for her than for anyone else.

Mum got worn out looking after three girls mostly on her own at Strathmore so we moved back to her parents' place in Miramar. This time we stayed in the main house, the sleepout too small for five of us. I changed schools and lost the friends from Taiaroa Street. There were always new friends to make, though, so my tears and protests were short-lived. Mum seemed to get comfort from being back with her parents. It must have been difficult for Dad though. He soon had the great idea that he would move to Australia, where work was better paid. He would send for Mum and us girls when he'd saved up our fares. Mum was desperate for a break and agreed. Tracey and I cried and performed about losing our Dad. I don't know if Mum believed he'd send for us; I was certainly sceptical.

Mum, Tracey, Shelley and I were still in Miramar when the Wahine storm struck in April 1968. That morning, despite the raging southerly, it was decided that us kids should attend school. Grandad drove us to the gates.

Trees had been uprooted and debris was being hurled through the air by the violent winds. The walk down the school driveway was sheltered, but once we got to the more open ground the storm was terrifying. Tracey and I were picked up by the wind and blown around the open playground in front of the infant classroom block. I tried to scream, but the words were blown away, leaving us soundlessly tumbling like pieces of litter around the schoolyard until a teacher struggled out and picked us up. The winds pounded the school, threatening to tear the building from its foundations.

We didn't have normal school; there were only a few kids in class anyway. The teachers put us all into the middle of a larger room, avoiding the windows and doors. The radio announced civil emergency information — houses were being battered all around us and people were told not to leave their homes unless absolutely necessary, as roofing iron was slicing through the air. We were apprehensive and mostly too frightened to cry. All the children at school that day lived locally and the radio kept relaying stories of the damage being done to houses in the region. None of us, teachers or kids, knew what we'd return home to.

When Grandad finally brought us home that day, the adults were grouped around the TV in the lounge. Even Grandma and Grandad Roche had come to visit. They lived about an hour north of Wellington, but they were at our house when I returned from school. We had always seen the Roche family as several social steps above Mum's.

Sometime during the afternoon Grandma Roche had needed to use the loo, which was a tiny room at the back of the house. Its roof, usually sufficient to keep out the elements, was leaking badly. Grandma had to take an umbrella in with her to keep dry. I loved Grandma Roche, but got more than a few giggles out of the mental picture of her wedged into that tiny loo, perching on the wet seat while trying to wipe her bum with a brolly in her hand. It was the only laugh we had that day. The house next door lost its corrugated iron fence — its sheets were hurled through the air past our lounge window. The major story, though, was of the inter-island ferry, the Wahine. It had foundered in the entrance to Wellington harbour with the loss of over fifty lives. We followed the live broadcasts in disbelief — this surely couldn't be happening in Wellington. The tension and sense of unfolding tragedy were immense. The day the Wahine sank is vivid in my mind — it has none of the blur surrounding other events.

In the weeks following the storm we heard from Dad. He'd found work in Whyalla, South Australia — a small industrial town on the edge of the Simpson Gulf and close to the desert. He said he was saving our fares so we could join him in the brick bungalow he'd rented, in a street of about thirty identical houses. Eventually he proved he meant it and sent for us.

We left to join him in December 1968. As we flew out from Wellington airport our former neighbours in Taiaroa Street waved a tablecloth out their front window at us. We were off to the Promised Land. I didn't know what to feel — I cried from excitement, but also from fear of not seeing my grandparents again, maybe ever.

2

We arrived in Adelaide in the late afternoon, tired and stiff from the flight. After a wander around the shops, where nothing was bought but a lot of incredulous gazing was done, we rang Miramar to let everyone know we'd arrived safely. Next morning we were reunited with our Dad. Tracey and I were delighted to see him and feel his scratchy chin as we kissed him. Shelley cried. Mum seemed reserved for a start, but we were soon all chattering together.

Dad drove us to Whyalla Norrie, to our semi-detached house at Baldwinson Terrace. The houses in our suburb had TV aerials several metres high so they could get a decent signal from Adelaide, the nearest city. Whyalla was hot, smelly and dry and had a main road with three lanes of traffic going each way.

The house was a cool refuge from the heat. It had a big kitchen, a lounge and three bedrooms, so I had my own room. The porch off the back was perfect for lying on at night, watching stars course the big, open sky. The smaller porch at the front became home to our dolls and toys. We'd each brought one special toy from New Zealand, having been promised new ones once we'd settled in. The back yard was bare, dry and full of nasty little prickles which thrived in the red dust. There was a wattle tree in the front yard with fluffy yellow flowers that made Mum sneeze. The family next door had kids our own ages. They had great toys, which they trotted out into their yard in a display of strength. The older brother, Simon, played the bagpipes, much to Mum's annoyance. It spoiled any chance of her weekend naps. I decided I liked Whyalla and thought we'd all fit in just fine.

Despite our hopes we still didn't see much of Dad. He

worked long hours in the Whyalla shipyards and drank in his spare time. He went hunting as often as he could; I can still smell the curing kangaroo and wallaby skins hanging in the back porch. He promised to teach me to shoot when I reached my teens.

Our first Christmas in Australia was peaceful. We shopped at New World, Whyalla, which had a large globe rotating above the car park. Mum bought three Mexican dolls for us girls. I got the boy doll, and Tracey and Shelley had a girl each, with different costumes. We called mine Pepe and Trace and Shell's Pepita as these were the only Mexican-sounding names Dad could think of. I also got a couple of books, which I secretly unwrapped and read in instalments behind the couch before Christmas came.

We seemed to be the proverbial happy family. Mum didn't cry as often and she was drinking less. There were no longer the parties we'd had in Strathmore. I had a pet goanna, a large Australian lizard, which I carted about all over the place. I think the poor creature was probably pleased to snuff it when it did — its life was a torment.

Things began to change though, slowly at first. With Dad away so much Mum felt restless, so she got him to teach her to drive so she'd be more independent. With the three of us in the back seat, not belted in, she started her lessons. It was only when she came to practise the emergency stop we discovered the danger: Tracey went flying into the back of the front seat and got a bleeding nose.

It was great at Fisk Street School. I got A's and had my stories displayed in a folder in the library — a big honour for such a junior student. My school photo shows an innocent girl, eyes full of dreams. My eyes are big, blue, untroubled; my smile as wide as it could be. I am wearing a pink dress with a row of daisies appliqued down the front — a present from Grandma in Miramar, who sent parcels of clothes regularly. I look like a girl in love with the world; a girl who expects that life will be kind.

Each morning before classes all the staff and kids would assemble before the Australian flag to salute it and swear allegiance.

I am an Australian
I love my country
I salute my flag
I honour my Queen
I promise to obey her laws

Most days I'd pledge this verbatim; however, if I was in a fiercely Kiwi mood, I'd alter the words to suit. At heart nothing would stop me being a New Zealander.

As I was "such a good girl" I got to be milk monitor for our class, which meant brief freedom each day before lunchtime, collecting the individual bottles of milk for each child. I watched a solar eclipse in the school playground one day, despite warnings from teachers that we'd go blind if we viewed it without special glasses. Later that year we watched the astronauts landing on the moon during a special assembly at school. The world was changing.

I had a crush on the headmaster at Fisk Street. I remember trailing him around the playground asking deep theological/philosophical questions like "If God made us, who made Him?" He couldn't answer that one.

At home we had a short-haired black-and-white moggy that we called Manu. We thought it was hilarious to have a cat whose name meant bird in Maori. We adored him. He disappeared one day. Mum said Dad had accidentally run him over. She changed her story a few days later to say that Dad had shot the cat in the kitchen, using the gun he used to shoot kangaroos. I could imagine the mess in the kitchen and felt sure Mum would have had to clean it up. Poor Manu — I couldn't believe he'd died painlessly. We cried and cried. We didn't get another cat while we lived in Whyalla.

Mum and Dad started fighting again. One night Mum wanted to go out and Dad wouldn't let her — he thought she was dressed 'like a slut.' All dressed up and wearing make-up, she stood at the back door, next to the shoe shelves; Dad was in the kitchen, by the vege rack. We three girls cowered under the table while Mum threw shoes at Dad and he pelted her with veges in return. She still went out that night. I cleaned up the mess.

Our parents' fights were frightening yet exhilarating. Sometimes we'd pass missiles to whoever was our favourite parent at the time. This was usually Mum. One night Mum locked the gate at the end of our short driveway just before Dad stormed out of the house. She knew that when Dad was in a temper he would reverse quickly out of the drive without checking behind him and she wanted him to crash into the gates on the way out. My two younger sisters were privy to this plan, but Shelley wrecked it by telling Dad. Tracey and I were furious with her.

Mum spent more and more time with her new friends having long, tearful discussions about how awful things were for her and how much she wanted to run away from Dad. Lots of plans were made for us all to leave, but were never acted upon. In childhood my favourite books became 'running away' ones. The passages I'd read over and over were the ones where the poor, ill-treated children laid plans to escape the clutches of their evil caregivers.

As the days passed, Mum became more stressed and unwell and plotted new ways we could leave Dad. One day she fainted. I found her on the kitchen floor and thought she was dead. I cried and shook her shoulder, shouting at her to get up. My tears turned to relief when she roused and got me ready for school. I told the school nurse what had happened, so she visited us at home later that day. Mum was embarrassed and after talking to her, the nurse assured me nothing was wrong. Several weeks later friends of Mum and Dad met us after school and took us to stay at different addresses where we remained for about a fortnight.

We were told Mum was in hospital, but nothing else. I enjoyed the luxury of being the only child in the house. I stayed with Aunty Vera and her two grown-up daughters, Sylvia and Merryl. I adored Merryl. She would have been in her late teens and rode a motorbike. Her thick brown bob of hair shone in the light and looked great, even when she'd just pulled her helmet off. Merryl took me under her wing: we rode her motorbike together and went swimming at the local pools. She let me sleep in her room and read her books. She had a collection of Ladybird books about famous and influential women, including Florence Nightingale and Marie Curie. I was transfixed. Merryl was awesome.

Inevitably we had to go home to Mum and Dad.

No one told us why Mum had been in hospital. After being ignored a few times, we stopped asking.

When I was ten a relative told me that Mum had been almost five months pregnant when Dad beat her so severely her uterus ruptured and their baby son died. Mum had haemorrhaged and needed major surgery. While in the Intensive Care Unit she had died and required resuscitation. Medical staff had advised her to press charges against Dad but she refused, telling everyone she loved him. She said to have lost a son was punishment enough for him.

He said he didn't believe the baby was his.

She could never again become pregnant.

My aunty told me not to question Mum about these events as it would be too upsetting for her. I wonder what she would have told me if I had asked. Dad gave me his version of events when I was 37 and trying to make some sense of my life. He said that the story I'd heard was untrue. He said that Mum was in the middle of another pregnancy. At first she was excited about it, as she enjoyed being pregnant and having babies. She was also delighted to be at the same stage of pregnancy as her younger sister Jenny, who was expecting her second child. As the pregnancy drew on, Mum had become more depressed and dissatisfied with her marriage. She felt trapped in Australia and thought another child would increase this sense of isolation. She tried to bring on a miscarriage with tablets, an act Dad discovered when he found her gasping and breathless in the bedroom one afternoon. She refused any kind of medical treatment. A few days later Dad returned home to find Mum bleeding on the floor, after trying to self-abort with a coat hanger. She developed septicaemia and nearly died. Their baby son was dead.

Dad said they didn't tell us the truth at the time as they considered us too young to understand. By the time we were old enough they assumed we'd forgotten the whole incident. When as an adult I asked Dad for his side of the story he was at first shocked, then felt betrayed. He looked incredulous. Had they truly believed Mum? Why had none of her family members ever confronted him about what he'd allegedly done? Why only talk about it behind his back? How could they have accepted him back into their homes without comment?

I still don't know what the full story was; perhaps the truth lies somewhere between the two accounts.

Life in Whyalla returned to our version of normal. Mum spent a lot of time in bed. She drank and smoked more than she usually did and cried constantly. The three of us spent a lot of time cuddled up with her in bed. We ate chocolate cake. Mum was good at making that — it was a real comfort food for her and the only thing I ever remember her baking. We'd usually eat the cake hot from the oven, with cold, creamy milk poured over it — yum.

As she got better Mum dug and planted a big vege patch in the back garden. She took pride in transforming the dusty, barren ground. The carrots and radishes never grew to any decent size, as we would pull them out, run them straight under the outside tap and eat them 'alive.'

We spent a lot of time with a family Mum met while in the hospital. Gladys was a deceptively frail-looking white-haired lady with a fearsome rage. She lived in a nearby caravan park with her divorced son, Stretch, a working class Pom with three children. Mum seemed more alive when she was with Stretch and spent a lot of time touching him, something she didn't do with Dad any more. Stretch had lank black hair straggled over his collar. His nose was sharp and his pale blue eyes small and constantly squinted against the sun. When he laughed it was wholehearted, head thrown back and decayed teeth exposed. I couldn't see what Mum saw in him. It made my skin crawl to see her kiss him. We called his mother Nanny White. Stretch's kids were Diane, aged between Tracey and Shelley, and Steve and Andrew, both younger.

The kids were skinny and dirty and their noses always streamed. No amount of feeding seemed to fatten them up. Diane and Steve had their father's thin nose and vaguely disappointed look. Andrew's undies always seemed to sag down to his knees and were full of poos or sodden with urine. He was blond with big brown eyes. He was cute, even though he stank and his tummy stuck out like the starving African kids on TV.

Stretch's parents Gladys and Duncan (Grandpa White) and his niece Joan lived in a caravan nearby. Joan was a few years older than me. The White family was quite a team. We loved playing with their kids and others we met at the caravan park. The Whites lived in their cars and caravans year round. It seemed a glamorous life — each day would feel like a holiday. I was jealous. When we first met them they were camped on the waterfront so we spent many hours swimming in the sea, fishing and catching crabs. It was a peaceful time, as long as we remembered not to tell poor Dad where we'd spent the day.

My eighth birthday arrived and Mum and Dad gave me the microscope I'd been begging for. Any time I refused to look after the younger kids Mum threatened to give my microscope to the Whites. I behaved.

Dad became more attentive — perhaps he was aware that Mum's affections had shifted focus. He would take one of us out on Friday nights to buy a small toy and a chocolate bar. He spent more time at home and we all watched telly together. He tried to teach me French and algebra at the kitchen table one day, but it didn't seem interesting at the time. The algebra was a confusion where x equalled 2 in one line and 6 in another. The French couldn't compete with the indigo sky outside the window, and who gave a stuff about Monsieur Jacques in the textbook? Hell, we were beginning to behave just like a real family.

One day Mum and Stretch went window shopping for an engagement ring. They said it was for a friend, but I was sure it was for them. It was one of those hot, clear days that made you want to stay inside. I didn't want to trudge around the shops with them, I wanted to be at home watching the cartoons with Dad, Tracey and Shelley. The jewellery shop was in a cool, dark mall. The jeweller put me on a seat in the corner to keep me out of the way as Mum and Stretch fondled rings they could never afford.

"Do you think she'd like this one?" Stretch passed her a sparkly ring.

"Yep." She laughed, the jewel on her finger shining in the light. It made the ring she always wore — the one Dad gave her when they got married — look dull and cheap.

The shopkeeper watched the adults closely. He'd sat me away from the cabinets so I couldn't nick anything. Stretch and Mum didn't buy anything and I bet the jeweller counted the rings carefully on our departure.

We managed to live this double life for several weeks. If Dad suspected what was happening, he didn't let on.

But one night we sat down to dinner. I was wearing my new swimming togs, bought by Dad a couple of days earlier. So far I had showered, played and slept in them, but hadn't been swimming. That would happen the following day when we saw the Whites again. Mum had cooked veges from her garden and some sausages. Dinners were getting better. I wondered if she was feeling bad about kissing Stretch instead of Dad.

I wanted the tomato sauce, which was at Dad's elbow.

"Can you please pass me the sauce, Stretch — oops, I mean Dad." Mum looked sick. Dad went pale then stood up, face flushing. He glared at Mum. "Get the fuck out." Food and plates flew. Mum packed our bags and we left, joining Stretch and his family in their caravan.

We obviously couldn't stay in Whyalla so the next morning we left in a convoy — Stretch and us, Nanny and Grandpa White and Joan, Joan's mum Lorraine, and Philip, Stretch's brother.

The adults didn't seem to know where we were going — we were simply on the road.

3

We travelled by day and slept by the road or in caravan parks at night. There were two adults and six children in our caravan. It was tiny; two single bunks at one end and a table and couch that folded out to form a double bed at the other end. There was never enough room, but we got used to being crushed in there together. Money was tight, but there was always enough for the pub or chippies or lollies. Tracey, Shelley, Diane and I spent a lot of time in gloomy pubs that smelled like the caravan — smokes, beer and urine. The three of us danced with men in the pubs while Mum and Stretch laughed and clapped. We liked it when they were happy. I missed Dad a bit, but enjoyed the lack of structure we now had. Sometimes I remembered him guiltily. Had it really been such a short time since we'd left him? While Mum, Stretch and the girls were in the pub, Steve and Andrew stayed in the car. Steve was three years old and Andrew about two. Sometimes we'd all be given money to sit in the car and eat lollies and stay out of the way of the grown-ups. We spent a lot of time at the side of the road eating lollies and ice creams. Our circumstances didn't seem strange and we never complained. It was life as we knew it.

After a few days we arrived at Bonney, a large saltwater lake in South Australia. We parked the caravan under a fragrant towering gum tree, which shed its bark in long sunburned strips onto the roof of the caravan. Kookaburras and kingfishers fought the pelicans for the pale, flapping fish that inhabited the lake. Several partially submerged trees a few metres from shore broke the water with pale ghostly arms. We swam, threw stones at birds, played and fought with each other. It was a paradise for the six travel-weary children. We made lots of effigies of Stretch's former

19

wife Kay and threw things at them. This made Mum and Stretch roar with laughter. Dad got off lightly. Tracey, Diane and I went to another new school, an hour's trudge around the lake. Mum skited to her friends about the distance we walked. The adults wouldn't drive us, saying there was no money for petrol.

Mum and Stretch still went out a lot at night. No matter how poor we were, the grown-ups could still afford a bar tab and petrol to drive to the pub. Who knows where the money came from? It wasn't from work.

There were no suitable jobs available at Lake Bonney. Mum, Stretch and us kids remained at the lake while Nanny, Lorraine and the others travelled further south. They would let us know if they found work; we would follow them then.

Our diet consisted mostly of bread and dripping. On good days there'd be golden syrup and maybe some pancakes that Mum made on the gas stove in the caravan. One morning Mum was making some toast in the stove, which sat at the foot of the top bunk, on which I slept. She was busy and asked me to check on it, but I was too slow, so she did it herself. As she opened the oven door, there was a large explosion and a fireball hit her in the face. She ran, screaming, from the caravan, with her hair and eyebrows burning. I yelled too, jumping down from the bunk and following her to the water. She threw herself face down into the lake, then returned to the caravan singed and slightly bald with no eyebrows, but otherwise okay. Fortunately she thought it was funny and was glad she was the one to be injured, not me. The smell of burning hair lingered for some time.

All our toys and books had been left in Whyalla. They weren't considered important, but I missed having things to play with and to read. One day I found a wind-up toy doll, her head missing. Some days later I found a toy duck head, similarly abandoned. I had a whole plaything. My wind-up human with a duck head went everywhere with me, until one day it too vanished. I was too used to losing precious things to cry.

We eventually heard from the other Whites. They had found work and lodgings on a vineyard in Barmera, a grape-growing region on the Murray River. We packed and moved again. Life was lived day-to-day, old friends and schools discarded without a backward glance.

Barmera was beautiful, an easy place to set up camp. The trip took us a couple of days, after stopping at every pub along the way. Mum and Stretch got casual work in Barmera as fruit pickers. They were away from the caravan for large parts of the day and although Mum looked tired, there was also a new radiance about her. She was no longer cooped up with a van full of kids, all wanting something from her. Although Nanny and the others had managed to score a house to live in with electricity, a bath and a toilet that flushed, we had to live in the caravan. We parked it outside an abandoned house about ten minutes' walk down the road from Nanny and the others

Our house was old, wooden and unfurnished and had no plumbing or power. Lots of the windows were broken and doors were missing. It had been empty for so long it was hard to tell which room had served what purpose. Our loo sat out on the decrepit verandah, in full public view. I was so excited to find it after weeks of using public conveniences or simply going in the lake. A real toilet, all ours, was precious. I sat down on the seat after wiping the cobwebs away with my skirt. I sat there, knickers around my ankles, singing as I peed. When I came to flush the loo, I realised my error. The toilet was not connected to any plumbing. Maybe there had once been the intention to plumb it in, but there it sat, a thing forgotten, on the porch of the old house. We used it anyway. It soon filled up. We tried to keep the lid down so the flies wouldn't get in it, but they did. We had the revolting task of perching over a rapidly rising pile of sewage, alive with pale, wiggly maggots when we used the toilet. The smell was awful.

To keep using the toilet seemed more civilised, somehow, than crapping on the ground or behind a bush. Eventually, the stench got so unbearable that Stretch buried the loo. We had to crap on the ground then. We used leaves to wipe ourselves once the old newspapers from the house were used up.

We were poor, but at least we had grapevines all around us. The fruit was abundant and we took turns at climbing trees for nuts. There were two immigrant families living near us. Mum and Stretch called them 'wogs.' One of these families — I think they were Yugoslav — kept us supplied with apple cucumbers and tomatoes they grew. The others plied us with watermelons. They were generous people and kept us far healthier than Mum would have managed on her own. We spent some time at their homes, which were clean bright places full of happiness and love.

Baths were infrequent and were taken in rainwater that had collected in a 44-gallon drum. We all shared the same water. I enjoyed being the eldest, as I got first turn. But we missed our swims in the lake.

One blistering day it was too hot for the workers to pick grapes, so the grown-ups drank big bottles of beer in the shade of the verandah. The smaller kids lay around, too tired to play, while I wandered off between the grapevines. I wore an old dress of Joan's that was too big for me. The armholes in the dress let what little breeze there was close to my skin to cool me down. Stretch's father Duncan (Grandpa White), and Philip, his brother, must have been looking for me, because they found me between the vines, hunting for old birds' nests, a favourite occupation of mine. They said they wanted to play — maybe a mothers and fathers game?

They smelled like smokes and beer, a smell I had learned to hate, because I associated it with sudden mood changes and other unhappiness. Philip took all his clothes off, saying he was too hot and Grandpa White started to undress, too. I sat on Philip's knee — something Joan did a lot — and he kissed me on the cheek. His face was wet and grimy and the hair on his chin was scratchy. He had nice eyes up close — not as squinty as his brother's, but the same faded blue. It seemed funny to be so close to him with his clothes off, but the heat was awful and he looked cooler without them. It dawned on me, slowly, what kind of mothers and fathers game they must be talking about. I saw Mum and Stretch doing it sometimes — they seemed to forget the old house had no doors or windows and didn't seem to care too much about the little kids who witnessed their noisy sex. Maybe they just liked it so much they forgot we could hear and see them.

Philip pulled my dress off over my head. I had no knickers on — I didn't have any that fit. He kissed my mouth. Grandpa White was now naked too. I couldn't hear the other kids or adults — it was so quiet that day — so hot and quiet. Even the birds and insects must have been resting. I felt funny in my tummy — scared and excited. I knew instinctively that what the men wanted was wrong, but I wanted to be a grown-up and it seemed that was what they were promising. Mum and Stretch seemed to enjoy this game. Philip said it could be our secret and I liked secrets. With so many of us in our little caravan, secrets were as rare as a cooked meal.

Philip lay me down on his clothes and climbed onto me. Stinky sweat was dripping off his chest and arms onto me as he reached between his legs and mine. As soon as he started to push between my legs I wanted him to stop — pleaded for him to. What Grandpa White and Philip did to me looked the same as what Mum and Stretch did, but it hurt and they wouldn't stop. When Grandpa White was in me — he held me on top of him, holding me hard with his twisted old fingers — Philip put his thing in my mouth and blood came off it, making me want to be sick.

When they'd finished, Philip kissed me then smacked me for crying and told me I'd get a real hiding if I ever told. They went back to the porch and kept on drinking. Grandpa seemed to be walking straighter than usual. They laughed as they walked. I put my dress on and wandered through the vines for a while. I cleaned up the sticky mess between my legs and cried because my dress was all dirty and it took ages to get things washed here. I spent a long time sitting in the shade, then walked over to Nanny's, telling her I'd fallen onto a stick. Nanny and Mum bathed me with salt and warm water and told me things would be okay. The water stung and was soon pink with my blood. They accepted my story; it was easier than confronting the obvious alternative.

Christmas came — the adults couldn't hide it from us. We learned about it at school and from the festive foil tops on the milk bottles that were delivered to the big house on the property. I would not let Christmas pass without pressies and nagged and complained until Mum and Stretch took us all shopping at the nearby town of Berri. Us kids were left in the car while they shoplifted gifts for us all. That year we got small, cheap and easy-to-conceal presents. Presents though. We were rapt.

We each got a toothbrush too. From an aunty in New Zealand we got green plastic tikis "to remind us where we came from" and rulers with strips of native New Zealand wood — kauri, matai, rimu and totara — in them. On Christmas Day I walked home from Nanny White's with my hands full of presents. I wandered onto a soldier ant nest and was bitten dozens of times. The stings were like hot little needles in your skin and when I jumped my tiki fell into the ant nest. It was lost for good, but my toothbrush was okay. I could clean my teeth properly again. As toothpaste was such a luxury, we used salt and rainwater. When there were no toothbrushes we used our fingers to rub the front of our teeth.

At the end of the Christmas – New Year period, Mum and us kids searched the streets for soft drink bottles that we could take in for refunds. We scavenged through people's rubbish while Stretch dozed on the verandah. We made enough money to buy ginger beer and orange cordial and little paper bags of lollies that looked like stones but tasted wonderful. It felt so good to have bought some treats — who needed bread when the world contained precious things like lollies? I made mine last as long as I could, taking tiny nibbles and then furtively hid the bag so the other kids couldn't find it.

When we got back to the caravan Tracey and I had the first drink of orange. It was disgusting — bitter, thick and horrible. Why did the rich people buy this stuff? Before the other kids tried any, Mum realised it needed diluting with water. It tasted much better that way. The ginger beer was yummy from the first though. We got drunk on it; we found we could act almost as drunk as a grown up after drinking ginger beer.

Shelley's third birthday was spent in the pub with Mum. Tracey, Diane and I joined them there after school. That day Mum and Shell held court, her fellow drinkers giving Mum their money to buy the "wee darling" a present. Of course they shouted the lovely young mother a beer too.

Shelley was cute. She had olive skin which had tanned darkly and big dark eyes. Her brown hair had lightened in the sun so she looked like a chubby sunburned angel. No wonder she was Mum's favourite.

Mum earned so much money that day she decided to try it again and again, each time in a different pub. We

25

sang "Happy Birthday dear Shelley" an awful lot that year. Had all the birthdays been real ones she would be about a hundred and six years old.

One night Mum and Stretch went out drinking, leaving us alone in the little caravan. I was awake, looking after the five younger kids, which was not unusual. This night, though, was different. I couldn't sleep; it was hot and the mosquitoes were whining. The little kids slept deeply, occasionally throwing an arm or leg out from the sheets they lay wrapped in. I would cover their exposed limbs, to avoid their being bitten too badly. It was lonely, being eight, with only the voice on the radio to keep me company. A newsflash caught my attention. A car ferry had sunk on the Murray River and people had died. I knew Mum and Stretch often took the car on the ferry to get to their favourite pub. I thought they must be dead, as they were usually well home by that hour. I could see myself bringing up all these kids on my own. There was no way I could let Duncan and Philip near them. The grown-ups finally crawled in just as the little kids were waking. They were pissed as chooks. They hadn't been on the ferry that sank but had heard of the tragedy. They hadn't thought I'd be worried about them, the inconsiderate bastards. For the first time I was angry with them. I wanted to knock their stupid drunken heads together.

4

The only way Tracey and I would survive our childhood was to bond closely. Shelley was never a real part of our unit — she and Mum were too close for that. Trace and I were physically alike, skinny and blonde with feathery fringes like toetoe blooms, but Tracey was a deep thinker and easily hurt. She hid behind her curtain of hair when upset or puzzled about something. She had an impish grin — it commanded her whole face, pressing her Kewpie-doll cheeks up and out — and crinkles around her dark blue eyes from forever squinting in the sun. Tracey loved animals and wanted a menagerie of pets. She dreamed of horses, whereas I wanted prissy ballerina dolls. In our games I led and Tracey followed. It was great to have such an eager understudy, she seemed a part of my shadow.

Tracey and I kept doing well at school. We could be kids there, not caregivers. We travelled on a school bus from the vineyard gate, which was at the end of a long drive.

There was a lot of wildlife in Barmera. Tracey saw foxes, but I never did. There were huge hornets with fearsome stingers. They were orange and twice the size of bumblebees. There were lots of horseflies that bit, and dozens of trapdoor spiders. We amused ourselves by springing their traps and watching them rush out to try and bite us. Once we saw a line of maybe a hundred caterpillars crawling head to tail. They were covered in stiff black hairs. Joan told us they were deadly poisonous — one touch and we were goners. No one was game to put this to the test.

One night in the old house where they went to 'do it,' Mum and Stretch found a snake. In a fit of gallantry Stretch cut the poor creature's head off. Or so he thought. It turned out he'd trimmed its tail. The snake died after sinking its fangs into the stump where its tail had been. They called us to watch its death.

Mum also found a live scorpion under the caravan step. I took it in a jar to school, where it wasn't well received. On getting it home I liberated it beneath the caravan, watching it disappear into the dust. Mum wasn't too impressed by my benevolence. We didn't see the scorpion again.

We also made our own raisins by drying grapes on the dusty ground. They made a good substitute for lollies.

It was a long walk into town where we bought groceries and alcohol. It seemed to take all day to walk there and back. When Mum and the little kids came we would hitchhike; otherwise I would trek it with Joan or Tracey.

One stinking hot day I walked to town and back to buy a loaf of bread. By the time I got home, I'd eaten about a third of it. I'd also lost my shoes, my only pair, somewhere in Berri. Mum didn't growl — she was too tired these days to growl much.

Life on the vineyard was still fun, despite the dangers and long walks to the shops. There were other distractions. I read a lot of old school journals. I don't know where the books came from; a kind teacher probably donated them. We had some excellent, caring teachers. One of them, who caught Tracey stealing another child's play lunch, didn't punish her for it.

Another of her schoolteachers gave Tracey a cat, a ginger tom she called Tractor, as it purred so loudly. The teachers must have realised the squalor we lived in — clothes and bodies always dirty, hungry and often exhausted. They helped out with small kindnesses.

I kept the kids amused at home with lots of inane running games. I don't know where our energy came from; we were all skinny little things with a woefully inadequate diet. We tried to keep as much as possible out of the grown-ups' hair, as Mum was tired again and cried easily, and Stretch was a shouter and whacker. We had little to do with the rest of the Whites now. I didn't have to go out of my way to avoid Philip and Duncan any more. We didn't see Joan either, which didn't matter, because even though she was older than me, she was pretty useless at looking after the kids.

When we ran out of food, Mum and Stretch ate dog biscuits. They covered them with tomato sauce and washed them down with beer. I tried the dog biscuits, but they were dry and salty. I preferred to stick to the fruit and nuts from the trees around us. The lack of food and amenities were having physical effects beyond mere weight loss. My teeth were dreadful. The Christmas toothbrush was the only one I'd owned in the twenty months since leaving Whyalla and it didn't last more than six months, despite my great care of it. I developed an abscess under one of my molars, which hurt badly. Mum assured me there was nothing that could be done about it so I learned to live with the pain. Mum wasn't well. She was tired and cried a lot. Sometimes she couldn't get out of bed to pick the grapes. She was snappy, too, which wasn't like her. One day something happened to Andrew and he broke his leg. Mum said a bed fell on him, but there were no beds in the house and those in the caravan were bolted down. Mum had to carry Andy several miles into the nearest town for medical care. She managed to borrow a pushchair from a church and wheeled him from doctor to hospital and back for X-rays and plastering. She was tired and grumpy by the time they got home, but she was exceptionally nice to us kids for a few days.

Mum had a huge surprise for us one day.

"It's about time you girls saw your father."

We were going to drive to Whyalla to pick up some things. Although I gave little thought to Dad, the idea of seeing him and our old house again was thrilling. Tracey, Shelley and I danced around the room holding hands. The other kids watched. They wanted to come too, but

Mum said no.

We had left real toys and proper books in Whyalla, and Mum thought we should go back and pick them up. I was looking forward to getting quality books to read again; I'd left some good ones behind. My bed there had a built-in bookcase where I kept a set of classics that Mum and Dad gave me one birthday. I so wanted to see, touch and smell my books again; maybe after all that I'd let myself read them.

Dad was out of town at a new job and was staying in a hotel at Port Augusta. Mum dropped us off to him there and went on to Whyalla alone. We spent the day with him in a hotel with a piano that played automatically. Dad was happy to see us and said he didn't want us to go away again. He didn't make much effort to keep us though, when Mum got back. I remembered something Grandma had always said: "Actions speak louder than words."

When Mum returned that night, it was with tickets for a ride on a small plane back home. In the plane she told us that Dad had given away all of our toys and books to the kids next door. We were terribly disappointed — getting our things back had been the main reason we'd travelled this far.

In fact Mum had sold everything in the house during her trip back to Whyalla. When Dad returned home from Port Augusta it was to an empty house, apart from a single bed that she left him to sleep in. All the money from the sale of Dad's and her children's belongings was spent hiring the small plane for our trip back.

Despite my usefulness as a babysitter, the decision was made to send me back to New Zealand. I wondered if Mum had decided I was trouble. The only thing that could have made her think that was the thing with Duncan and Philip, but I'd never told her what really happened. I was to travel alone and return to live with my Miramar grandparents while Mum, Stretch and the littlies were to stay in Oz. I was glad to be leaving, as I missed my grandparents terribly. I would miss Tracey a lot and felt sorry for her because she would now have to do all the babysitting.

It was exciting flying from Adelaide to Sydney to Wellington by myself. Mum bought me Poems to Read to Young Australians to occupy me on the plane. I'd just about memorised the book by the time I got to Sydney. A stewardess gave me two more for the second leg of my journey. I was flying Air New Zealand so I was given a big plastic tiki to replace the one the soldier ants had stolen. The stewardesses fussed over me and brought me anything I asked for. One of them let me give the lollies out at the end of the flight.

My life seemed to be changing for the better.

I felt so lucky.

5

The second I arrived at the airport my Miramar grandparents scooped me up, covering me with kisses. They hadn't changed much at all. Grandad smiled broadly, his black-framed glasses riding up on his cheeks as he did. He was a kind man with a gentle face and lean build. People felt comfortable around him. He had thin grey hair, more prolific around the edges of a central shiny patch, disguised by judicious combing. He always smelled nice too, like those pink 'smoker' lollies which he sometimes kept in the pocket of his cardigan. Grandad would never have smoked though — he had these lollies for the taste, not to disguise anything. Grandma was motherly, cuddly, strong. She had wavy grey hair and a big bust like a shop verandah. I loved to cuddle Grandma. She had a few pale pink fleshy moles on her neck and I pretended not to watch my baby cousins trying to pull them off when she held them. I felt so safe with my grandparents.

They made a huge fuss of me at the airport and exclaimed at how much I'd grown. They were horrified at my 'green teeth' and blamed the acid from the grapes. The dental nurse at Miramar Central School removed my rotten molar and I scrubbed at my remaining teeth until they shone.

Miramar was heaven. Food was plentiful, as was adult supervision, safe love, privacy and real books and toys. Schooling was regular and encouraged not just because it gave the adults a break. I missed Mum, but her loss was more than compensated for. She sent regular letters from Oz, which included lots of tales about their travels. Once she sent a leg from a huge spider they found in the car. The letter described the leg as thick as a matchstick and as big as a wishbone, but it must have been confiscated by Customs, as it didn't arrive. I didn't miss life on the road. The stability

I now had felt far superior. If I could have Tracey with me, things would have been totally perfect. I went to Sunday School — Grandma and Grandad were Salvation Army soldiers — and made friends there. For the first time I was able to have friends to visit, although I rarely did. I had lost the habit of making close friends. What was the point when I stayed nowhere long enough to maintain relationships.

Grandma came from strong Salvation Army stock and her faith provided her with a sense of love and duty. Her ability and desire to nurture made me feel at times like the most loved little girl in the world. The house she lived in was built when she was ten, to be the home of her father, five brothers and herself. Her mother had died suddenly, leaving this ten-year-old the 'woman of the family.' The house had four bedrooms and was of weatherboard construction, with the south-facing wall clad in corrugated iron. The section was large, with a big shed and the sleepout at the rear where I'd spent my early life. When Grandma's brothers left home, she married my grandad, Cliff. Grandma and Grandad had eight children of their own, starting with honeymoon twins. Mum's kids were the third generation Grandma had mothered, all in the old house in Miramar.

Life with my grandparents was paradise. I had lots of clean, fresh clothes. My hair was clean and tied back with ribbons and elastic bands with coloured bobbles on them. I walked home for lunch every day. Grandad brought chicken pies or filled rolls home with him. Meals were regular and healthy.

We had holidays at Diamond Harbour near Christchurch, staying with Grandad's sister Aunty Gwen. We'd catch the car ferry to Lyttelton then drive around the coast road to Aunty Gwen's. She had an outside toilet and I spent a lot of time looking under the seat for the redback spider I was certain must live there. One time I did catch

33

a weta in there.

At Easter, Grandad would drive the three of us to Lake Rotorua where we stayed in a motor camp. The moon always seemed to be full and the poplars lining the road had crisp yellow leaves that shone silver in the moonlight. We always had a hut close to the lake. It was beautiful.

During other school holidays I'd help at Grandad's factory. My grandparents owned and operated a soft-furnishings business, where they made high-quality eiderdowns, curtains and covers for chairs and lounge suites. All of their daughters, including Mum, were accomplished machinists. I loved to help although I was more than likely a big nuisance to the workers.

News trickled in from Australia. My old family was on the move again, having travelled by caravan to Sydney, where another new life beckoned. They seemed happy and, in their own way, settled. Things seemed cosy from a distance, yet I didn't want to join them again.

One night my grandparents took me to the airport. They said we were going to meet an uncle who was flying in from Australia. In those days there were no flight tunnels connecting planes with the terminal building and you could go outside to watch passengers disembark. While waiting for this 'uncle' I saw a couple and five little children disembark.

"Look," I said to Grandma. "That could be Mum and Stretch and the kids." It was. They had borrowed fares from one of Mum's sisters and come back to live. The 'uncle' had been a red herring, probably used in case my family didn't actually turn up as arranged. The fares for two adults and five children would have bought an awful lot of booze and dog biscuits, after all.

Somehow we all fitted into the house in Miramar.

Mum and Stretch soon started to look for work. They bought The Dominion every morning and searched for farm labouring work, as this would guarantee us a home and income. Mum helped pay our way by sewing for Grandad. Tracey, Diane and I attended Miramar Central School. One school day we all travelled by train to the Wairarapa where the adults had a job interview. We were all well scrubbed and behaved like angels, while Mum and Stretch were tidily dressed and sober. This ploy must have worked: we were soon on our way to live at Papatahi, a Merino stud farm on Western Lake Road in Featherston.

Time for another new house, another try at being a family and another wrench from my grandparents. I didn't know how it would all turn out, yet I couldn't refuse to move. Perhaps it would be all right this time.

Stretch was hired as a farm labourer at Papatahi and Mum was to care for the house and cook meals for the shearers. It was a big farm with several workers' houses in addition to the big homestead where The Donalds — always pronounced with capital letters — lived. Our place was the nicest I'd ever lived in, a white house with dark blue trim and tons of room. There was a curved gravel driveway in front and a garden with well-tended shrubs surrounding a large, semicircular lawn. As we were shifting in, three neighbourhood girls who were swinging on our gate greeted us. Gail, Vicky and Arlene Stewart became good friends. They lived just down the road from us and had their own horse, which they could all ride. I — not yet a farm girl at heart — was impressed by this. They also had a caravan in their front paddock, so we had some common ground.

We enrolled at Featherston School. The school bus left Papatahi at 7.30 each week day morning and returned us home around five. To reach the bus stop we had to walk for about fifteen minutes along a road over which giant macrocarpas arched. The walk was eerie in the half-dark of winter — we would run along the stretch between the trees then.

The school days were long, but good. I was near the top of my class at everything and scored 98 percent for a spelling test. I spelled catarrh and typewriter wrong; what did Standard Two kids know about catarrh? — I thought the teacher said 'guitar.' I was in the school choir and the orchestra in which I played glockenspiel and recorder. My teachers were Miss McLachlan and Mr Connor. Miss McLachlan was Maori and taught me poi and action songs and an ever-greater love of reading, while Mr Connor was a Pakeha with a moustache. His favourite phrase was "all that jazz." They were great teachers.

The farm was wonderful. I spent hours lying on my back in paddocks dreaming, searching under dry old cowpats for ladybirds, scavenging at the farm dump, building huts from haybales, collecting discarded cicada shells, wandering in the bush, balancing and rolling on old 44-gallon drums, and climbing on massive vines with the older farm kids while trying to dodge the wetas. We had a sheep called Doctor Taylor; a calf called Pinocchio and a pony called Peanut Butter that we never learned to ride.

Home was peaceful initially; but changes crept in. There were shouting matches between Mum and Stretch, plates of food thrown at us when we dared to ask why we had to eat Weetbix for dinner while they were eating roast meat and veges. No one noticed my good marks any more, but I still worked hard for them. School was my island of calm, predictable and safe; home was far from either.

Stretch whinged a lot. He didn't like New Zealand; Papatahi was too far from the pub; the farm work was too physical. He started to beat Mum up. She in turn would hit Tracey and me. We took our frustration out on Diane, Shelley and Steve. Andrew was too cute to hit, so he was usually spared. Hitting wasn't our only revenge — we were subtler than the adults. One day when Diane was out of bed, Tracey and I tipped a pint of warm water over her bottom sheet and mattress then told Mum she'd wet the bed. Mum was furious — she knew the bed was dry when Diane got up — the "filthy, lazy little bitch" must have climbed back in to piss the bed rather than go to the toilet. Diane was thrashed and Trace and I had to expend little effort over it at all. That would teach her for telling tales on us.

The adults' violence escalated. Oh, for Whyalla's flying shoes and vegetables — here it was knives and furniture. Even the new lounge suite that they'd bought on credit got bashed about. We kids spent as much time as possible outside, in the bush, at the dump, or at the Stewart's place. We played together well and conspired against the adults. We were a mutually protective unit at times, not always rotten to each other. We tried to be good, but sometimes even perfect behaviour wasn't enough. It was impossible to predict the way the adults would react to us and this was extremely confusing and unsettling.

One night Stretch got particularly pissed and beat Mum like never before. Screaming drunken abuse he pulled the phone out of the wall and up-ended couches and other furniture. As Mum was pushing us into our bedrooms he drew a large and heavy knife — the one he used to slaughter cattle with — from a drawer and threw it at her. She ducked and it sank deep into the kitchen wall just above her head. As Stretch lunged after the knife, Mum fled.

Tracey and I got the little kids into their rooms before heading to our own. Tracey saw Mum climb out of the bathroom window — I didn't. Stretch followed the two of us to our bedroom, grabbed me and twisted my left arm up behind my back. He kept asking where Mum was. Although I told him I didn't know, he bent my arm higher and higher behind my back; I was certain he wanted to break it. Eventually I was on tiptoe, blubbering and snotting all over the place and he let me go.

We all stayed quietly in our rooms that night. In the

morning Mum was bruised and subdued and had bald patches where Stretch had pulled out her hair. She swore Tracey, Diane and me to secrecy before she let us go to school. She made no other mention of the night before. Stretch acted as though nothing had happened. I only told the Stewart girls what had happened; they only told their mother. Mrs Stewart was worried about Mum and approached her about the beating. Mum waited till Mrs Stewart left before she thrashed me. I curled into a little ball on my bed as she sobbed and slapped and punched me all over.

Before I knew it I was back living with Grandma and Grandad in Miramar.

The morning I was to leave Papatahi I got up early and wandered in my pyjamas over the paddocks to collect mushrooms for Mum and Stretch's breakfast. It was a cool, clear spring morning. The dew hung heavily on the fences and around the edges of the new mushrooms. I climbed over the wire and wandered through the paddocks for the last time. I was careful not to pick any toadstools; I didn't want to poison anyone. I got home before Mum was up and put the mushrooms on the bench. I went back to bed, listened to the birds outside and to the younger kids beginning to stir in their rooms. It was a special morning.

6

For another nine months or so the others remained in Featherston. Occasionally I saw them, but it was as though Featherston wasn't my home any more and those people weren't my family.

In Miramar I woke to the sound of traffic and the National Programme on the radio. In Featherston the magpies, sheep and cattle provided a gentler wake-up. My grandparents' house smelled of hot porridge, not smokes and the grown ups didn't get up grumpy or headachy like they did in Featherston. Grandad's cat 'Minnie', wasn't as exciting as the lambs and horse I'd left behind, but there was no point lamenting their loss.

Eventually Mum and Stretch split up and he and his kids returned to Australia. I hated him — he hurt my Mum, my sisters, his own kids and me. Mum, Tracey and Shelley came back to Miramar and we all lived again at Grandma and Grandad's place.

Dad came back to New Zealand to live. He had a new girlfriend, Helen. Tracey and I liked Helen. Some weekends we would ride our bikes from Miramar to visit her and Dad. Mum didn't mind; she was either at the pub or in her bed, anyway. Often she would have Shelley as company. I deeply resented her status as favourite, but was glad I didn't have to spend all my time in that dark, smoky room.

Shortly after Shell started school, Mum decided on a whim to holiday in Auckland with some friends. She planned to travel by overnight train and take Shelley with her. It wouldn't matter if Shell missed a few days school — she was only five. Shell made the most of this coup. Mum wanted her, not Tracey or me, to go away with her. She packed her bag a couple of days before the big trip and talked about it incessantly. The day of the holiday arrived and Shelley returned home from school excited and chattering. Mum was out — she spent her days in the pub — but had promised to pick Shell up at the front gate in time for their taxi ride to the railway station. Tracey and I tried to ignore her as she piled her bag and pillow inside the front gate and sat on them, keeping watch for Mum. She sat there for three hours, long past the time Mum should have arrived. She was still there half an hour after the train would have pulled out. Forlorn, but still hopeful, Shelley had to be coaxed inside as night arrived and the temperature dropped. She didn't cry. I felt certain I would, had I been the one abandoned like that. Mum had changed her mind about taking her baby, but didn't think to tell anyone she was holidaying alone.

Mum helped out at the family business, but often couldn't get herself out of bed to go to work. She spent days in bed sending Tracey and me to the shops to buy her Twisties, Coke, curry and rice rolls, Milky Bars and cigarettes. She was taking drugs, too. She smoked a lot of dope and took all sorts of different coloured pills which she washed down with booze. Milky Bars are still my food of choice, but after half-swallowing a drowned cigarette butt years before, I never caught the tobacco bug.

Mum slept in a small dark bedroom off the kitchen. The window frame was rotting and the only window had long been nailed up. There was a large tree right outside the window, so although it faced northwest the room got little natural light. Mum's room had a spooky feeling. Great-grandad died in there from a massive stroke. Despite this, visiting children gravitated to see their Aunty Pam. Mum was a kid magnet. She could be fun and always had time for a cuddle and a story for visiting children. She especially loved my cousins with the big brown eyes — Phillip, Lynne, Julie and Melita. She told them they had "cows' eyes." I wanted brown eyes so badly; Shelley had brown eyes and she was Mum's favourite. Tracey and I had blue eyes like our father, while Mum's were hazel.

Mum's room was filled with music and incense and a couple of brass Buddhas. There was a poster of Desiderata — "Go placidly amidst the noise and haste…" — on the bedroom door and tapa cloth covering the walls. She taped black adhesive footprints to the ceiling. One night when she was stoned she stood on her bed and wrote swear words on the ceiling using a black felt pen. There were several instructive books in her room; I read The Exorcist, Drum and The Happy Hooker before I started high school.

Mum loved dogs. Her puppy, Tala, lived in her room. Tala was constantly horny. He was often worse after Mum got him stoned by holding a burning joint under his nose. He always seemed to have an erection, which he liked to rub against furniture, carpets and people's legs. I was disgusted and decided to teach him a lesson. Grandma's brothers had owned a slug gun, which they'd used to shoot sparrows. I was entertained for several months by using it to shoot glass-headed dressmaking pins at flies on the wall. Although no Annie Oakley, I have to admit I was a pretty good shot. This day I loaded the gun with a pin, but in such a way that the round pin head would shoot out first. The plan was to hit Tala's exposed penis with the blunt end of the pin, stinging him and maybe discouraging his constant display. Unfortunately for Tala, things went awry. The head shot off the pin as it flew out of the gun and the metal shaft entered and lodged deep inside his penis. He jumped, yelped and whimpered pitifully. His penis retracted quickly and he limped into Mum's room where he remained, rather less excitable than usual.

A day or so later Mum noticed a trickle of blood coming out of his urethra and when she saw he couldn't walk properly and howled when he tried to pee, she took him to the vet. Tala needed an X-ray, followed by surgery to remove the mysteriously placed pin. Everyone was bewildered by his injury. I didn't own up. Happily to say, Tala returned to being his normal male self before long.

Tala was one of the few animals we owned who didn't just disappear one day or get run over. Mum had him put down a few years later when one of her boyfriends decided he didn't like him.

If Grandma and Grandad were away on the days Mum found the energy to go to the pub, she'd leave us alone or with some flaky friend. One night she left us with a young bloke she'd just met. We were aged maybe nine, seven and five. We'd never met this guy before, but he worried me. Life had taught me to view men with suspicion. Within minutes of Mum's departure he ran himself a bath, undressed fully (making sure we could see him) and asked the three of us to come into the bathroom and wash him. I refused, but couldn't stop Tracey and Shelley who giggled and soaped the creep down. I left the room in disgust and still feel ashamed that I left my little sisters in there. How could Mum have exposed us to people like him? In later years when I thought about these times, my museum nightmare sprang to mind: Mum too busy with her friends to notice what was happening to her children. At least I hoped she was too busy to notice — that didn't seem as mean as realising what was happening in our lives and simply not caring about it.

Grandad was looking tired. One day in August 1972, he phoned from his workplace. Grandma answered the call. He had collapsed at work with terrible pains in his chest. He'd had a massive heart attack and was admitted to Wellington Hospital.

Grandma was frantic. As she sped us off to school she let us know it was all the fault of us girls for misbehaving that morning. We'd made our poor Grandad so stressed his heart stopped working properly.

After a few days we were allowed to visit him in hospital. It was scary seeing our Grandad so pale and sick and propped up on pillows. His room was full of cards and flowers, sent by all his children and grandchildren. I gave him a special pottery plaque I'd made at school. It had a religious theme — a hill with a cross on it. Grandad thought it was hilarious — I'd given him a 'get well' headstone. He spent two weeks in hospital and began to look rested. We looked forward to having him home — we'd never, ever be naughty again.

A few days later at teatime, we girls were sent to a neighbour's place, because Grandma, Mum and some aunties were called to the hospital. Grandad died that evening of further complications from the heart attack. He was 54. Uncle Andre said it was Mum's fault, for not helping at his business enough. Nobody blamed Grandad's coronary arteries, his diet or the stress of running a small business alone — it's so much more satisfying to have a person to get mad at.

I was sent to stay with Dad's parents at their property in Te Marua until the day of the funeral, which was held at the Salvation Army Citadel in Vivian Street.

"Poor Grandma has got enough to do without running around after you!" was an aunty's explanation of my dismissal.

It was always fun staying at Te Marua, as my grandparents lived next door to a nudist camp and I lived in hope of seeing a real, live, nudist. It never happened. Dad picked me up from his parents' place and drove me to the funeral. My aunties and uncles cried and cried. So did Mum and us kids, and all the other grandchildren. Grandma was too upset to cry much — poor, poor Grandma.

I got lots of cuddles from teachers at school — they knew who my real support system had been. I had lost my rock, the one man I knew would never hurt me or abandon me. I was ten years old and bereft. Grandad was the first person I was close to who had died.

Grandad's business, Capitol Furnishings, was closed down. Mum and her sisters worked hard to clear orders. Grandma was lost. Grandma and Mum both kept diaries and wrote vastly different descriptions of Grandad's death. I discovered these a couple of years later, while snooping. Mum said he had looked horrible, with his face "purple, yellow and contorted"; Grandma said he finally looked "very peaceful."

I became terrified that I would see a dead person. In my prayers each night I'd ask that we have no prowlers, but if one did enter the house, that they'd leave alive and the family be left unharmed. The thought of finding a dead person in this safe place was too much to deal with.

7

Life was sadder and quieter without Grandad. I missed the little things, such as him using his electric razor in the kitchen each morning and pretending to shave my chin with it. His smiles and cuddles. Minnie the cat missed him too. Grandad used to play a game with her each lunchtime. After eating he'd race her up the back yard and tease her as she climbed a tree. He'd always preface this with "Let's play, Minnie!" She'd start running when he said that. He looked happy and not so old when he played with the cat.

Grandma was sad too, she wasn't ready to face life without him.

A few months after Grandad's death, I was sitting at the dinner table at Grandma's, minding my own business, when my attention was grabbed by a headline on the back page of The Evening Post: 'Boredom Led to Booze — Booze Led to Buckets.' The news item told the story of one Pamela Mary Roche (actually Mum's middle name was Joan) who had that day, in an extremely inebriated state, lit a fire in a rubbish bin in Cuba Mall, one of the main shopping streets in the city. The dreadful woman then sat on the flames, burning her behind. To gain some relief from her scorched butt, she took some beers and climbed the buckets of the Cuba Mall fountain and sat in the topmost bucket singing lurid songs and drinking. There she remained entertaining the shoppers until the police arrived. She wouldn't move on request and stomped on the hands of cops who climbed up to escort her down. She attracted a large crowd and most of them seemed to her to be on her side.

I read this story aloud and was ignored. I then read it louder, with particular emphasis on the name of the heroine. There was dead silence in the kitchen as the adults turned to stare at me. I was told to shut up and go to the lounge to watch telly. The grown-ups turned to the back page to read it for themselves. I watched the TV as instructed — the network news was on and the incident was mentioned on that. My Mum was famous! I never knew whether the 'Mary' was a journalistic error or an attempt by Mum at some anonymity. I still feel proud of her when I walk past the Cuba Mall fountain. That was some feat! Here's to you, 'Pamela Mary'; as far as I know your stunt has never been repeated.

Mum made a brief attempt to get well. She checked into Kensington House, a fashionable treatment centre in Kensington Street, Central Wellington where she received addiction counselling and love. She also turned religious while in there. I loved visiting Kensington House; it was everything my grandparents' house wasn't. It was 'The Dawning of the Age of Aquarius' and the staff had long hair and wore caftans and love beads. There were guitars playing in the lounge areas. The people who worked at Kensington House seemed ethereal, yet grounded. Mum was relaxed and happy and almost 'normal.'

Sadly, her recovery was short-lived and she returned to being the constantly tired, frequently drunk, depressed and thoughtless woman we knew so well. One morning the police found her sitting on the Porirua Railway Station and brought her home. She had rips in the legs of her jeans, which were blood-soaked. She sobbed as she told us she'd been sitting at the station when some gang members had accosted her and repeatedly raped her before cutting obscenities into her thighs with a knife and razor blade. She said the police didn't believe her and had been horrible. She pulled the bloody jeans over her damaged legs. Carefully etched into her skin were the words 'fuck me' and 'fucken slag.' The words were carved into her in such a way that she was the only person who was likely to have put them there.

She cried more, babbling about the bastards who hurt her. We all cried with her. The police said later that someone had witnessed her attacking herself with a razor blade, her jeans around her ankles. Who knows if the rest of her story was true? Did she know she'd hurt herself? Had she been raped? Poor, tortured Mum — she had so much mental pain.

We occasionally saw Dad when he came round to Grandma's to give Mum a maintenance cheque. Those cheques he remembered to sign would often bounce. Mum cashed the cheques at the local dairy or butcher shop and was humiliated when they bounced, so she began to avoid contact with these places. This confined her more to home and meant that Grandma, Tracey and I were the ones that had to give her the news — another cheque had been returned by the bank.

Mum drank, smoked and cried a lot.

After she was widowed, Grandma spent more time staying with her other children scattered all over New Zealand. The poor woman needed a break more than anything, yet was lumbered with a dependent daughter and her offspring. When Grandma left, she would lock her bedroom door after storing her precious things in cardboard boxes in there and hope and pray the house would be in one piece when she returned. It usually was.

With Grandma away Mum had rowdy, drunken parties to which her rowdier, drunken friends came. The police were frequent and uninvited guests. Once they bashed down Grandma's bedroom door to search her cardboard boxes for stolen property. Mum pleaded with them to leave Grandma's things alone. She was extremely upset when they didn't listen to her. Grandma was none too impressed either. She swore she'd never go away again.

Another time when the police arrived in force to tell Mum to "turn it down", they found her alone in the kitchen listening to a transistor radio. I guess the neighbours had become hypersensitive.

One morning, laughter and the sounds of heavy objects being dropped on the floor woke me. Mum and some mates had burgled a service station while her children slept in the house alone, and scored cigarettes, cash and dozens of cassette tapes. I was rapt to see the tapes. I'd been working part time up at the Salvation Army shop behind Grandma's place and had saved enough money to buy a cassette player. We could never afford to buy tapes — now I had heaps of them. We opened the first cassette case — empty. All of the boxes were empty. I was so disappointed.

With Grandma away, drugs became a part of our daily life. The house reeked of dope, a smell that seemed to cling to the curtains and furnishings. Mum's friends brought cocaine and heroin and there were always pills. Mum even took the Doloxene, a very strong painkiller prescribed to me after I broke my nose at school. Her arms bore clusters of bruises when she could get herself injectable drugs; it seemed access to illegal substances was never a problem. I don't think Mum felt she was betraying Grandma by using her house in this way. She was depressed and disorganised and having fun, in the best way she knew how.

Another morning when Grandma was away, Mum woke Tracey and me to help her hide things she'd stolen in a burglary at the local doctors' surgery. She led us to the back yard. Dumped just over the back fence were needles and syringes, pills, a blood pressure cuff and some other things I didn't recognise. Tracey and I buried most of the needles and syringes under a bush on a piece of empty land next to the lamp factory on Tauhinu Road. This place, although open to prying eyes, seemed the best place to put them at the time.

If it wasn't drugs, it was booze. Mum's second home was the pub and we often spent weekends and evenings home alone. If we wanted something, we had to remember which pubs Mum was currently banned from and phone all the others. I had memorised the phone numbers for the Clyde, the Panama and the Royal Oak, among others. Sometimes my sisters would go to the pub with Mum and would sit in the carpark in her current boyfriend's car. I was sick of that, and usually refused, staying at home alone reading.

If Grandma was home, we'd be dumped on her. I loved Grandma and preferred her company to Mum's, but my real wish was to live with Aunty Jenny and Uncle Dave. They had three kids and lived on Rotoroa Island in the Hauraki Gulf. I secretly hoped something would happen so I could live with Jenny and Dave.

Mum had friends who owned a café in Courtenay Place. They served meals like wiener schnitzel with mashed potatoes and tinned veges, or crumbed fish and chips with salad. The café had mirrors on opposite walls, so you could see yourself reflected to infinity. Mum liked to dine there and probably rarely paid. She had charisma and radiated the feeling she'd do anything for anyone. We were always told our Mum would "give the shirt off her back" for someone in need. She was generous to her friends, to her nieces and nephews and to strangers. If we passed a drunk in Courtenay Place or near the Basin Reserve — the cricket ground where the drunks all slept, in those days before night shelters — she'd give them her last coins for a drink. She'd also line the three of us up and make us kiss them. Mum's kind of generosity was appreciated by those who didn't depend on her for protection, for safety, or for any kind of moral or other guidance. She was too sick to be depended on. You had to live with her to realise this.

Mum occasionally took us to eat at her friends' café. We'd always order schnitzel, eggs and chips. It felt so posh to eat in a restaurant.

One Friday night when Mum was out, Grandma took us

in to town for late night shopping. There was no weekend shopping then, so Friday night was the main chance for working people to spend their money. Town was always full on Friday nights. When we went late night shopping we usually went to the Farmers' cafeteria for sandwiches and juice, but this day Grandma took us to Mum's friends' café as a special treat. Our dinner was lovely and as we left to walk to the bus stop in the near dark, we saw a drunken, dishevelled person lurching down the street in our direction. Grandma shepherded us together as the drunk stumbled along the footpath. As the person neared us, we realised to our horror that it was our Mum. Shelley called out to her. Recognising us and possibly even more horrified than we were, Mum spun around and tried to run back up the street away from us. She was drinking from a bottle and had another in her pocket and as she lurched her way up Courtenay Place, booze splashed from the bottle in her hand and foamed on the footpath.

Grandma was mortified and broken-hearted. I felt sad, angry and contaminated by the sight of my drunken, disintegrating mother. Shelley cried. We went home on the bus, then straight to bed.

8

The needles and syringes remained hidden for a couple of months until Mum phoned from the pub one evening and told us to dig them up and put them under her pillow. We did as we were told. But someone must have overheard Mum, or seen us digging the gear up, because the cops arrived shortly after and searched the house. They found the needles and syringes and Mum was back in court.

The morning of her case, Mum brushed her hair away from her face and put on make-up. She wore a long blue paisley skirt and white blouse and had a blue enamel cross around her neck. She was dressed like other people's mums. She walked back and forth between the court waiting room and the nearby public toilet. She rested her cigarette on the edge of handbasin, took some blue capsules out of her pocket and turned on the taps. She cupped water into her shaking hands and used it to swallow the drugs. She couldn't swallow pills dry when she was frightened. She smoked non-stop, lighting one cigarette while the last was still burning on the edge of the basin. The room was shrouded in a blue-grey haze. The downers didn't work because Mum vomited repeatedly from fear.

"I won't go away — I'd kill myself before doing time. Oh Laurie, they can't send me away." I hugged her. There was nothing to say.

Soon it was time. I sat outside the court with one of Mum's friends until the case had been heard. Mum had apologised to the GPs whose rooms she'd burgled and this went in her favour. The judge, worried about the effect any imprisonment would have on her daughters, let her off with a fine and a warning.

Shortly after this court case, Mum was admitted to

51

the Wellington Hospital Psychiatric Unit under the A & D (Alcohol and Drug) Act. Kids weren't allowed to visit their parents there and we wanted to see our Mum. Shelley especially needed to see her. One afternoon Grandma and Aunty Trish smuggled us up to the psych ward window to see her. The place looked full of loopy women. It was scary seeing them all together. They crowded, grinning, to the window to smile and wave at us. Mum was at their centre. She smiled too and kissed Shelley through the glass. I held back, feeling shy at seeing her there. My Mum wasn't crazy. It was great to see her, and brave of Grandma and Trish to take us there. Mum apparently felt a lot better for having seen us.

When Mum got out, she stayed at home more. She made light of her hospitalisation and used to skip around the house holding our hands singing 'They're coming to take me away, Haha!!' Another favourite song of hers was 'Brain Damage' by Pink Floyd. The lyrics are suitably 'Mum': 'The lunatic is in my head; You raise the blade, you make the change; You rearrange me till I'm sane; You lock the door and throw away the key; There's someone in my head, but it's not me.'

That song can still make me cry.

While Mum fought her demons, Grandma introduced us to angels. Tracey and I threw ourselves into all the Salvation Army activity open to kids our age. We sang solos in church, believing our words made their way directly to Heaven. Shelley was Mum's girl, spending her time in Mum's poky little bedroom. We smugly believed Shelley would go to Hell.

Tracey and I were Junior Soldiers, members of the Singing Company and ace timbrellists, wielding our ribboned tambourines with skill and enthusiasm. We dressed like the other girls, played like them, moved in the same formations as them. For a few precious hours each week we felt the same as them.

We both did double timbrels, marching to brass band music while shaking and waving a timbrel in each hand. We were hot. Our Timbrel Brigade travelled to Christchurch, where we performed dressed in black skirts, white blouses, white knee-high socks and black shoes. The ribbons on our timbrels were white and we performed under ultraviolet light, so all the white in our uniforms luminesced. Too cool. Music, coloured ribbons and our faith in God made a shining counterpoint to some of the other parts of our lives.

I took lessons on the tenor horn, aiming to play in the Miramar Salvation Army brass band. We also did the Sunday School thing and attended Girls Brigade on Tuesdays. This side of our lives contrasted starkly with life with Mum and lessened our time at home with her. It fulfilled different needs for all of us.

Tracey and I found some of our timbrel marches on an old record of Grandad's. We wanted to be the best and practised our moves in the lounge with Sally Army brass band music playing loudly on Grandad's old radiogram. Using Grandad's things made us feel close to him again. The timbrels must have driven Mum mad, but she didn't complain much about it. We were in full cry when the cops came one day to search Grandma's house. Mum was in a good mood and didn't mind showing them through. They popped their heads into the lounge, but didn't come in when they saw what we were up to. The cops looked bemused and one laughed when Mum told him to be careful, or Tracey and I would have him converted before he left the house.

Mum was becoming noticeably sicker. She was committed to the Porirua Psychiatric Hospital under the A & D Act when I was eleven. She hated being locked up and tried to escape at every opportunity. She was eventually locked up in Lomond, Porirua's high security unit.

We visited Mum a few times at Lomond. It was horrible seeing her locked behind two sets of doors. I remember fear fluttering in my throat and stomach while we sat in the waiting room. There was a reproduction of a sombre old English painting on the wall. I tried to lose myself in the scene of cows, haystacks and carriages. The dark shadows in the picture could hide me from view and make this place invisible.

I couldn't tell anyone I was afraid. That would seem disloyal to Mum.

More often than not Grandma and Aunty Trish went to the hospital alone. I used that time to terrorise my sisters, especially Tracey. Often I'd chase her around the house hitting her with the jug cord. I wanted them to feel the same turmoil I was experiencing. Somehow they always forgave me.

Mum wrote us letters, always addressed from 'The Funny Farm.'

Many years after her death I saw Mum's psychiatric records. They revealed that she'd received multiple bouts of electro-convulsive (shock) therapy during her time in Porirua Hospital. I don't know if it was just coincidental, but the ECT was given when she was brought back to the hospital after escaping. If the shock treatment was punishment for running away, it was a lousy sort of punishment.

9

I was now thirteen and enrolled at Wellington High, a large co-ed school in central Wellington. I loathed shorthand and typing with a passion but took it because Dad's girlfriend said it would guarantee me a job. I loved French, although it was likely to be of no practical use at all. We had to adopt French names for our language classes: I was re-christened 'Juliette.' I felt different in those classes — mysterious and worldly.

Most of my time in the third form was spent hanging around with the school stage crew and writing, directing and acting in plays. I was obsessed by acting and the stage, and convinced I was going to become a famous actress. I read the 'Blue Door Theatre' books repeatedly and all the books on stagecraft I could find.

With my friends Julie, Lee Ann and Geraldine I adapted a melodrama called The Mask and the Face. I was the lead girl Savina, and the others played my husband Mario and lover Franco. We sat in the school library with pens and paper, arguing over lines. We'd take turns jumping up and acting out our parts, quietly enough that we weren't asked to leave.

Our play was a hoot. We performed it at our end-of-year school function to an audience of over six hundred and it seemed to go down extremely well. We had our script assessed by someone at the Hannah Playhouse, now Downstage Theatre. Their assessment took three weeks to arrive. During this time we had fantasies of rave reviews and were terribly disappointed when a teacher passed the official report to us. The experts thought our play "a bit melodramatic" and didn't want to use it. We consoled ourselves, saying what did they know, anyway?

At that end-of-year function our whole music class

sang a song from Oliver — 'I'd Do Anything.' We were all supposed to sit along the front of the stage dressed as grubby urchins; everyone but me did. I wore a white, floor length caftan in a thick, yet clingy material. The caftan had a hood and a blue embroidered panel surrounding the plunging neckline. I had borrowed it from one of Mum's friends and thought I looked a million bucks — no more grubby urchin for me. I took my place on the stage with the rest of my classmates and sang as though I meant it. I don't think anyone growled; if they did, I wasn't listening. I was going to be a famous actress one day. My English teacher had told me I wrote like an angel, but I thought I'd act. More people would notice me that way.

Mum was still erratic, doing drugs, drinking and smoking excessively and going out with different men. I was more sophisticated about it now. I told kids at school that Mum took drugs. Some of them wanted to come home and see for themselves, but I didn't let them. Mum would have gone mad.

Walking across the school grounds one day I came across a wild rabbit. We'd always had animals around and while I loved them intensely, I had a compulsion to be mean to them at times — smacking them or pulling their tails. Sometimes I just forgot about them, like the cage of mice left in the sleepout for a couple of weeks while we went on holiday. After not being fed for several days they got hungry enough to chew through the wooden door of their cage. Mum convinced herself the drug squad had freed them while executing a search warrant. She was furious. Never mind the chewed up door — the incident was further proof that the police were assholes and out to get her and her children.

The rabbit I caught must have been sick because I was able to outrun it. I took it home to protect it from dogs and put it in a big cage I'd made in the back yard for some short-lived guinea pigs. I fed my rabbit heaps, hugged it and loved it. It would lie in my arms and let me stroke it. It was dependent on me, unlike a cat or a dog.

One day I was hugging my rabbit in the sleepout when I realised I had never been cruel to it. That wasn't good enough; I picked it up by the ears and slapped it a couple of times before biffing it back into its cage. This didn't mean I loved it any less, it merely brought my rabbit into line with the other things I loved and with the way I was loved.

The bunny died when Mum and some of her mates set a pig dog onto it one drunken night. It wouldn't have had a chance. I woke to see the torn wire at the front of its empty cage. Mum said it was an accident but I didn't believe her.

Wellington High was a school that encouraged us to think and act 'political.' The teachers tried to instil a strong sense of social justice and we were encouraged to attend protest marches if we could demonstrate a true and accurate knowledge of the cause that was being espoused.

I attended a number of protest marches, including the 1975 Maori Land March. Pupils from Wellington High joined the throng just north of Wellington and journeyed with them to Parliament. The elders in the group, moved by injustice to grief as much as rage, were powerful figures.

Poverty had played a big part in my life; I had experience of abuse and other social ills. As a stroppy thirteen-year-old, I wanted justice; surely it could be found in a group of like-minded, slogan-chanting people. In later years I also marched for free access to abortion, in opposition to the SIS Bill, and the Springbok tour of 1981.

I was a difficult thirteen-year-old. I was always getting up Grandma's and Mum's noses by being lethargic, lazy and mouthy. I was depressed; they didn't know about the 'suicide attempts' that I'd made periodically since I was nine or ten. Once I sliced a mole off my tummy with a steak knife, thinking I would immediately develop cancer and die. I drank a mouthful of iodine ('Poison S2 — Not to be Ingested') from a bottle in Grandma's cupboard. Another time I swallowed handfuls of pills from the kitchen cupboard and spent the night vomiting. The grown-ups were unaware of my misery and were pissed off with me. Grandma kept telling me I was fat, ugly and stupid and my breasts were too big. Every second guy I passed in the street let me know how top-heavy I was; I didn't need reminding at home. Mum gave me a good black eye just before school one morning for drinking the last of the milk.

Ignoring the real life soap opera at home, my escape was to be found on the stage. One Saturday morning I was locked in Mum's bedroom by her and Grandma to stop me going to a play rehearsal. I don't think they believed that was how I was spending all my time. The window was nailed shut, so there was no way out. The harpies sat in the kitchen, just outside the bedroom door, ending any thought of escape. They chatted and laughed over their cups of tea. I prayed they'd choke. I spent my time in Mum's room biting the beads off a blue bag she had given me and spitting them onto the floor. I hated them both.

One weekend morning when Grandma was away, I was enjoying a lie-in. Tracey shared the big side bedroom with me and she and Shell were already up and about and making a fair amount of noise. Mum wanted a letter posted. I rolled over to face the wall again and groaned.

"Laurie, get up and post this for me. It's important."

"Get one of the others to do it — they're up."

"Get up and post it now!"

"Couldn't Tracey do it?" I started whining, but my question was reasonable. My sisters were awake and aged eleven and ten — perfectly capable of walking a hundred metres to the post box.

Mum went crazy. Was she withdrawing from drugs?

Was she depressed and irritable?

She pulled me out of bed and to my feet, then shoved me to the floor. Her strength was surprising.

She knelt astride my chest, grabbed me by the throat with both hands and started to strangle me.

Her grip tightened — my face was hot and my head tight and heavy. My blood pulsed loudly in my ears. I looked her in the eye, absolutely stunned. She glared back.

She was mad and I was going to die there on the scruffy old carpet where Mum played as a child.

She yelled, "Having you ruined my life!"

I couldn't answer. I tried to keep watching her, but my eyes were bulging and I couldn't think well.

Although outwardly calm, I was panicking.

My vision went grey then black.

When I came to, Mum and my sisters were gone. There was no note, nothing to tell me when or if they'd return. I had a thumping headache and my neck hurt. I was tearful, confused and furious; I couldn't believe my mother had tried to murder me.

I grabbed an old suitcase of Grandma's — I was going to run away. Grandma was on Rotoroa Island with Aunty Jenny. I'd catch a train, then hide on the boat and go to them. I pulled clothes from my drawers, stuffing them into the bag.

I'd make Mum sorry. I'd call the police and have the crazy bitch locked up.

In the end I was too tired to do anything. I cried in bed, then fell into a sleep where I was surrounded by sharks and Mum wanted them to eat me.

My neck was circled with deep red marks that faded throughout the day. Late that afternoon she came home from wherever she'd been and cried all over me. I was still sleeping. She was drunk. She'd told some of her mates what she'd done and a succession of them visited that night to inspect the damage and ensure I wouldn't 'tell.' They were relieved that there was only a faint mark on my neck and a red streak in my eye where a blood vessel had burst. I was quiet and uncomplaining. I went to school on Monday as though nothing had happened. I was becoming good at ignoring my own pain and fear; I'd had a lot of practice.

10

Mum soon had a new boyfriend, her last. His name was Rodney, and unlike the other men who came into her life, Rodney looked like a stayer. They spent hours together at the pub or in the sleepout where Mum stayed. Rod liked Tracey and Shelley as they were more amenable and less likely than me to challenge him or Mum about anything. I had joined the Young Nationals, a conservative political group, in the lead-up to the 1975 general election. My newfound political leanings lasted as long as that election campaign — I had only joined because a friend encouraged me to — but they felt sincere at the time.

Rodney was a Labourite. I pretended I didn't care that he hated me.

For my fourteenth birthday Mum gave me a silver cross to hang around my neck. She gave it to me in the sleepout as I sat on her bed in the gloom. Rodney hadn't stayed that night. As we walked down the section towards Grandma's house Mum reached over and ruffled my hair and smiled at me. I can see her so clearly, copper tints in her mousy hair, loops under her hazel eyes from not enough sleep, and love in her expression. I felt Mum was truly seeing me that day.

The week after my birthday I got a letter from Aunty Jenny and Uncle Dave. They were now living in Parnell, Auckland, and wanted me to come and live with them so I could finish my schooling in a more supportive environment. I was so excited — my dream of living with them had been realised. I moved to Auckland in mid-December. It was the move I had most looked forward to in my whole life. I travelled by train to Auckland. Grandma waved goodbye at the station. Mum stayed at home in bed.

After my departure Mum and Rod moved into a flat in

Newlands. Tracey and Shelley lived there too. They could all play happy families now I was out of the way. Like me, though, Tracey and Shelley spent their Christmas holidays with other families.

I loved it with Jenny and Dave. They were the Salvation Army Officers in charge of the Bridge Alcohol and Drug Rehabilitation Centre at Churton Drive, Parnell. They had a four-bedroom house on the property and I got to sleep in my own bedroom again. There were three kids in the family: Denise, Mark and Leanne. They made me so welcome it was humbling.

The first week I was there Aunty Jenny took me shopping to buy fabrics I liked. She sewed me dresses, bought me new shoes, put make-up on me and told me I was pretty. I felt grown up and treasured. Maybe I wasn't fat, ugly and stupid after all.

Jenny and Dave loved one another and their three kids. They didn't ever fight or yell. They didn't drink or smoke; they took no drugs; they listened to their own kids and me, and cared about what we thought. They modelled the behaviour they wanted their family to live by. Meals, each beginning with grace, were eaten as a family at the dining table. The evening meal ended with a Bible lesson. Each day had a consistent pattern, which was alternately comforting and stifling.

Letters from Mum dropped regularly into the mailbox. Her phone calls came weekly, always when Rod was out of the house. She seemed sad that Jenny was doing more for me than she ever had and I couldn't help rubbing it in. I think she missed me. She told me about her little flat and how proud she was of having sewed the curtains and bedspreads herself. She seemed happy enough. I tried to brush her off — I was having a happy new life of my own and didn't want or need to hear about hers. That part of my life was over and I didn't want to look back.

Christmas came and went. It was sunny, fine and settled. There were a lot of presents — all paid for — and hugs, and lots of love. Grandma came up to stay and we all took the Sally Army boat over to Rotoroa Island for a real family holiday.

I loved the island. Jenny and Dave lived and worked there for many years, leaving for the mainland when their eldest daughter neared her teens. I'd spent a few holidays there, usually with Grandma, but once with Mum, Trace and Shelley. The island is owned by the Salvation Army and operated as an alcohol and drug rehab centre for men. It is dry (in the teetotal sense), which is probably why Mum didn't like it much — when she visited there she spent the whole time in bed, reading.

The island is in the Hauraki Gulf, close to both Waiheke and Pakatoa Islands. It is hot, clean and idyllic. There is a sense of time moving more slowly there.

Staff and visitors use Ladies' Beach — patients are barred from there. I spent whole days on Ladies' Beach with my little cousins, watched over by the adults. It seems no other beach in the world has the same warm, golden sand and azure sky. No shells seem to have the beauty and fragility of those washed up during my childhood days there.

We swam at Ladies' Beach and fished from the wharf, which was always crowded. The men receiving treatment for their alcohol addiction had spare hours to fill in. Those who didn't sunbathe at Men's Beach, fished. We hung lines over the edge of the wharf but never caught anything worth cooking. My small fishy contributions went to the feral cats that haunted the Island.

That year's holiday was full of walks and swims and hunts for fan shells for Grandma, who was collecting them to decorate jewellery boxes.

It was 1976. January 16 was my cousin Denise's birthday.

We spent most of the day at the beach. I was working on a script for a 'Star Trek' type play where I, of course, was to play the lead female role. I called my character Galadriel after Tolkien's Queen of the Elves. I was engrossed in my writing but managed to drag myself away for swims and walks on the beach.

The next morning after breakfast we were all sitting in the lounge planning the day. Would we walk, swim, or collect crabs and shells? The phone rang and was answered by Aunty Jenny. She said hello to Aunty Trish in her usual animated manner, then went quiet. We all froze — something was wrong. Jenny crumpled a little. She looked at the ceiling, biting her lip, then transferred her gaze to Grandma, ignoring the rest of us who were also watching her. "Sit down, Mum. I've got bad news. Pam's passed away."

Mum was dead.

Grandma sank heavily into an armchair, covering her face with her hand. She looked old, so old. She seemed smaller, diminished in a way I had never seen before. A wail, long and loud, came from deep inside her. Jenny replaced the phone and moved, weeping silently, to her mother's side. I felt cold and dead inside. Surely this must be wrong?

Denise, Mark and I were ushered out of the room. We walked to Ladies' Beach. It seemed like I was in a dream or a play — it was all so unreal. My feet hit the sand heavily as I walked, my footfalls repeating the word dead, dead, dead. The beach was beautiful. The sun still shone, the sea still beckoned and the gulls still called, but the holiday was over. Things would never be so carefree again. I had a deep sense of guilt and self-hatred — I believed that if I'd been with Mum, she'd still be alive.

Mum was such a complex character; so much fun at times, so loving and protective. So keen to educate and pass on her sense of wonder and delight at the world. I remember her waking me at different times to watch a comet or an electrical storm with her. She'd lead her three girls in wild dances in the infrequent Whyalla rain and roll with us in the 'green New Zealand grass' if we found any on our travels in Australia. She'd hold our hands in town and skip down the street with us, or go 'people spotting' where we'd observe strangers and decide what they were like based on what we saw. I still find myself doing this at times.

She could be a great Mum, but her other side was never far away; she could be indifferent, suddenly violent and horribly cruel.

Tracey was overweight as a child and Mum would sing 'Roly Poly' to her while cuddling her in bed. Tracey is now underweight and keeps a tight rein on her eating. She says she's terrified of 'losing control' and becoming fat again.

Mum loved us but would leave us alone at home or have us babysat by abusers so she could go drinking with her mates, to whom she was intensely loyal. She would keep us home from school to keep her company while she skived off work. When I was twelve she told me — with a needle hanging out of her arm — never to try drugs. A year later she told me not to use "any old crap" but to come to her and she'd make sure I got "decent shit."

My feelings about her were ambivalent but her death hit me hard. I suffered immeasurable guilt.

11

It was years before I knew the full story of Mum's death. She had been on parole and one of her conditions was that she keep out of pubs. She'd fallen and broken her wrist and had been to Wellington Hospital to have it plastered and to pick up a script for painkillers. Mum had chalky bones in her wrists; as a teenager she started deliberately breaking them to avoid school and other tasks she found unpleasant. As an adult she spent a lot of time with casts on. Sometimes she broke bones simply to get painkillers. She'd grow sick of the casts within a few days and would cut or soak them off. Her bones never had a chance to heal properly.

On her return from the hospital, newly plastered, she had stopped off at a pub for a 'quick one.' She was recognised by an off-duty cop who told her to leave. She pulled a pocketknife on him, was arrested and charged. Bailed pending a court appearance in a day or two, she returned to her little flat.

There were no kids there and no Rod. Tala her Golden Labrador had been put down because Rod didn't like him, so the flat was empty of all life. Did she feel abandoned? She had a bottle of barbiturates from the hospital — over six hundred of them according to the coroner's report.

Mum went to bed and took a handful of pills, washing them down with milk. She wrote a letter to her brother David (not Jenny's husband) asking him to care for Shelley while she went away for a while. She rang Aunty Trish a couple of times in a disturbed state. Before she slept she went to the neighbours' place. She was agitated and told them she'd be going to jail and her kids would be taken from her. The neighbours tried to calm her down and sent her home. She went back to bed, maybe took some more pills and went to sleep. Alone. Forever.

She was thirty-two.

Some hours later Rod returned to the flat. He'd been out drinking and had forgotten his key. He climbed in through a window and found Mum dead in bed, her body covered with pills from the spilled bottle, a half-empty pint of milk at her side. Rod called the police, who took Mum to the mortuary where Trish identified her. Trish then called us at the island.

After the doctor saw Grandma, Aunty Jenny organised the boat to take us from the island. There was talk of bringing Mum back to Rotoroa for burial. Grandma was grief-stricken. I was numb. Uncle Dave drove us from Auckland to Wellington.

I don't remember arriving back at Grandma's place. Tracey was already there, as were many of Mum's brothers and sisters. Shelley was in Christchurch with an uncle and wouldn't return until after the funeral.

Some of my aunties stripped the place where Mum had lived and died. I'd never seen the flat and they dismantled it without giving me the chance to see the place she'd been so proud of. This was probably the most upsetting thing to happen in those first days. I didn't confront them; it was too late by then. And they were just doing what they thought best.

Mum's possessions were taken to the sleepout and piled in the main room there. I spent about an hour lying on her bed, smelling the tobacco and her 'Mum' smell in the dark green curtains and bed linen, remembering how proud she'd been of sewing them herself. I cried there for the first time and rocked myself, wrapped in her blankets and my memories of her.

Michael, Mum's youngest brother, found me there and led me back to the house.

Mum's body was with the pathologist and hadn't yet

been autopsied, so no date could be set for a funeral. It was decided I should go to Papatahi to stay with Aunty Liz and spend a couple of days in peace there. That time passed quickly; I read and wandered around the farm, visiting my favourite places from all those years ago. I gave up my script; I didn't feel the least bit like the invincible Galadriel. Besides, that all seemed too juvenile now.

I felt empty and small and terribly guilty. I convinced myself I could have talked her out of dying. Perhaps she'd overdosed because she felt abandoned by her daughters? Mum had been sick and I'd failed in my responsibility to her. How could I ever forgive myself? This forgiveness eluded me for over twenty years.

We returned to Wellington after a couple of days. The family was still making a huge fuss of Grandma. I couldn't understand it; she had eight children and only one of them had died; we had only one mother, who was gone forever — surely that meant our loss was about eight times as great?

Uncle Dave and Aunty Jenny took me to the funeral home to say goodbye to Mum. As we pulled into the carpark we noticed a group of plainclothes cops in the burger bar across the road, who seemed to be watching us. Uncle Marau, himself a former cop, called Central Police Station to complain. The cops still wouldn't leave Mum alone.

Mum was in a room by herself in an open coffin. She looked pale, cold and lonely in her new white nightie. Her hair was shoulder length and coppery and longer than I remembered. She'd lost weight. I stepped forward to touch her face. Uncle Dave appeared behind me and placed a hand on my shoulder; I thought he wanted me to step away so I did. He only wanted to comfort me but inadvertently stopped me from saying a proper farewell. I'd said goodbye to Mum so many times before but this was the first time I truly didn't want to leave her. I wish I could have kissed her goodbye, smoothed her hair, touched her face.

I had wished for Mum's death on occasion, and even rehearsed it a few times already in my mind. I think this helped me through the period immediately following her suicide and added a sense of unreality to it. In public Tracey and I were both matter-of-fact that Mum had died, and in front of strangers acted with indifference we did not feel.

The funeral was short. Uncle Dave gave a moving tribute and didn't make her into someone she hadn't been. No one was told how perfect she'd been; her faults were well known to us all. Tracey stayed at Grandma's with an aunty; Shelley was still in the South Island. I was Mum's only girl to say goodbye and perhaps the one she would have least wanted there; hadn't she sent me away time and time again? Some of her mates sat at the back of the crematorium, barely recognisable in their good clothes and sobriety. I was glad to see them.

That night Tracey and I sat on the lounge floor reading through the sympathy cards. This way we learned that some of Mum's drinking buddies had collected a few dollars for Tracey, Shelley and me. We were offended that the money went towards her funeral expenses and wasn't given to us directly. It was good to see the number of cards we got, though. It reminded us that Mum was loved by a lot of people. I wondered if she knew that when she was alive.

The day after the funeral I drove back to Auckland with Uncle Dave. He was a wonderful loving man who had a deep intuitive understanding and great compassion; I loved him dearly. When I got back to my bedroom in Parnell I set up a little shrine to Mum. In the top drawer of my dressing table I placed the silver cross she'd given me for my fourteenth birthday, the death notices from the newspaper and the order of service from her funeral. To these I added her last letter to me; she'd written it on toilet paper a few days before she died.

Uncle Dave came into my room and saw my shrine. Placing his hand on my shoulder, just as he'd done at the funeral parlour, he called me Laurie. That had been Mum's name for me so I asked him not to use it any more, without telling him why. I think I hurt his feelings but wanted to reserve that name for Mum's use only; I was her Laurie Kim and no one was allowed to take that away from her.

While in Auckland I attended the Salvation Army with Jenny and Dave. I still had some religious beliefs and prayed that Mum might take the place I would no doubt earn in heaven; I was certain she'd never make it without my assistance. I planned to be especially good so she'd spend eternity happily, and maybe somewhere along the way I'd earn enough credits to join her when my turn came. It was hard, though, to be pure in mind and deed each day when there was possibly no reward in it for me. It wasn't long before I was misbehaving again. If Mum was counting on me to spend eternity singing with the angels, her rest will have been short indeed.

•

Mum died twenty-four years ago and I'm at last becoming aware of her as a person; she was flawed, sad, special and full of need. When I think of the day at the funeral parlour I replay it in my mind. This time I touch her. I see myself as if in a dream. I reach for her, lift her from her casket and hold her close. I rock her and stroke her forehead, and tell her that I'll miss her. In my mind she is small so I can hold her easily. I'm smaller too — a little girl cradling her favourite doll. There I sit, a young child, maybe three or four years old. I'm in a little rocking chair cradling my dead mother doll in my lap. I rock her and croon to her. I brush her hair — shoulder length and coppery — back from her cool forehead, an act she performed for me several times in my short life. She is so fragile, cold and vulnerable, my dead mother doll. I hold her and rock her for a long time, my tears falling on her porcelain face, pooling in the sockets of her eyes. It is as if she cries with me. Then when I am ready, I kiss her forehead and lift her gently back into her coffin. I am once again fourteen and she is thirty-two.

Who was she, this mother? When I'm lonely or sad I miss her and cry for her. Although at times she was an appalling mother, she's the only one I ever had and I know she loved me.

She was so many people: the woman who woke me to listen to the thunder, the one who danced in the rain, the fearless climber of fountains and the one who staggered drunkenly down a busy street to escape from her children. Or is she the one who sat on my chest and tried to squeeze the life from me? Or maybe the woman who on a warm November morning reached over to me and smiled, tousling my hair?

I now know she was all of these people and she probably felt as confused about her many facets as the rest of us did.

12

Two weeks after Mum's funeral I began fourth form studies at Epsom Girls Grammar School. EGGS was completely different to Wellington High School. All the girls in my new class seemed rich and most of them snooty as well. The curriculum was standard, but the methods of teaching differed greatly and I thought the new teachers were awful. Although the school's entrance exam placed me in the top class, my marks slipped. Living in a happy well-adjusted, functional family was not the panacea I'd imagined. The love of Jenny, Dave and their children was not enough to compensate for the sense of dislocation I felt.

How could the sun still rise and fall when my life was suddenly so different? I spent hours in my room memorising passages from Shakespeare. My favourite line was Lear's uttered at the death of Cordelia. "… No, no, no life. Why should a dog, a horse, a rat have life and thou no breath at all …"

I grieved deeply and secretly for Mum. I wasn't aware how affected I was by her loss. I was rude and insolent to my teachers, even stunning myself at times with my cheek.

I was the worst girl in the school. It wasn't that difficult.

Miss Coulter was my French teacher. She wore Cleopatra kohl on her eyes. She was ancient and always wore a long fur coat and thick black stockings, whatever the weather. Her black and silver hair was pulled back into a bun. In Miss Coulter's class we stood and read aloud from crusty old plays, all in French. Everyone knew I wanted to be an actress; Miss Coulter was pretty theatrical herself. As it's hard to act well in a language you barely understand, her classes made me feel like a failure at acting as well as French.

The things I'd been good at and proud of at Wellington High were failing me here. I was despairing.

My first real run-in with Madame came on April Fool's Day. Miss Coulter was trying to be funny and made a comment to the class about students faking dental appointments on April Fool's Day. I muttered something about this not working for staff as they all had false teeth.

Miss Coulter took offence to this comment and pulled herself up to her full five feet four inches before kicking me out of class. I flounced off to the bike stands, climbed aboard my big yellow chopper bike and pedalled off. I didn't return to school that day. I cycled around the Auckland waterfront in my uniform, just daring someone to ask why I wasn't at school. I had dark thoughts about Madame; I'd get even — I'd find a way to wreck those ugly black stockings.

My best friend Cathy sat next to me in French. She hated Miss Coulter too. Cathy and I cooked up a plan and unfortunately shared it with the whole class. I was to stand up during the next French lesson, say I felt unwell and dramatically faint at Madame's feet. Cathy would throw water from her drink bottle over my face to 'bring me round', but would make sure the bulk of the liquid splashed down Madame's legs. The old bat would have to remove her stockings then. The time for the heinous act arrived. I stood up looking suitably pained and the class erupted into giggles. Miss Coulter glared and before I had a chance to throw myself at her feet, kicked me out of the classroom. Then to add insult to injury she had me banned from the sick bay.

I made a genuine effort to participate in her class one day. I asked what I thought was an intelligent question: "Does France use the metric system yet, Madame?". She ignored me so I repeated my question a little louder. She spat, "They invented the metric system, you stupid girl," and henceforth pretended I didn't exist. Zut alors! And I had been so good at French at Wellington High.

My chopper (a big yellow boy's bicycle with a banana seat and macho handlebars) provided transport to school and back. I preferred riding to catching the bus; it gave me privacy, independence and exercise. I would cycle to school each morning on my bike singing Helen Reddy's 'I am Woman.'

The two terms I spent at EGGS were painful for my teachers and for me. I was fourteen, an awful age for anyone. My Mum had just died; I'd almost been murdered the previous year; I was in a new family, new town and new school. Of course I was distressed. My teachers were aware of some of these things; some of them made allowances.

One day I came into class late, and unusually for me, I entered quietly.

The teacher, a nice young woman, was at the front of the room and had just taken the roll. She was unaware I had come into the room and continued to speak to my classmates.

"I know we put up with some bad behaviour from Lauren. Things are hard for her. Her mother committed suicide a few weeks ago. It'll take her a while to settle in."

She took a breath, as though about to say more, when she noticed the discomfort of some of the girls in the front row. She turned towards the door and paled, then flushed to see me standing there.

I found a seat and did my lessons quietly, aware of the mostly supportive stares from the girls sitting near me.

I hated that school, but in spite of it all I made some friends. Cathy was gorgeous. Blonde with green eyes and an American accent, she'd lived all over the world, including Mexico and Burma. She was a Bay City Rollers fan and introduced me to their music. Angie was pretty too; she had shiny dark hair and a beautiful smile. She was fun and a talented pianist. Together she and I wrote a musical called 'Life.'

A small group of us developed code names based on our initials and wrote messages to each other in an old exercise book. We flung it around the classroom to one another while the teacher's back was turned. We wrote secret messages and plans in the book as well as highly uncomplimentary personal remarks about our tutors and their teaching methods. Our form teacher, who obviously wasn't as blind as we thought, confiscated the book during a maths lesson.

It had just landed with an audible thwack on my desk.

Mrs Rapson spun around — quite a feat for one who looked to be at least a hundred years old — grabbed the book and placed it on her desk, which was right next to mine.

Now I was in trouble, as were my co-offenders; she'd recognise their handwriting. The book contained language and sentiments not fit for the elderly, let alone the girls from EGGS.

I caught the eye of Jenny, one of the others who wrote in the confiscated volume. She skimmed one of her other exercise books across the floor. I managed to switch it with the incriminating document while the old dragon was writing on the blackboard.

Mrs Rapson was livid. She was certain she'd captured a prize far more valuable than another girl's exercise book. She yelled at me anyway. I paid her back by tipping a soft drink into her open briefcase later that week.

While all this was happening at school, the churchy side of my life trundled along rather different lines. I enjoyed spending time with a more mixed group of people. We had a Youth Group weekend trip to Turangawaewae Marae at Ngaruawahia. We were told we were only the second Pakeha group to get permission to stay there. It was a huge honour and a lot of fun.

Despite agitating by one other girl and myself we were segregated overnight, boys in one sleeping hut, girls in another. We slept on mattresses on the floor, rows and rows of restless bodies, snores and coughs punctuating our sleep. Meals were varied and the food plentiful and the people of the marae generous and patient. Between scheduled lessons and activities we walked along the banks of the Waikato.

I had my first real kiss on that weekend, with a boy from my youth group. I'd never noticed him before he invited me to join him in the back of a bus where a few of the older kids had gathered for some chaste fumbling. It was dark in the bus and other teens rustled and tussled. He kissed me wetly on the lips for a few moments, then put his tongue in my mouth. I was astonished. Did the church allow people to do things like that? It wasn't nice, so I didn't mind if it was banned; I had no plans to do it again in a hurry.

The next day the new 'couples' went for a walk on the bridge over the Waikato. The boys piggybacked the girls across the bridge. The boy I'd been kissed by the night before was a lot shorter than me so I piggybacked him instead. We never spoke to one another again after that weekend.

Apart from school and church there was the Bay City Roller fan club. On Saturdays around a hundred BCR fans met in an old building in Shortland Street, downtown Auckland. I walked there from Parnell in as much tartan as I could muster.

In the room next to our meeting place a band called Dragon often practised. Although their music was good we thought it wasn't a patch on the Rollers. The guys in the band were good-natured and put up with us with considerable grace.

The fan club was a great diversion from real life. It was

run by 'Granny-fan,' a woman in her 60s. We got a lot of media attention — there always seemed to be a print, radio or TV journalist around. We taped 'Roll Over Rocktober' jingles for Radio Hauraki and plotted publicity stunts. One of my ideas was to kidnap Andy Shaw — a kids' TV host — while he was on air. Andy wasn't too keen on this idea and refused politely. Getting to talk to Andy in person was reward enough for me anyway.

13

I loved being the centre of attention. When Auckland Salvationists staged the rock musical Spirit I was near the front of the queue for a part. The musical — based on the Acts of the Apostles — was full of singing and dancing and would be an acceptable outlet for my theatrical streak. I have always been slightly uncoordinated but didn't want to admit to that then. I gained a part and put all my study of stagecraft to good use, positioning myself upstage at the apexes of imaginary triangles so I'd draw the eye. Unfortunately the woman who was directing the production knew all these tricks and thwarted me, placing me at less conspicuous spots on the stage in the hope that my lack of coordination would be hidden.

I had two speaking parts and was able to take centre stage for a few precious minutes. I loved it. We played at Auckland Grammar's Centennial Theatre for a week, then toured to Whangarei and Dannevirke for one show in each town. While we were playing at the Centennial Theatre I met Laurence, a pretty boy the same age as me. He worked the lighting for the show and was as into drama as I was. We exchanged hurried glances, my cheeks feeling as flushed as his. My heart beat painfully when he was near, confusing me. I'd never felt this kind of attraction for a boy before. One of the girls in the cast told me Laurence fancied me. I stammered that I thought he was cute too, but neither of us ever got the courage to ask the other out.

Aunty Jenny, with her wonderful singing voice, shone on centre stage. She was to perform a couple of numbers but she became unwell a couple of months before opening night and had to pull out.

Aunty Jen had always been a human dynamo, racing from one activity to another. Now she was pale, lethargic and stressed. She'd been working hard for the Army as well as caring for her own three kids and me. She was fading fast.

I was catching the train to Wellington (Wellington! Home!) to spend my May school holidays with Aunty Trish and her family in Wainuiomata. As I left the house in Parnell, Aunty Jenny was lying on the couch. Uncle Dave had just called an ambulance to her. She had her period and due to a blood clotting problem was literally bleeding to death. She looked awful, but I was so excited about returning to Wellington I paid her little attention.

"See you in two weeks. Love you." I kissed her cheek and ran for the door. Free! I felt like an expatriate in Auckland, all my thoughts on the mythical perfect homeland whose shores I'd been all too willing to escape a few months earlier.

I took the day train through the North Island. A beautiful trip but my mind was less on the scenery than the promise of arrival at my destination. The train sang 'Wellington, Wellington, Wellington' as it sped along.

In early evening we passed through a series of tunnels before entering the city I'd been longing for. Aunty Trish was waiting for me at the station. I remembered to tell her that Jenny was sick. Trish phoned Auckland when we arrived back at her home. Jenny was hospitalised and having a blood transfusion. She was connected to drips and other tubes and had had several tests. She was near death.

That night I shared a bedroom with my cousins Lynne and Phillip. Leaning against the wall in that room was an oil painting of Aunty Jenny. It was extremely unflattering and had a spooky, almost luminous face and eyes that followed you everywhere.

"That is so creepy," said Phillip, echoing my thoughts exactly. We turned the picture to face the wall and prayed hard before we went to sleep.

Jenny recovered. The next morning Aunty Trish was

irate that we'd turned the painting around and put it in her own room for the rest of my stay.

Grandma said she blamed me for Jenny's illness — caring for me had been far too hard for her. How many deaths and illnesses is one child supposed to be responsible for? I didn't feel I was to blame for Jenny's state. I still blamed myself for Mum, though.

Being back in Wellington was intoxicating; I was unhappy in Auckland and blamed the city itself for this. I guess it was easier than facing the real reasons — Mum's death and my guilt surrounding it and simply being fourteen — these things conspired against me.

I saw Grandma and Tracey again and some of my old Wellington High classmates. Before a week was over the holiday began to drag. Wainuiomata, although part of greater Wellington, was a long way from the parts of town I wanted to see. I didn't have enough money to catch a bus into town and felt trapped in the backblocks. The Wellington friends I'd dreamed about had moved into new cliques. I didn't fit with them the way I once had. Tracey and I didn't get on the same either. I was disappointed and became pouty and rude to Aunty Trish. This resulted in a hiding from Uncle Marau. Despite my loneliness in New Zealand's biggest city I found I was actually looking forward to getting back to Auckland.

The train trip back to Auckland was confusing. I felt torn between my old life and new. When in Wellington I had begun to long for Auckland and the peace of an ordered environment. When in Auckland I dreamed of Wellington. Would I ever be happy where I was, or was I condemned to always pine for what I couldn't have? The prospect of a whole life of not quite belonging was dismal. I felt subdued on reaching the other end.

To cover my confusion I retreated into a fantasy world. I made up stories about anything. One of my silliest was woven around Dad's younger brother who lived in California. He pumped gas in a petrol station there but I liked to believe he was an agent for all the biggest Hollywood stars.

The story went like this: my uncle had met The Osmonds and told them about his poor recently-bereaved niece in New Zealand. The Osmond family wanted to help me out and invited me to stay with them for a few months at their home in Provo, Utah.

I concocted this elaborate tale and shared it with anyone under the age of fifteen who'd listen to me.

I wanted to be part of a big, happy, supportive family and since the Waltons weren't real I had to choose the Osmonds. I was actually living in a real family for a change but my mindset hadn't caught up with that fact yet.

There were times I almost believed I was going to live with the Osmond family. I soon threw them over totally, though, for the Bay City Rollers. The Rollers seemed like much more grown-up icons somehow.

The Rollers provided new ways for me to get into trouble at school. EGGS had a hideous blue and gold towelling romper suit we had to wear for phys-ed. I chose to wear my BCR fan club T-shirt over the top of it. Not allowed. Another day I wore stripey BCR socks with my school uniform instead of the regulation light fawn — that earned me a detention.

I still missed Wellington dreadfully. When I was alone in my room I'd sing to myself songs like 'I Wanna go Home' and 'Country Road, Take Me Home.' If I was ever travelling on the motorway I'd look out for Mount Wellington signs and screw my eyes up so only the last word on them was visible.

Aunty Jenny was much better but not as vibrant as she'd been. She seemed to have moved down a gear or two and spent less time running from place to place. She told me a couple of times how much she missed my Mum. I hadn't given much thought to her grief until then. Coming barely eighteen months after Grandad's death, Mum's had struck her hard. I felt a new respect for her after thinking about that.

The second term arrived and was no improvement on the first. School was a drag. Monotonous, meaningless classes were sandwiched between brief periods of freedom. I couldn't see the point of school.

One highlight was a Shakespearean play performed at the Centennial Theatre at Auckland (Boys) Grammar School, to which all the local high schools were invited. Of course the girls' schools attended a different session to one the boys went to. They didn't want us to catch those boy germs. Laurence, the boy I had met during Spirit, was up in the lighting box during the performance our school attended. I saw him and sneaked up there to watch the show among a group of boys. I still blushed and stammered around Laurence but couldn't pass up the chance to thumb my nose at the stupid school system. I sat next to him in the lighting box, my heart racing and my spirit freer that it had seemed for ages. It was completely innocent; the only physical contact between us was an accidental, but electric, brushing of hands, but I felt wicked as all hell for being there.

I could see the auditorium clearly and saw a few of my classmates nudging one another and pointing me out. I'm sure they were dreadfully disappointed that none of the EGGS teachers noticed me there and ordered my removal. At the end of the play I rejoined my class for the walk back to Epsom. I'd showed them.

Despite the disappointing 'triumphant return' to Wellington, I still yearned to go back there. The annual Salvation Army Congress was held there. Jenny (now fully recovered) and Dave were attending and as I was from

Wellington, I was certain I'd get an invite too. I would of course attend the Congress functions, but I'd make a greater effort to see my old friends. I plotted and planned. I was in for a big disappointment. Congress was during the school term and I had spent the May holidays in Wellington. I was being selfish expecting too many holidays. I had to remain in Auckland.

Aunty Jenny arranged for me to stay at The Grange, a Salvation Army Girls' Home in Epsom and attend school from there. It was only for a few days and Aunty Jenny said I could attend the Roller fan club, as usual, on Saturday. This promise sweetened the package a little.

Things went okay at The Grange until Friday night, my third night there, when I mentioned my planned fan club visit. "Oh, you're not going there," said the Salvation Army Officer in charge, who refused to phone Wellington to check if I was telling the truth. Her assumption that I was lying stung me into action. Oh yes I am going there, I thought to myself as I went to bed.

The next morning I got up with the other girls, gathered my things and was out the door before breakfast. I walked to the fan club, had a great time and decided I was definitely not returning to The Grange. With an audience of several approving girls I made a few obscene calls to the officer in charge there, so she wasn't expecting me back. I went instead on the train with Nadira, a former classmate of mine, to Granny-fan's house north of Auckland. She knew I was doing a bunk and phoned The Grange to let them know I was safe. The officer spluttered that she'd never even heard some of the words I'd used over the phone that afternoon. I was doubtful of the truth of that statement but felt victorious. I had slapped a few faces and made my point about being left behind. I read a book of stories by O. Henry which Granny had placed by my bed.

Before I could sleep I had to make a decision. Would I

apologise to Jenny and Dave and return to their place? I felt I'd hurt them enough. I wanted, though, to move on. I just had to return to Wellington. Nadira concurred. The next day I went to stay with Nadira's brother and his boyfriend in central Auckland. This was my first conscious experience of 'gayness' and I found it fascinating. The guys were great to me and let me phone Dad from their flat, even though it was a toll call.

Dad agreed I could come to live with him and his girlfriend Helen in their flat at Lyall Bay, a Wellington suburb. He sent me a plane ticket. I was going home.

14

Dad met me at the airport with a hug and no lecture. Helen had made me up a bed in their spare room — another room of my own. Tracey was still living in Miramar with Grandma while Shelley was living in the Hutt with Aunty Trish and Uncle Marau. Our little family had been through so many combinations that this didn't seem unusual. Our relatives had divided us up in the way that most suited them and we were grateful that they wanted us at all.

As I was only fourteen I was under the legal school leaving age, but it was near the end of the school year and I argued all the classes would be studying for exams which I'd be unable to sit, so I talked my way to freedom. During the day I'd read or wander around catching up with old mates. I also spent time at Grandma's.

Abba's 'Dancing Queen' was Number One and the Bay City Rollers got a fair amount of airplay too.

The Rollers were due to arrive in New Zealand at the end of 1976 for a series of concerts. On their arrival in Auckland the band was interviewed by Dylan Taite, a television journalist. The Rollers walked out on this interview when Mr Taite asked something offensive related to the Rollers not sanctioning a New Zealand fanclub.

It was so unbelievable that the Rollers were in New Zealand and not half a world away. Even the sun shone brighter with them here. New Zealand felt gripped by Rollermania.

The morning of the Rollers' arrival in Wellington a group of about twenty of us Rollermaniacs waited at the airport all tartaned and scarved and ready to prostrate ourselves at the feet of our idols. We were photographed by some baffled Japanese tourists, then told by airport staff that the Rollers had been met on the tarmac by a limo which had whisked them to their hotel. We left disappointed and caught buses to the James Cook Hotel. As we were conspicuous in our tartan outfits and spiky hair we weren't able to get into the hotel itself and had to amuse ourselves by standing outside the lobby and gazing up to the hotel windows. The Rollers were on the second-to-top floor and their windows were under the letters 'HO' and 'TE' of 'James Cook Hotel.'

We saw them and screamed; they waved to us, we screamed even louder. We tried to get to them but the police and security guards repelled every attempt. It was wonderful.

I told lies to the massed girls: "Yes, of course I was at the Auckland concert — I fainted three times — Les smiled at me when they were playing 'Dedication.'" Blah blah blah. My lies made me feel important.

We gave radio and press interviews from our spot outside the hotel. I lied some more. I was good at this.

I spotted someone I had been to school with entering the hotel. Her mother was a member of house management at the James Cook. She took my tartan scarf and posters from a couple of the other girls and promised to have them autographed by the Rollers themselves. She returned an hour later. Only one of the items had been signed — my scarf! My tartan scarf — usually tied to my left wrist — grubby, stained and signed by the Rollers! I could never ever take it off again.

Sadly for me I was such a liar that no one (except those who were at the hotel that day) ever fully believed me.

The night of the concert, crowds of tartan-clad teens and pre-teens bussed or were driven to the Wellington Showbuildings. We pounded on the closed doors, chanted and screamed. "We want the Rollers, we need the Rollers, give us the Rollers." We thought they were much bigger than Jesus.

The doors finally opened and we rushed in. There were seats set out for us, in front of which was a small clear area. Closer to the stage a big wooden barrier had been erected to keep us away from our idols. Before the opening act we were told by security that we were to remain seated at all times or the concert would be called off. Yeah, right.

The opening act was a local band called Billy Starr. They were okay but definitely not the real thing. We cheered heartily at the end of their set in celebration that they'd finally finished.

Then lights dimmed, there was movement on stage — and there they were — Les, Eric, Derek, Woody and Pat, the new guy.

As the Rollers took the stage, police and security guards filed between the barrier and the stage and formed a second line of defence. Gee, they must have been scared of us.

No one stayed seated — we all rushed the barrier, pushing against girls who pushed other girls who got squashed against the wooden wall in front of the stage.

Some fans fainted and were dragged over the barrier by police and security guards. The St Johns Ambulance team attended and cared for anyone hurt in the crush. They were kept busy.

Some girls managed to get to the stage, to be tackled by police or roadies before reaching the band. Oh yeah, they're really here. It's really, truly the Bay City Rollers.

The next morning, ears still ringing from the night before, I hitchhiked with a friend from Grandma's place to the James Cook. We were hassled by the guys who picked us up ("Why chase those dorks when there are good Kiwi blokes like us around?") but they ended up dropping us where we wanted to go. The Rollers were leaving later that morning and we had to be there to say good bye.

This time our heroes walked right past us — I could have reached out and touched Eric, but I was too busy squeezing my legs together so I wouldn't wet my pants.

I had ordered a taxi with a couple of other girls. Our driver was in position to pull out directly behind the Roller's limo so we could race them to the airport. A Radio New Zealand journalist outside the hotel cornered me though, and never being one to pass up a chance at self-promotion, I gave an interview. "Yes, we are rapt in the Rollers … I certainly did spend all night here outside the hotel … I was at the Auckland concert too but the Wellington one was better."

I ran to our cab and we sped off. We remained two cars behind the Rollers all the way to the airport; the taxi driver seemed even more disappointed by this than we were. We didn't get to talk to our heroes at traffic lights, but hell, I was on National Radio!

15

Life after the Roller concert was boring, boring, boring. We needed to do something; we needed a fan club. I started one.

I put notices on the walls of all the major record stores in central Wellington asking Roller fans to contact me if they wanted to join. I put Grandma's phone number on them as I was back living with her. Helen had got sick of coming home to find me wearing her clothes and perfume and had asked me to leave.

The phone rang day and night with girls (mostly) wanting to join up. Initially I had them send their membership money to Granny-fan in Auckland. She then sent them down their badges and T-shirt. Soon, though, I decided to collect the dosh myself — after all, this was *my* BCR fan club. This was a mistake. Disgruntled fans and their grumpy fathers began to complain when promised badges and certificates failed to arrive. Granny-fan bailed me out.

I began to spend my days hanging out at Radio Windy and 2ZM where I begged the DJs to play more and more Roller music. More often than not I got my way — even the National Programme played their music sometimes.

The Rollermaniacs met on Saturday mornings above a dance studio in Courtenay Place, central Wellington. We'd get together and swap posters and gossip and dance to Roller music. We became well known and got invited as a group to the re-opening of Ziggy's, a disco in Vivian Street. We did our special Roller dances all dressed up in the gears. We were hot. We also spent a lot of time at Avalon TV studios during the taping of live segments for shows such as *Ready to Roll*, the weekly Top 20 music show.

One of our big adventures was kidnapping a Radio Windy jock after he made disparaging remarks about us on air. We grabbed him from the foyer of Radio Windy after his shift one Friday evening. His punishment was to spend the weekend at the house of Terri, one of the Roller fans, and four or five other Rollermaniacs including my sister Tracey and me. Our plan was to subject Johnny to non-stop BCR music, to help him appreciate its artistic merit. When he met Terri's mother, an attractive single woman, his punishment melted. Rather than being handcuffed to a chair for 48 hours listening to BCR music he spent his sentence in bed with Terri's mother. We were treated to their muffled sounds from the bed on the mezzanine floor above us.

Johnny did call his station and describe his imaginary punishment in a series of hourly bulletins. It was good publicity for the fan club and for Radio Windy.

Some little trauma or other triggered one of my fantasy phases again. It was becoming apparent to me that these lapses in reality took place when I was stressed or upset. This time I became the illegitimate half-sister of Eric, my favourite Roller. As proof of my heritage I would flash my blue eyes; they may have been similar in colour to Eric's but any resemblance ended there. In a strange twist to this story, I began to say that my half-brother had sent me an engagement ring from Scotland — talk about mixed metaphors. Fortunately I grew out of the need to lie. The scruffy-looking ring which I'd found in Grandma's garden was returned to that spot after too many people questioned its authenticity.

I was fifteen and ready to get a job. My reluctance to go anywhere without my personally-signed tartan scarf caused some difficulties so I eventually retired it from my wardrobe.

My first job was working as a cleaner at Wellington Hospital. I swept and washed the main corridors before graduating to ward work. The wards were more fun as I got to interact with the patients. It was my job to keep the ward clean and provide patients with food trays at meal times and with tea and coffee.

I was in awe of the nurses. They were so knowledgeable and professional. One was kind to me when I discovered an old woman had died in her bed ("Excuse me nurse, I can't wake Mrs Thingie up for her cup of tea"). I wanted to be a nurse but thought I wasn't clever enough; perhaps I could be a nurse aide instead? The doctors were on a different plane entirely. I think cleaning staff were invisible to those gods who seemed to possess power over life and death and were obviously far superior to us ordinary people.

I eventually left the hospital, tired of being bossed around by my supervisor. Although I knew I was thick, she seemed even stupider to me and I felt she shouldn't have been giving me orders.

It also felt like the right time to find someone to have a proper sexual relationship with. I had the idea that it would be hideously embarrassing to find my soulmate and be sexually inexperienced for 'him.' I needed some practice and fast. I settled on a DJ from 2ZM. I spent hours each day sitting on the stairs at Broadcasting House watching him work through the studio window. He looked like Roger Daltrey from The Who, with long golden curls and a sexy smile. He was about six years older than me. When I thought he was beginning to tire of my attentions I deliberately stayed away from the studio for a week. When I resumed my vigil he was all mine. He'd missed me. He invited me to his flat for a drink and we ended up in bed. In answer to his question about whether or not I'd 'done it' before I said, "Of course, with two other guys", thinking that made me sound worldly. The sex wasn't memorable. When I got up in the morning he'd gone to work and left $5 on the bench for me. I didn't like to ask what the money was for but took it anyway.

God had no real place in my life now. The religion that

had been important to me had been supplanted by cynicism. I was a rebel with few clues and the tattered remains of a moral sense. All I wanted was to have fun.

I went on the dole for a while. Tracey had also left school by now so we'd visit the Labour Department together. The rest of our time we spent sunbathing on the roof at Grandma's — all slathered up with cooking oil or baby oil. It wasn't a bad life. We were both utterly unskilled, totally free and getting paid for it. We were part of the minority that gives the unemployed a bad name. We loved it.

I was still doing fan club stuff when I got my second job as an office junior at an appliance repair company — the fan club cost money. I lost that job when I decided on a whim to relocate to Auckland. I had the idea to move one day, a train ticket the next. I can precisely place this visit to Auckland because while I was walking up Queen Street to see Granny-fan, a newsflash announced the death of Elvis.

I wanted money and Auckland was an even harder place to find unskilled work than Wellington was, so I soon headed back to Grandma's. I'd avoided Jenny and Dave while I was up there. I felt uncomfortable about the way I'd betrayed their hospitality but not ready to apologise.

On my return to Wellington I got a job as a life claims clerk at Commercial Union Assurance in central Wellington.

I was going through a self-conscious period and couldn't bear to travel on buses — I was sensitive about my developing body and worried everyone would look at my breasts — so decided I'd walk to and from work. The nicest way to get there was around the waterfront, a seven-kilometre journey, so I began each working day with a two-hour walk and ended the day with a similar hike home. To go with this new exercise regime I decided I should drastically cut down my eating to make my curves less obvious. I was walking four hours a day, using the stairs rather than the elevator at work (my office was on the tenth floor) and eating probably fewer than five hundred calories a day. I was obsessed. My weight plummeted and I was delighted. For four months, rain or shine, I did this and only stopped when I found myself unable to stand, let alone walk.

16

Shortly before my sixteenth birthday, while walking to work, I saw a large red ship berthed at the Overseas Terminal. *Coast Guard* was written on her bow in huge white letters and she bore the crest and colours of the United States Coast Guard. The *Polar Star* was beautiful. It was one of those summer mornings where the sky was almost purple and you know it would be sweltering. The *Polar Star* shimmered in the heat. I was entranced.

There were a few newspaper articles about the ship. She was an icebreaker and berthed in Wellington so her crew could have some R and R and restock the ship before spending summer in the Antarctic. She was here for a week and Wellingtonians were encouraged to phone the 'Dial a Sailor' hotline and invite crew members home for some Kiwi hospitality. I decided to round up some friends and visit the ship. It was so big, clean and full of Americans. Mum had taken Tracey, Shelley and me to visit a US Navy warship once. This seemed more relaxed. I joined some of the crew in laughing at the girls who'd got themselves all dressed up in order to catch a sailor. Spiky heels and big hair on a wharf just didn't look right.

The American sailors seemed a nice bunch. Not one of them put the hard word on my friends or me; it was fun being around them.

Just after the *Polar Star* left Wellington, the US Coast Guard cutter *Glacier* pulled into port. The *Glacier* was smaller and older. I made friends with two crew members, Bill and Mark, and took them home to meet Grandma. Bill was older than Mark — slim, blond and rugged. His smile was open and disguised a smarmy nature, which I didn't recognise at the time. Mark had darker hair, was more clean-cut and tended towards tubbiness.

Bill and Mark had hired a little red Mini and often

picked me up on my walk home in the evenings so I could take them sightseeing. During one roaring southerly we went to Island Bay and drove up a hill to a new housing development, Southgate. There was still a lot of empty land there and we walked over an exposed section and leaned our bodies into the wind. We tipped over at least 45° to the horizon at a point where the land dropped steeply away. It was exhilarating and amazing to get so much pleasure from such an uncomplicated act.

I missed Bill and Mark when they left and wrote many letters to them while they were on the ice. Before they left Wellington Bill told me he fancied me and would send for me on his return to the States. I didn't take him seriously but he didn't realise that. It led to an interesting misunderstanding a couple of months later.

I loved my job at Commercial Union. I'm sure I was a pain at times. I was still keen on the BCRs and kept a poster of them sellotaped to my desk. I was obsessed with my weight and didn't mind who knew about it. I was good at my work, though, so they didn't have too much to complain about. Part of my job was to prepare life insurance claims before sending them to the actuarial department for further assessment. I would send messages in code to the guys in the next office each time I sent files across to them. There were soon secret messages in all sorts of codes and languages passing between the actuarial and life claims offices. It made the working day go faster for all of us. It was a happy time, enjoyable and busy. I was discovering an active mind and was realising that some people found me interesting company.

The BCR fan club wasn't so busy any more; I needed a new challenge. Doctor Hook came to town and listening to their music on the radio I felt I could grow to like it. I hung out at Radio Windy while they were doing an interview there and introduced myself to the band as they left the studio. They were nice and didn't mind at all if I started a club for them, especially as I seemed so experienced at such matters.

I scored free concert tickets for Tracey and me and we set about finding out all about Dr Hook so we could start a fan club. We searched through magazines and newspapers and learned all about them.

The concert was great — we stood right at the front, cheered and yelled like we'd loved them for ages. We liked their song about 'teenaged, blue-eyed groupies', although we had no plans to bonk band members — Dr Hook wasn't that kind of band, nor were we those kind of girls.

We saw them off at Wellington Airport. They felt like old friends. My favourite band member was Dennis Locorriere, while Tracey fancied Willard Henke. Reading an album cover we learned that Willard came from Flagstaff, Arizona. We set about tracking him down. The phone directory gave us the number of the only Henke living in Flagstaff. We dialled it. A girl answered the phone; we'd been given the number of Willard's former wife and were speaking to the babysitter caring for their daughter. Mrs Henke was at work — would we like the phone number there? Sensitive souls that we were, we phoned Mrs Henke at her work and obtained her ex's unlisted phone number and address.

Willard got a few frenzied letters and phone calls from us. He even sent us postcards when the band was on tour. We felt so special. Willard thought it was hilarious that some fans from New Zealand had tracked him down, something that no US fan had ever done.

January 1978 arrived. I was still gainfully employed, skinny and living with Grandma. Part of my pay (I earned a whole $90 a fortnight) was going to repay Grandma for a hefty phone bill I'd clocked up calling Arizona, Scotland and Canada. It had become my habit to look through the penpals columns in fan magazines and try to phone interesting-sounding people who advertised in them. I had a regular phone pal in Vancouver until Grandma realised and put a toll bar on her phone. I had to write to Judi after that, much to my dismay — having a pen pal seemed pedestrian.

In mid-January *The Evening Post* carried a small notice about the *Polar Star*. She had experienced engine difficulties in the Antarctic and her tour had been shortened. She would be back in Wellington in a few days before returning to Seattle, her home port.

I was excited. Although I had no friends among the crew of the *Polar Star*, the visit promised an interesting diversion.

The day the *Polar Star* arrived I sat on a desk in the Commercial Union office watching the harbour and Overseas Passenger Terminal. I was beside myself with excitement watching the ship berth. She was so big and beautiful.

The *Polar Star* was in port a week. The next day after work and each day after that I boarded the ship and made new friends. Americans were so cool — I just had to go to the States one day.

On the fifth day I jokingly told one of the sailors that I was going to stow away on his ship. He laughed. As I left the ship that night the captain was standing on the quarterdeck.

"I'm stowing away to the States on your ship."

He smiled. "Are you now? All right then."

Poor man, I'm sure those words haunted him in the months to come.

That night at Grandma's, where I was sleeping in Mum's old room, I had a long think about things. Life in New Zealand was going well for me but it was a little tame. Why shouldn't I stow away? I was brave enough and it was only a twenty-day voyage. I'd get to see America and I wouldn't have to save a cent for airfares. I'd just bought a few new books — *The Narnia Chronicles* as a boxed set and the complete set of Mum's favourite author, Jacqueline Sussan — an eclectic selection. I had new books to read on the ship so I wouldn't get bored. The more I thought about stowing away, the more sense it made.

By the next morning my mind was made up.

17

The first thing to set the plan in action was to see my manager at work.

"Things are turning bad at Grandma's place. I have to leave Wellington tomorrow and move to Auckland. Can I please have my final pay?"

He seemed surprised by the lack of notice and tried to persuade me to stay. I said I'd remain until the next day and was paid up until then. With my final pay I bought two identical red, white and blue tote bags, a torch and some batteries. I felt prepared for my journey.

After work I went to the *Polar Star* and over a card game on the mess deck I announced my plan. Only one guy seemed to take me seriously and motioned me to shut up and see him later. His name was Joe. He was from Salem, Oregon, and at twenty was already a big bear of a man. I warmed to him immediately.

When we were alone he asked if I was serious. When he realised I intended to do it, he promised to help. I think the same imp which wanted me to seek excitement spurred him on. He didn't seem to have any problems with the Coast Guard; in fact he seemed to love his job. It was Thursday evening and the ship was leaving port on Saturday morning. I was to meet him on the mess deck after work on Friday and we'd take it from there. I was on my way.

I packed my tote bags on Thursday night and had another look at the calendar behind my bedroom door. Counting off the days from 20 January through to 9 February reassured me. Twenty days was not too long to stay in hiding. Besides I'd probably get caught by the end of that time and returned to New Zealand.

Friday morning I said goodbye to Grandma rather offhandedly. She didn't ask why I was taking the bus that day rather than walking. Nor did she query the two tote bags I was carrying. Tracey was still asleep when I left. Never mind, she'd have tons of time to catch up with what I'd done.

As I left Grandma's I said a silent goodbye to her house, doubting I'd ever see it again. Despite the shelter it had provided me for long periods of my life, I wasn't at all sad to be leaving it. I tried to imprint it on my memory, however; the green house on the corner with the browny-red roof, the flowering pohutukawa in the front and the big yellow Salvation Army home on the hill behind it.

I worked at Commercial Union that day in a daze. Nothing seemed important. My co-workers were sad I was leaving and I had a couple of offers of temporary accommodation. I smiled sweetly and said I was well set up, thanks, and I'd send them a letter from Auckland. I couldn't tell them what I planned; they would have narked on me before the ship even left the harbour.

At 5pm I left to walk to the Overseas Terminal. On my way there I dropped off one of my bags at an office on the wharf.

I met Joe as arranged. He seemed surprised to see me but at no stage tried to back out of his promise to help. He hid my bag and I returned to the wharf for my second one. I deliberately chose identical bags in case someone noticed me taking two bags aboard and became suspicious. We had a couple of Cokes in the mess and Joe showed me to my new home; a high ledge, hidden near the ceiling of the turbine room. It was hot, bright and noisy, but I knew I could handle it. This was my big adventure and I wasn't going to let mere discomfort put me off enjoying myself. Another bonus was that I wouldn't run my torch batteries down; it was bright enough to read twenty-four hours a day in here if I wanted to.

I slept well until 4am when Joe and another crew member woke me. A rumour had gone around the ship that there was a girl in the engine room so they decided to shift me to a safer location before the ship was inevitably searched.

We crept through the sleeping ship to the forward deck upon which the bridge stood. As I ducked to enter the space under the bridge I turned to look at Wellington. It's a beautiful city and looked its best that clear still morning. The glass-like harbour reflected the city lights and the towering bush-clad hills which loomed dark from the water. Over my right shoulder I could see the Point Jerningham lighthouse flashing its warning. It crossed my mind that it might be telling me not to leave New Zealand. That light was my last glimpse of home for four months.

Once we entered the space under the bridge we had to crawl about ten metres to our left where there was a tiny compartment through another small hatch. This fan space was to be my home for almost three weeks.

The space was narrow — less than my height — and the ceiling was too low to allow me to kneel or stand. It was a long space though, almost the width of the ship. My helpers had placed a mattress, pillow and blanket there for me.

The mattress had to be wedged across the narrow compartment, otherwise it would have rolled with the ship. Icebreakers have rounded hulls to allow them to ride up onto thick ice before crushing a way through it, so they tend to roll a lot at sea. As I was near the top of the ship this rolling motion was exaggerated. As the mattress was folded into this gap I was unable to stretch my legs out while lying down. When I sat on the mattress my head grazed the ceiling of the space; there was no way to get completely comfortable.

Where my first hiding place had been bright and noisy, this space was pitch black. No light entered and sounds were muffled. I hadn't brought a watch with me — there was no way to tell whether it was night or day. I was alone. I interpreted the flutter in my heart as excitement. There was no room here for fear. I unpacked my bags to check on supplies. Two pairs of jeans, four T-shirts, three pairs of socks (including stripey BCR ones), three pairs of knickers, one spare bra, deodorant, large hoop earrings, ten books, a torch, six spare batteries, a box of tampons, my contraceptive pills, shampoo, toothbrush, tissues, a Bible, a diary and a pen; quite a haul. The Bible was a comfort, a stand-in for a teddy bear. Grandma had given it to me during my first real flush of religion. Although I claimed to no longer believe in its writings, I found the presence of my Bible reassuring. In my pocket I had forty New Zealand dollars. I was ready for anything.

I slept awhile after the sailors left. They'd provided me with a can of Coke and a large preserving tin to use as a toilet. I woke the next morning to the feel of the ship pulling away from the wharf. The adventure had begun. I opened the Coke to celebrate — having located it with the torch — and tried to suppress my excitement. As this was the only food item I had I saved about a third of it. I wrote in my diary that "this was to spare me the psychological problem of being left with nothing to drink." I settled the can behind my bags and started to read.

Despite my mattress being wedged across the width of the fan space, when the ship got out of the harbour I began to slide — back and forth across the long space. Nothing I could do would stop it. I sat myself on the cold, hard floor and waited for some assistance. Joe turned up a few hours later and went away to get a rope. He used this to secure the mattress to a post close to the starboard side of the ship. He told me the ship had been searched before leaving port and the turbine room had received special attention. The officers were now certain no stowaway could be on board. I would be safer to remain under the bridge though. There was far less chance of being discovered accidentally there. He also told me that my current hiding place was between the bridge and the captain's cabin so wherever the captain was, he wasn't far from me. This wasn't reassuring. Joe also brought another big tin, this one full of drinking water. He gave me sandwiches too. He was going to look after me well.

After he left I got back to reading. I'd finished *The Lion, the Witch and the Wardrobe* and thought I should start on the Jacqui Sussan books. *Valley of the Dolls* was the first I picked up. Its story of drugs and sex reminded me of Mum.

Over the next few days I adjusted to the motion of the ship. My mattress now stayed put but it wasn't comfortable lying on the rope. I took my pill conscientiously and used my toilet tin to pee in. I was far too embarrassed to poo in the tin which Joe emptied overboard every three or four days.

Joe visited me daily, usually late at night or early in the morning, because he didn't want anyone to see him entering the space under the bridge. He always brought food but I wasn't eating much so most of it ended up in the rubbish bag.

After a week of not washing, my hair was feeling greasy and revolting. I was dying for a shower but we couldn't risk me leaving my space. Once when half asleep I poured shampoo into my drinking water and tried to wash myself, using tissues to dry up. I then had no drinking water until the next day when Joe visited.

I got my period about a week into the trip. My tampons joined the uneaten food in my rubbish bag, wrapped in sheets of apricot-and-white tissue paper, as I wasn't exposing Joe to them either. When we crossed the equator Joe told me of the maritime tradition that accompanied this milestone: any sailor who was crossing the equator for the first time had to crawl through all of the ship's rubbish to the feet of a crewmate who was christened 'King Neptune' for the day. The initiate then had to kiss Neptune's bellybutton. As far as I knew I was the only person on the ship on their virgin equatorial crossing, but they held the ceremony anyway. I cringed at the thought of someone slithering through the ship's garbage to Neptune's belly button with a tampon caught in his hair.

Having no way to tell the time of day was disorienting. Sometimes it seemed Joe visited twice in one day. Other times the gap between visits seemed huge. I was reading my books at a fast rate and had finished them by the time my journey was half over. I wrote in my diary that *Once is Not Enough* was "an A1 book."

My little space was starting to smell ripe. I was the most likely source of the smell, followed closely by the rubbish bag and pee can. My urine smelled awful; this wasn't surprising as I was eating little and because of this my body was probably producing a lot of chemicals.

Near the end of the trip there was a time when Joe seemed to be away for two or three days. My water had run out, I was dry and thirsty and had even been tempted to drink my urine for some refreshment. I crawled a little way out of my compartment so when Joe arrived I'd see him sooner, and lay on the cold floor. It felt great to be able to straighten my legs out. I spent a couple of hours stretching my body and enjoying the air, which smelled much fresher than that in my space. At last someone opened the hatch under the bridge and turned on a light. It wasn't Joe — I'd been found.

The sailor crawled away from me initially, then turned back and rubbed his eyes.

"My God it's true, it's a girl."

I remembered seeing him in Wellington before our departure and he recognised me too. He told me there was a bra pinned to a ship noticeboard with a sign 'The Phantom Stowaway?' next to it. He asked if I was missing a bra. I wasn't. I told him how thirsty I was and he promised to bring me a drink. He left, leaving the light on, to return a long time later with a paper cup of water. He'd been so worried about being spotted entering the fan space with the drink that he'd had to walk around the deck several times before it was safe to bring it to me.

Before he left he kissed me. I smelled and looked terrible and my breath was probably disgusting too. This was the beginning of my education that a man would fancy anything, in any state, if he'd been away from women for a while. I wrote in my diary that he was a "ferocious kisser."

Joe appeared shortly afterwards. It had been two days since his last visit. He was keen to have sex with me (either he could tell one of his crewmates had kissed me or he was too far from land also). I had already decided I liked Joe enough to have sex with him but had wanted to be sure I felt safe with him first. This seemed as good a time as any, although it did give further proof that men aren't too fussy about who and what they will sleep with.

As he was leaving Joe warned me that another sailor was going to visit my space the next day — Frank, the man who'd brought me to this compartment early on my first morning. He had to perform some routine maintenance and I was not to be worried about seeing him.

That night the sea was rough. I was perched on my mattress peeing into the toilet tin when the ship rolled alarmingly. As the ceiling was so low it was a performance having a pee — it was impossible to sit straight so I crouched and slouched over the can. It had to sit on the mattress; otherwise it tended to slide across the floor. This night the ship lurched, I lost my balance, my toilet tin tipped over and urine soaked the mattress. I managed to turn the mattress over but the ship gave a repeat performance and anything remaining in the tin splashed on the other side. My last few days aboard were spent lying on a cold, stinking, piss-soaked mattress. I was glad I still hadn't had a crap in my tin — if I had, that would have made an even worse mess.

Frank appeared a few hours later bringing me a can of drink and some advice. We were now less than a week away from Seattle and he was worried about me. Did I know what I was letting myself in for? Did I have some place to stay? What would I do when I disembarked? Did I know what a pimp was? I knew the answer to the last question — everyone who's been to Sunday School knows that a pimp is someone who tells tales on somebody else. I nodded my head vigorously and fortunately didn't open my mouth. He would have been more worried if he'd had any idea how naïve I was. He didn't mention the smell in the fan compartment, which must now have been extremely unpleasant.

Three days before we arrived in Seattle, Joe asked me if I'd like to stay with him in Oregon. I was delighted. I'd thought about hitchhiking to see my uncle in California (the one who didn't know the Osmonds), but this was a better plan. We decided we'd head straight down to Salem to see Joe's folks, then plan what we'd do. As he spent a lot of time either at the Coast Guard base or at sea, Joe didn't have his own apartment yet. He was sure his family would love me.

We docked in Seattle. As the ship had been away from home for several months there was a big welcome waiting. From my space under the bridge I could hear loud music and cheering. The pier was crowded with family and friends welcoming their boys home — and unbeknown to them, one bedraggled girl.

We needed to wait until things quietened down a little before I could be set free. I had to leave the ship while there were still civilians aboard, but couldn't risk being seen coming out of my space while there were too many people around. It was a tricky manoeuvre.

Soon it was time. Joe and one of his friends assisted me from the fan compartment. When it came time to get up I found I couldn't easily stand. My calves were weak and cramping and it hurt to bear weight on them. I looked around me. It was early evening and the light seemed muted compared to that in Wellington. I sat on the deck while Joe concealed my tote bags in his luggage. His friend supported me as we walked from the ship. I heard him tell someone I was his girlfriend and on drugs.

I must have looked awful. Three long weeks of grease on my hair and skin; dirty clothes that were now far too big on me; my lips cracked and bloodied where I'd chewed the dried skin from them; my legs barely able to hold me upright. Joe still found me attractive though. He'd obviously been away from women far too long.

Joe called a taxi from a booth on the pier. The roads were huge and packed with enormous cars all driving on the wrong side; there wasn't a Morris or Mini in sight. We drove to a hotel on the waterfront and Joe checked us in after telling me to keep out of sight. We rode up in the elevator with a well-dressed woman who was on her way to the cabaret being held on our floor. She couldn't keep her eyes off me and melted against the back of the lift to get as far from me as possible. At least she didn't hold her nose.

The two things uppermost in my mind were a toilet and a shower. I had begun to feel like I'd never be clean again. I took my time over both and afterwards felt fabulous.

I'd shrunk a lot. My hipbones jutted out and I could remove my jeans without undoing them. I could see a marked difference in my shape when I looked in the mirror. Tracey would be jealous.

Joe ordered us a meal and bottle of wine and I called Wellington collect. Tracey answered the phone. Grandma was worried about me — she was keeping Tracey awake at night by listening to religious radio till all hours. Trace hadn't been sure where I'd done a runner to and had wondered if I was back in Auckland. Hell no, that was far too tame. I'd been there, done that.

Despite the food and wine I couldn't sleep. I looked at the Seattle shoreline all lit up through the window. I watched TV — even the ads were amazing. The one I remember most was for Nivea skin cream and involved a family dressed as jars of moisturiser, dancing across the floor.

Nivea, Nivea, Nivea
From your head down to your toes,
You've just got one set
Of permanent clothes.

It was a strange little ditty from my wonderful new land.

The hotel hired fishing rods to guests who wanted to fish from their window, but it was too late for that. Maybe I'd just go for a hobble downtown... I stayed put, eventually curling up behind Joe. The mattress was long, soft and dry. I was clean, fed and back on land. I'd made it.

From all accounts I was a welcome baby… at first

Mum with the three of us, at Miramar

Happy days — with my parents at a friends' wedding

At Miramar Central School, aged five

Our front yard at Whyalla

My favourite pink daisy dress

Caravan kids: in our brand-new nighties sent by Miramar Grandma

I got to know Dad again at weekends

Farm kids in the wide-open Wairarapa spaces

A 'monument to Mum' — the Cuba Mall bucket fountain

This photo was taken a few days before Mum died

Well, at least I had a brief career as an angel — I was Gabriel, centre back, in a school play

When I started the fan club I even had the Rollers' names embroidered on my sandshoes

photo courtesy Evening Post

AOTEAROA
NEW ZEALAND
Places mentioned in the book

Cape Reinga

•Whangarei

•Hauraki Gulf

Auckland•

Ngaruawahia•

Rotorua •

• Napier

•Dannevirke

Waikanae•
Paekakariki•
Porirua• •Upper Hutt
•Masterton
• Featherston

Wellington

Miramar - North Wellington
Strathmore - West Wellington

Christchurch• •Lyttelton

•Dunedin
University of Otago

This passport photo was taken in prison. I look unhappy because it was the third attempt at taking my photo - the first two times the camera broke and the prison officers laughed at me!

With Christopher

A touch of glamour from the San Fran days

Urging co-operation with the police (just as well the spelling police weren't around)

photo courtesy The Dominion

*Going back as an adult
student was a culture shock,
but it turned my life around*

Paulie at five months, 1985

The A & E crew after a long night
photo courtesy Louise Goossens, Wellington
School of Medicine

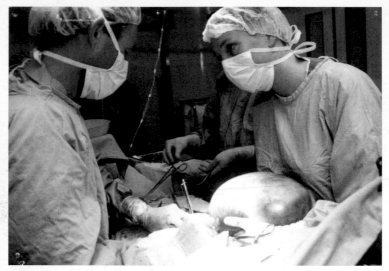

That's me on the right behind the mask - and thankfully not my ovarian cyst!
photo courtesy Louise Goossens, Wellington School of Medicine

Political lobbying during the Smoke-Free Environments Act debate. Presenting Hon. Simon Upton with a certificate
photo courtesy Louise Goossens, Wellington School of Medicine

Entering a new life
photo courtesy The Evening Post

18

Next day we took a Greyhound bus to Portland, Oregon. I had problems in the Greyhound depot drinking from a milk carton — we only had milk in bottles in New Zealand. My jeans had holes in the knees and people stared at them. Maybe things weren't going to be so simple after all.

From Portland we travelled to Salem, to Joe's family home. I had imagined we would describe our daring voyage from Wellington and have a few laughs. This was not to be — I was to tell his parents I was eighteen years old and had flown to the US to join Joe in Seattle. This was a big disappointment; some of the gloss went off our great adventure when I realised that it had to remain a secret.

Joe's family was lovely. His Mum made us up a bed together with no hassles and left us mostly to ourselves.

I was glad to have a rest as my calves were swollen and sore and I'd begun to get pains in my chest when I took a deep breath. I thought nothing of this; I thought anyone who hadn't walked for three weeks was bound to be breathless and sore, after all they would be unfit. Years later I learned that the combination of prolonged immobilisation and the contraceptive pill was a recipe for blood clots in the leg. These of course can break off and travel to the lungs; and if big enough, can kill. Fortunately I must have only been throwing off small clots as I didn't keel over dead. But it was a few weeks before my legs and lungs returned to normal.

A couple of nights into my stay Joe and I went to visit some friends of his who lived in a converted garage. We drank beer and mellowed out listening to the soundtrack from *Saturday Night Fever* which was number one at the time. I felt so grown-up. I had a man who said he loved me, beer and new friends with fine taste in music.

A couple of days later after a few drinks and with prompting from Joe's sister-in-law I let slip that not only was I an illegal alien but at sixteen I was two years under the age of consent. Jail bait! Joe's mother was horrified and upset that we'd lied to her. She phoned my uncle in California and arranged for me to stay there. To show there were no hard feelings she bought me a box of chocolates and some glossy magazines to read on the bus.

Joe was sad to see me leave and promised to keep in touch. He told me that he loved me. It made no difference; I was back on the Greyhound, this time headed for San Francisco and the home of an uncle I didn't know.

Uncle Dave is my Dad's younger brother and had lived in the States since his youth. He was the only person in my extended family with a tertiary education so I had always been in awe of him. Grandma and Grandad Roche kept a photo of him in graduation gown and mortarboard on the wall of the bedroom I slept in when I visited them. I thought he must be so brainy.

Uncle Dave was waiting for me at the bus station. We recognised one another at once. He was a shorter, stouter, balder version of my Dad. His face wasn't as battered though — Dad's face has been somewhat beaten about by life and circumstance. He was fun and wanted to hear about my trip to the States. He smoked a joint and offered me some as we drove to his place in Pleasanton. I refused. I'd never smoked before and didn't want to cough and choke and look like a dork. I said something pompous about learning from my mother's mistakes and wasn't offered any weed by him again.

As we drove past San Francisco Bay I looked around for the Statue of Liberty. I didn't know that it was in New York. I could see Alcatraz, though, and the Golden Gate Bridge, which were consolations. San Francisco was breathtaking.

Uncle Dave was married with one and a half kids. Justin was his infant son and Aunty Carol was pregnant. She had loads of pregnant friends — the house pulsated with hormones. Suddenly babies seemed very attractive.

I made a few friends my own age and attended high school as a visitor for two days. The students were voting for their Prom Queen, which seemed so typically American. The girls wore make-up to school and seemed much more sophisticated than Kiwi schoolgirls. I couldn't compete with them on that level so I found another way to make my mark, because make it I must.

I started to hang out with a bunch of boys. We did naughty things like climbing onto the roof of the local primary school after dark and drinking beer. We were real outlaws. I told the boys that New Zealand was a nation where free love was encouraged and I was just the girl to teach them all about sex. I was still on the pill so mistakenly felt that promiscuity held no dangers.

I missed home a lot and began making phone calls again. I rang around the radio stations in Wellington to speak to the DJs (including my five-dollar man), phoned my old high school (where I had Tracey called out of class so I could have a long chat to her) and called my phone pal Judi in Vancouver.

I ate a lot too. While on the *Polar Star* I obsessed about food and about having free access to a fridge. I'd compiled lists in my diary of the food I could cook (not much) and what I'd have in my fridge and pantry when I got to land again. This obsession continued when I got off the ship. I ate enough food for three people and went to fast food restaurants at least twice a day. My weight ballooned. I had no money and paid for my binges with cash stolen from a jar in David and Carol's bedroom. I wandered around San Francisco. I'd catch the BART (Bay Area Rapid Transit) train that travelled under San Francisco Bay, then roam around the city. I met a young man who offered to show me the 'real' sights and took me to Polk Street, the gay area. The place was crowded with interesting and exotic people. We entered a disco/bar called Busby's where the bartender asked me if my breasts were real and raised his eyebrows when I told him they were. I travelled on the cable cars, ate at Chinatown and did the touristy thing. I loved it.

19

One day I phoned the Coast Guard base in Long Beach, the home port of the USCGC *Glacier*, and learned that the *Glacier* was due back in port in three days time. I telegrammed Bill, the sailor who'd told me that he'd send for me on his return to the US, and told him I'd arrived on the *Polar Star* and would meet him at Long Beach when the *Glacier* berthed.

I was going to be on the move again. It was 30 March 1978. I planned my departure from Pleasanton to coincide with the absence of David and Carol. Sneaking around had become my way of dealing with things.

I left them a note apologising for the phone bill that was due to arrive and for stealing money from their room. I wished them well for the future and said I'd be in touch. I enclosed a poem from Tolkien's *The Lord of the Rings*, leaving out a few of the refrains as I wanted it to read in the way I'd have said it:

> *The road goes ever on and on*
> *Down from the door where it began*
> *Now far ahead the road has gone*
> *And I must follow, if I can.*
> *Pursuing it with weary feet*
> *Until it joins some larger way*
> *Where many paths and errands meet*
> *And whither then? I cannot say*

Tolkien had the right words for the way I felt back then. It was as though I was on a mystical journey of the type he wrote about.

I caught a bus to the BART station and headed for Daly City, the furthest point south the train ran. I planned to hitchhike down the West Coast to Long Beach, south of Los Angeles. As I took the bus to the BART station I was humming a few lines from 'Landslide,' a Fleetwood Mac song. The words were about getting older and time making people bolder. I felt I was getting older and wiser, even at sixteen. I had no idea how much I had yet to learn and how soon my education would start.

It was raining when I started to hitchhike. I had a waterproof jacket that Joe's sister-in-law had given me, but wasn't thrilled by the weather. I got my first ride quickly and had a no-hassle trip with a French woman who took me to stay with her family in San José. Next day she gave me $20, a map for the next part of my journey and a sun hat. I'd told her I wanted to hitch to New York, and live in Grand Central Station, so would pass through Death Valley — the hottest, driest place on the continent.

My next ride took me just north of Monterey where I met a couple of young guys who took me out for a meal. It was hard to turn offers down as I had no money and no prospects of getting any. The guys seemed nice enough. They assured me they both had girlfriends and invited me to stay the night on the couch. I accepted on the condition they'd drive me to Carmel the following day. They did. I was motoring towards Long Beach, down the Pacific Coast. The sea that washed the beaches here also touched New Zealand's shores. I felt a kinship with the people who lived along this route and connected with home when I paddled in the surging waters.

Monterey and Carmel were lovely, lots of trees and rugged coastline. It was April 1st, bright and sunny. The world seemed grand. I was free and felt ten feet tall and bulletproof. My aim for the day was to get to Los Angeles if possible, otherwise Santa Barbara or Santa Cruz. Things were going well.

I had a list of rules for hitchhiking. I would never get into a car if there were more than two men in it. I would never allow myself to be separated from my bag. And I would never, ever get into the back seat of a two-door car. These rules had served me well and they allowed me to feel a measure of control at all times. Things had been so easy though — I was feeling cocky. Who needed such a restrictive code? It was just making things more difficult, slowing my progress. I needed to relax. When a two-door car with three men in it pulled over I thought, why not? The front passenger took my bag and placed it in the boot. I didn't protest. He beckoned for me to get in the back seat with his mate. I did.

I estimated the guys were in their thirties. They all had dark hair and were neatly dressed and clean-shaven. But though only mid-morning they were drinking wine — this didn't fit with the rest of the picture. They weren't visibly drunk though — I allowed this to reassure me. I told them I was heading for Los Angeles and foolishly, that I was an illegal alien. The men told me they were from Yugoslavia but had lived in the US most of their lives. They were friends who did everything together, they said.

It wasn't long before I realised I'd made a mistake accepting this ride. The men kept drinking. I refused their offers of a mouthful or two "to loosen me up." They started to talk about sex. Did I like it? Was I good at it? What did I like the most? I was uncomfortable with the questions but wanted to appear 'a big girl' and tried to shrug them off. It dawned on me then — maybe the reason I'd had no hassles before this was due more to my rules than my luck. Maybe I'd made a mistake... I felt the first stabs of fear.

The man in the back seat shuffled over next to me and asked for a kiss. When I refused he grabbed my breasts through my shirt, mauling me. It was hot in the car and there was no way out. He pulled my shirt open to show his mates. His breath stank of wine — he was drunker than I'd thought. The front seat passenger had turned around and was encouraging him. I still thought I might talk my way out of it. I swore to myself that if I got out unharmed I'd never do anything so stupid again. I'd be good, really good. I might even go to church again. *Help me God.*

Mr Front Seat told me to remove my clothes. My heart sank. I didn't know what to do — I was outnumbered and trapped in the back of the car — should I do as they said? I tried to turn the situation around — "Come on, guys, I don't want to do this, why don't you just drop me off?" Mr Back Seat laughed, "We're just going to have to rape you then, aren't we?" He used the word 'rape' a lot — he obviously got off on it.

He undid my jeans and pulled them and my knickers off over my shoes. I tried to cover myself with my hands. I was embarrassed as well as frightened. He thought that was a huge joke. My clothes were thrown to Mr Front Seat, who made a show of sniffing my panties. My face was so hot and I felt so humiliated. I was now naked — Mr Back Seat liked to see skin. I tried to curl up on the seat, protecting my self as much as possible, but he hit me a few times with the back of his hand. I decided to lie limp instead and escape into my mind.

I was back in New Zealand. It's cool in April there, maybe raining lightly — not this inescapable heat. I wondered what Tracey was doing and whether she missed me. I hoped she'd never find herself in this situation. I hoped she'd never do something so stupid. I tried to forget what was happening to me.

The car was getting hotter. My heart was racing — I'd never been so frightened in my life. My head was pushed against the side window as Mr Back Seat started touching between my legs. His hands and fingernails were filthy — they were the only parts of him I recall clearly. He inserted a finger into my vagina and said to his mates, "I smell hot pussy." I wanted to die. Mr Front Seat was feeling left out of the action; so was the driver. They pulled down a side road to the shore where they took turns watching each other rape and sodomise me. Mr Back Seat was vile. He taunted me, "You haven't been doing this for long, have you, bitch?" At one time I'm sure a fourth man joined in — I can remember seeing two lots of two men at the beach, although the fourth man wasn't in the car at any time. Where it had been hot in the car, it was breezy at the beach. I was terrified we'd be seen. The fear of yet another person being a witness or accessory to this degradation was too much. I felt sure that if someone saw us they were not likely to call for help — a Good Samaritan seemed far too much to hope for. Besides, I'd walked straight into the situation. Some people would say I'd asked for it.

When they'd had enough the driver and his passengers took me back to the car. My clothes were in there and I was sure they'd let me go, now they'd had their fun. So I didn't make a run for it.

I got back into the car. A different man was now in the back with me. I asked for my clothes and he refused, saying that if I kept asking for them they'd be thrown out the window. I lay down again in the back and sobbed. I felt filthy and extremely stupid. He began to rape me again. I tried to daydream and ignore what was happening to me when a searing pain made me look down. He was raping me with the wine bottle — the base first. I couldn't stop looking — there was blood on the green glass of the bottle — it looked so big and hurt so much. I was wrenched back to reality — New Zealand impossibly far away, perhaps I'd never see my home again. I yelled with pain and fear.

I was now too aware of my surroundings. I saw we were headed north again — the sea was on the wrong side of the car — although the driver denied this when I protested. I started to think they weren't going to let me go — maybe they were going to kill me and dump me somewhere along the coast. I had no ID, no one here to identify me if I died, no medical insurance and no one to turn to. I wasn't so clever after all ... I pulled myself up, terror of a lonely death providing the motivation I needed to get the hell out of there. I leaned across the seat in front of me, my arms over the driver's eyes. I was crying, babbling and conscious of blood running down my thighs. The driver couldn't shake me off and neither could his mates, so he pulled the car over. He threw me my clothes and told me to "get the fuck out." One of my shoes hit me in the face. The driver seemed shaken. I dressed while he stood beside the car and smoked and the other two whispered to each other. Was it a trick? Was I safe? Would I ever get home? When I was dressed and on the footpath the driver took my bag from the boot and threw it at me.

As they sped off down the road I was so relieved they'd gone that I waved goodbye to them. It seems such a stupid thing to have done but I felt incredibly lucky to be alive. It was now early evening. My ordeal had lasted several hours. As an illegal alien I couldn't tell the police what had happened — I was on my own. I also had a terrible fear that anyone who learned what had happened would blame me for it.

I stood by the side of the road looking after my attackers, fearful yet almost resigned that they would return for me. I was sore, terribly sore, from the tears and bruising between my legs and grazes on my body from stones and gravel. I was emotionally numb. I had flashbacks to Nanny White's place, but didn't know why — the memory of that childhood abuse was still murky. I wanted a warm bath to wash the dirt and blood away, and I wanted my Mum. Although I made no conscious effort to block out the rape I found it retreating to some dark place near the back of my mind. It didn't remain there long enough.

I had to put my mind and energy to getting a ride out of

118

there. I was injured, alone and afraid. The one comforting thought I had was to getting to my friends at Long Beach and resting awhile. The only way there was to hitch a ride. There was no other option. I picked up my bag, limped across the road and began hitching south again. A road sign read 'San Luis Obispo.'

A pickup truck stopped and offered me a lift to Santa Barbara. The driver was a gorgeous young male who introduced his passenger as "my boyfriend Michael." They obviously wouldn't be interested in me. There was another hitchhiker sitting on the back of the truck. I joined him there and talked about inconsequential things like the weather and the beauty of the coastline. I didn't mention the trouble I'd had, explaining my limp as a sprained ankle. Each mile took me further from my attackers. Behind us was a truck carrying food for McDonald's. We wrote a note "Two cheeseburgers and some fries, please" in black felt pen and held it up for the trucker to read. He slowed down as he passed and waved and tooted at us. We thought it was a great joke. Our driver stopped at a roadside stall where Michael bought us saltwater taffy. The contrast with my last ride was extreme.

That night I stayed at the home of my fellow hitchhiker. We had a beer and retired early to his room. I didn't know what I'd do or say if he wanted sex, but knew I couldn't trust "no" again. I was terribly confused and scared — I wanted some closeness and felt afraid to sleep alone yet didn't want sexual intimacy. My rescuer — that's what he has grown to symbolise — didn't touch me all night or make any sexual advances to me, for which I was more grateful than I ever remember being. I loved him for it. His sensitivity to my vulnerability that night has made his brief presence in my life unforgettable.

20

Next day I hitched to Los Angeles. I had wadded up a couple of socks in my underwear to help soak up the blood still oozing out of my wounds. Leaving Santa Barbara I had jaywalked in front of a cop — a provocative act in the US, but never remarked upon in New Zealand. He came after me on his motorcycle and asked for some identification. I had mentally rehearsed my answer to this.

"Sir, I'm an exchange student from New Zealand doing some hitchhiking before I start classes. I've posted my passport and other documentation to my destination in Long Beach, so I'm afraid I have no ID on me." So far, so good. He looked me up and down and asked why I had crossed the road against the lights.

"Sir, I've only just arrived here from New Zealand which is a little island in the South Pacific. We don't have any traffic lights there."

He looked at me as though I must come from a primitive place. He was probably impressed by how quickly I'd learned to speak American. He leaned closer to me and spoke slowly. "Here's the rules, miss. G is for green, and G is for go, so if the light is green you can go."

I smiled sweetly. "Thank you, officer. I'll make sure I stay out of trouble now."

He touched his motorcycle visor and drove off. Another good deed in the life of a California Highway Patrolman.

I arrived in Long Beach the day after the *Glacier*. It was no trouble to get on board and meet up with Bill and Mark. Bill seemed stressed about my arrival. Hearing I had no place to go he got me a meal in the mess and offered me a place to stay. I could sleep on the floor of his radio room on the ship. Bill was a radio operator and had a small workspace aboard where no one was likely to enter. I stayed there for two nights and spent a third night dozing on the beach with Bill in a sleeping bag. We were afraid of being spotted by the military helicopters that flew overhead, so sleep was difficult.

During one of my days in Long Beach Bill took me for a walk in a park. He was embarrassed but blunt.

"Look, Lauren, I don't want to do this but I suppose I should marry you since you've come all this way to be with me."

I told him I was far too young to marry and settle down. I had places to visit, people to see. His relief was palpable. I told him I'd been raped. He said he wasn't sure if this story was true because I wasn't "acting right" about it. Is there a right way to act when something so wrong has happened? Anyway, it was time to move on. I left Bill and the *Glacier*. Bill bought me a ticket to Flagstaff, Arizona, where I thought I'd drop in on Willard from Doctor Hook.

I travelled to Flagstaff by Greyhound bus. The other passengers on the bus were wonderful. A young guy was concerned that I wasn't dressed warmly enough. He took off his woollen coat and gave it to me along with his address in Pennsylvania in case I cared to return it one day. His friend said I needed something to protect myself with. He took a knife and sheath off his belt and presented them to me. Nothing had prepared me for the generosity of most of the people I met in America.

My bus got in to Flagstaff at about ten at night. I was tired and sore and didn't want to wake Willard, so got a $17 motel room. It was snowing and freezing so I wound the heating right up and had a long hot shower before going to bed. I was alone and it felt sweet.

I spent two days with Willard. He lived with two other guys in a small apartment. He had a gold record on the wall — the only indication that he was a successful musician. He took me to see the Grand Canyon and the Painted Desert and took me to a restaurant where we shared a big clam pizza. We slept together each night and he gave me my first orgasm. He was gentle, slow and despite my fear of never wanting to have sex again, he made me feel perfectly relaxed and desirable. My physical injuries were healing well, although I was still bleeding.

Willard told me the band was due to give a concert in Texas and then they were returning to New Zealand for a tour. "Well, then," I thought. "Time to get to Texas, girl. You've got a concert to catch." Bugger the New Zealand concerts, though, I wasn't ready to go home.

The next morning I hit the road again. It was snowing lightly but I was warm in my new woollen coat. I felt confident and in control again. Texas was a long way but I knew I'd get there okay. I had three days to do it. This time I would keep to my hitching rules though. I had hidden reserves of courage and naivety which allowed me to keep moving. Freezing with fear at this point was not going to help me. I was too far from home to chicken out now.

I felt safer with my hunting knife which I wore under a long sweatshirt. I was certain I would use it if provoked but hoped I wouldn't need to. I walked to the outskirts of Flagstaff and bought an early lunch at McDonald's. My ride from Arizona to Nevada and then on through New Mexico was with a trucker driving a big rig. I slept in his bed behind the cab. When he woke me for breakfast at a truck stop I went to grab my knife but it was gone. I was suddenly fully awake and scrabbling through the bedclothes for my 'protector.' The trucker was bemused and before he stepped away asked, "Who are you?" I found my knife and sheath in the blanket. They must have come loose while I slept. This made me realise I wasn't fearless all the way through. There were cracks in my armour.

From New Mexico I got a ride with a businessman who dropped me at the outskirts of Dallas. On entering Texas I had a sense of deep foreboding that something was going to happen to me there — that somehow I wouldn't be leaving Texas. I told myself not to be so negative. This sense of fear whittled away at me though, making me realise that I wasn't as in control of things as I was pretending to be.

I decided to hitch right into Dallas. A man in a suit stopped for me. He told me he was a police officer, could tell I was a runaway and wanted me to accompany him to the police station. I refused after he was unable to show any ID. He assured me he'd be right back after he returned to his office to get it. I didn't see Mr Fake-policeman again. A woman picked me up within five minutes and drove me to downtown Dallas. I wasn't far from 'Six Flags Over Texas', a fun park where Doctor Hook was due to play two concerts.

I phoned Willard at his hotel. He'd checked in but wasn't in his room. After getting directions at a burger bar I walked to the hotel to find him. It was a beautiful day, bright, still and over 90°. When I reached the hotel the other band members were grouped around the pool, drinking from tall glasses. I greeted them all by name but they didn't recognise me as the girl from Wellington, a whole world away. Willard was in his room playing guitar and singing. He seemed amazed to see me. Why would no one believe what I was doing?

Dr Hook performed two concerts back-to-back that night. I arrived at the venue in a limousine with some of the band members and sat on the edge of the stage while they performed. Between concerts I stayed backstage talking to the band. Ray Sawyer, the lead singer, thought the story of my travel to the States was a tall tale but in the second set when the band played 'Only Sixteen' he dedicated the song to me. He said he was playing it for a certain girl "because when you're only sixteen and leave your home, you forget to plan how you're going to get back there." I was delighted.

I learned that the band was leaving to tour New Zealand in six weeks. I felt homesick and, for the first time since leaving home, wanted to return. I'd have to wait until the *Polar Star* went back to the ice and catch a ride with them. There seemed no other way.

That night I couldn't find Willard and had nowhere to sleep — I had assumed I'd be staying with him. I didn't want to bother any of the other band members. I only had a few dollars, certainly not enough to pay for a room in that hotel. I wandered into Reception and asked the young duty manager if he'd let me into Willard's room to retrieve my bag. After I explained why I needed to do this he agreed and used a passkey to gain access to the room. When I told him I was homeless he offered me a room to stay in free of charge as long as I left the next morning.

When his shift ended after midnight he let himself into my room. I hadn't thought that I'd have to pay for my accommodation somehow.

I didn't want sex, I wanted to sleep. I pulled out my knife and held it on the pillow. He saw it as he undressed. He called my bluff — "Okay then, stab me." I tried but couldn't. He shrugged. "You could have just said no." He dressed again and left the room. I knew that No wasn't a reliable defence, despite his comment. It hadn't got me far in California and it would be a long time before I could trust that word to work again. I didn't sleep well that night but wasn't disturbed again.

So much had happened to me in such a short time. In many ways I was a small, frightened girl miles from home. The situation began to feel beyond my control. I couldn't rid myself of the feeling that I wouldn't leave Texas alive. I needed help. Although I hadn't felt able to rely on him before, I thought I'd call my Dad. I tried to place a collect call to him. When the operator asked my father if he'd accept a reversed charges call from his daughter in the US, he refused. "I have no daughter in America."

I asked her to try again. Again he refused. I had spoken to Dad from his brother's place in California — he knew I was in the States. I began to cry, "Dad, I'm in a bad way, I've been raped, I want to come home." I thought he heard me, but perhaps it was a bad line. He replaced the phone after saying a final No. I felt my link with home had been cut. I cried and cried. I felt so alone and so far from help. So much for my new invincibility.

21

I went to the hotel coffee bar for breakfast and sat alone. On some of the tables were small piles of coins, tips for the waiting staff. I helped myself to about $5 which I used to buy a coffee and a sandwich. I cried some more. I felt utterly trapped and could see no way out. I didn't want to hitchhike again; I had the feeling that this time something terrible would happen. The reality of my predicament had finally got to me. Rape and beatings were no longer theoretical things that happened to other girls. I was still bleeding from the injuries I'd received. There were also unseen injuries assaulting me from the inside.

As I cried into my coffee a man who'd been sitting at one of the nearby tables approached me and asked if I wanted to talk. I told him what had happened when I called Dad. "Don't worry," he said. "Come home to me and my wife, we'll sort out what happens from there."

When we left the coffee bar I left a $1 tip, pretending to myself that it was the thought that counted even though I had stolen the money from the waitresses in the first place.

We went home to the man's place in Fort Worth. He said his wife and child were at church, perhaps we could "lie down together" until they got home? I burst into a new round of tears. It seemed everyone in the world was only interested in one thing from me. He left me to my tears but he was pissed off.

That afternoon some friends of the family came to visit and took me to stay with them. They also lived in Fort Worth and had three kids, two of whom were close to my age. Gwen, the wife, looked startlingly like Barbara Eden of *I Dream of Jeannie* fame. Her husband Joe was tall and Italianate. The kids, two boys and a girl were lovely. No one expected sexual favours from me. I told Gwen and

Joe the whole stowaway story from start to finish. They offered assistance, advice and a safe base from which to continue my travels. I was free to stay with them as long as I needed.

Gwen had recorded a couple of country music songs and was bubbly and full of fun. She introduced me to her friends, including a DJ at a Fort Worth radio station. He interviewed me on air about New Zealand before trying to grope me in the studio.

Gwen liked the idea of adopting me and began to tell people I was her long-lost daughter. She introduced me like this when she took me to a Dallas bar called The Silver Saddle. I wore the clothes she'd bought me — tight jeans and a T-shirt with *Afternoon Delight* printed on it. She bought me some bleach for my hair. Instead of lightening it had turned it a strawberry-blonde that still looked nice. I got horribly drunk on pina colada and had a hangover the next day. I was having a great time — I could get used to living with this family. Joe, Gwen and I still talked about what I should do, but never reached any decisions. They made toll calls to the New Zealand Consul in Los Angeles who could not assist me without involving the US authorities. I was stuck. Joe and Gwen seemed keen on adopting me so all was not lost. Now I think they meant adoption in a casual sort of way. I took them literally then and began imagining myself with a long Italian surname. Why not? I'd been in lots of different families up until now.

One morning Gwen woke me. "There are some men downstairs who want to talk to you." She and Joe had become worried about me — a kid so far from home —and had phoned the Immigration and Naturalisation Service (INS) for advice. The INS had contacted the FBI who sent the two agents. I was questioned. They asked if I would voluntarily leave Gwen and Joe's place and enter custody while the authorities sorted things out. I was worried about overstaying my welcome in the house so agreed I'd leave the next morning, no hassles. This would give the authorities time to sort out my future.

That last night at Joe and Gwen's place things were relaxed. The FBI had arranged that I would be held in the Tarrant County Juvenile Detention Centre until my status as an illegal alien was sorted out. The family made a big fuss of me. The little girl wanted me to take her teddy bear with me so I wouldn't be lonely. Gwen bought me some lollies to eat and promised she'd accompany me the next morning if she was allowed to. I was worried about leaving but had reached the end of my reserves and wanted someone to take full responsibility for me. I needed a rest. I slept well that night — the best sleep for ages.

The next morning two INS agents picked me up to drive me to 'Juvie' — the girls' name for juvenile detention. They were pleasant guys and seemed moved by my situation. They had a disconcerting habit of speaking in Spanish when they didn't want me to know what they were saying. As Texas is close to Mexico the bulk of the 'illegals' the Texas INS dealt with spoke Spanish, so the officers needed to be fluent too.

Gwen hadn't been allowed to come with me and I'd left the teddy behind so I was going to be on my own. I ate my lollies in the INS van en route to my new home. I kept telling myself I could handle Juvie, whatever it was like, but I was still apprehensive. My confidence had waned over the past three months. I wasn't the same cocky kid who'd stowed away. I was about to be locked up with some seriously bad girls. It was scary.

We went to the Immigration and Naturalisation Office in downtown Dallas before going to the juvenile detention centre. INS officers and the two FBI agents questioned me again. The FBI men wanted the names of the people who helped me into the States. I gave them my most winning smile and said I couldn't give them names as I didn't want anyone to get in any trouble, but yes, I did know who had helped me and I'd written about them in my diary. The agents asked for my diary but I refused to hand it over. They didn't take it from me but hinted they would the next day if I didn't co-operate. They were always pleasant, as were the immigration officers. I'm embarrassed at how easy it was for them to get information out of me.

We were soon off to my new residence. Tarrant County Juvenile was a dark, unfriendly place. As we entered the foyer we passed a woman who was talking to her weeping teenage daughter. The girl wanted to come home but her mother refused. "You will stay here until you've learned your lesson about running away." I was shocked — didn't everyone run away?

On arrival at Juvie there was a pile of paperwork to fill out. The INS guys then left. I was taken into a small cell and told by a female guard that I was to be strip-searched. "All clothes off, back to officer, touch toes, squat down, spread buttocks; same again, facing officer this time." When she was happy that all of my orifices were empty of knives and guns I was allowed to dress while she went through my bag. Everything in there (including my diary, knife and sheath and a bundle of dirty underwear) was examined and inventoried and I had to sign for them. They were held until I was allowed to leave.

I was taken to a room where about twenty other girls, most of them black, were watching television. They'd already had their dinner, but when I was given some sandwiches and a piece of fruit a couple of the girls asked if they could have it. They were bigger and looked meaner than I was and I didn't feel like eating so I handed it over. I started to cry again and this time couldn't stop. I sat in a corner of the room and wept — huge sobs and copious tears. My emotional time-bomb was beginning to tick faster. When one of the girls asked what my problem was I spluttered something about getting other people in trouble and being many thousands of miles from home. "Could you be quieter about it, girl, I can't hear the TV," was her reply. No one could stop those tears and it's probably best they didn't stop — I was overdue for a good howl.

That night I shared a cell with another girl. Our room had two single beds, a toilet and a washbasin. There was no privacy for the loo. We were locked into our cell and told we'd be kept in there in the morning if there was any noise after lights out. I asked my roomie if they meant that. "They most surely do," she replied, "and I'll be really pissed if you fuck things up for me, get the message?" I did. I was quiet, even before lights out. What was I doing in this place and how soon could I get out? Too soon, I found out the next day.

The following morning after breakfast we had art therapy. We had to paint a picture, with text about our feelings. I'd read books so I knew how to play these games. I drew a big thundercloud all grey and black covering the whole page. At the lower edge I added the last line of Mum's favourite Pink Floyd song in big purple letters: *everything under the sun is in tune, but the sun is eclipsed by the moon*. Let the silly social workers figure that one out.

Lunch was in the same room as breakfast. Our cutlery consisted of a plastic spoon and fork, whatever we were served. They didn't want any of us bad girls stabbing each other or the hired help (especially the hired help!)

That afternoon I was picked up again by the immigration guys and returned to their office. They had lots more questions. I spent the day describing the fan compartment in which I'd travelled to the States and telling them what they might find remaining there. I even told them the serial number stamped onto the mattress I'd lived on and the fact I'd written on the compartment wall in ink: *I stowed away here 20/1/78 to 9/2/78.* I had also left behind a sock bought in my Bay City Roller days (red and black stripes) and a silver hoop earring.

They wanted to read my diary. I said they could as long as they didn't give any names to the FBI guys. Stupid, stupid, stupid. I didn't want to get anyone in trouble but was naïve, exhausted and overwhelmed. It had been a long few months.

My diary was photocopied and read by several of the officers, who seemed to find it amusing. The diary had started life as an exercise book in which I collected words I didn't know. I loved to read the dictionary and had set a target of learning five new words a day. I was up to the letter 'B', having culled unfamiliar words from a baby Oxford. The words 'arable' and 'avarice' were among those on the first page. The INS officers who were reading my journal asked me to explain the meaning of the word list.

I was sitting in an office eating a sandwich and writing out the numbers from one to a hundred in binary when the FBI returned. The agent who sat next to me was friendly, clean-cut and intrigued by the numbers on the page. He told me he'd been speaking to the captain on the *Polar Star.* My story had been checked and they had confirmed my presence in the fan compartment. When I asked what the captain's response was he shook his head and smiled ruefully before saying, "No, not my ship. Please God, not my ship." I felt sorry for him, a good man with some silly girl spoiling his chances of promotion. It was just meant to be a laugh.

One of the Immigration guys called the FBI agent aside and showed him an entry in my diary. He returned with a female INS officer. "Lauren, could you tell us about this, please?" He looked at the floor, obviously disturbed by what he'd read. I looked at the page in his hand, it had been written a little over a week earlier. "I'm still bleeding from when all those men raped me and I'm still sore, too — very sore. I've been so stupid."

I blushed and said I didn't want my rape to become public knowledge. He promised it would remain confidential unless I wanted the police involved. I didn't want to live through that ordeal again. No thank you. The agent's main concern was that sailors on one of the ships (*Polar Star* or *Glacier*) might have carried out the assault. I told them that any activity on the ship had been fully consensual and that my attackers had been civilians.

I cried again — there were too many tears to hold back. The officers left the room. I locked myself in. I curled into a little ball and rocked back and forth sobbing. I wanted my Mum and I wanted to go home. Despite repeated knocking on the door I refused to open it. I needed to be alone. When I did open the door I was covered in a red blotchy rash from crying and looked pitiful. I got a hug from one of the female officers and it was decided we'd stop for the day. My diary was returned to me.

The media had been alerted about the teenage stowaway in Texas and there was a lot of interest in the story from America and New Zealand. I was photographed leaving the INS building that day walking between two armed officers to their van. On the way back to Juvie they began speaking in Spanish again. I knew they must have been talking about me as there were only the three of us in the vehicle. The only word I understood (from *Sesame Street* Spanish classes) was *mañana* — tomorrow. I asked what was going to happen to me tomorrow and they said I must have misheard them. But the next morning when they picked me up they brought all of my stuff from the Juvenile Detention Centre with them. Apparently I had too many rights in Juvie. My tell-all diary couldn't be examined at the convenience of the officers dealing with my case so the authorities had decided I should be transferred to Dallas County Jail. Once there they could examine the contents of my bag whenever they wanted. I didn't want to go to jail but no matter how much I complained, the issue was settled.

22

We entered the jail through a downstairs carpark and rode up to the police station area in a lift with some uniformed, armed police. I felt small and extremely young. One female officer saw my look of dismay and misery and misread it as hostility. "You better wipe that look off your face, young lady, or you won't last long in here."

There were armed cops all around me and, incongruously, a group of well-dressed school kids of about my age who were being shown the sights. These kids filed past me as I was having my fingerprints taken and having regained my sense of humour I let out a low, throaty growl as they passed by. It was gratifying to see them jump.

When all the paperwork was done I was placed in a holding cell with several other women. I was the youngest there by far and I seemed the least stressed. The other women were all well-dressed and looked wealthy. I had on my grubby jeans and 'Afternoon Delight' T-shirt. They didn't seem like the kind of people you'd expect to see in a cell. I was interested in what had brought them here. They ignored my polite questions until eventually one of the women (who all seemed to know each other) told me to shut up. I curled up in a blanket and lay down on a bench at the back of the cell. It sure was a busy place.

Before long I was taken out again and escorted to my new room. I got a cell of my own because of my age. The downside was there was no telly in the single cells and the lights were left on twenty-four hours a day. But I would be safe there. The state had hired a lawyer for me and he seemed a nice young guy. It was too late for advice relating to my diary but he promised to represent me the best he could in the immigration hearing set for the following day. The big decision I had to make was whether or not to fight expulsion from the States. I told him I was ready to go home. He seemed relieved with that. Next up I was asked if I minded giving an interview to one of the Dallas daily newspapers; a reporter was waiting to see me. The next morning I got a big write-up in the Dallas *Times-Herald* and the staff at the jail began calling me "Miss New Zealand."

The set-up in the single cell unit was simple — there were two lines each of about six or eight cells facing one another across a corridor which had a locked door at its end. Just before this locked door was a single shower unit. We were allowed out of our cell once or twice a week for a shower, supervised, as an inmate had hanged herself from the showerhead using a torn-up towel some months earlier. Each cell had a bed, stainless steel lidless toilet and washbasin which were all crammed in. The whole corridor-facing wall of the cell was barred and the locked door at the end of the corridor had a window in it. Privacy wasn't an issue — there wasn't any. We were locked up all day and night. My cell must have backed onto a bigger, communal one because I could hear a television going but it wasn't loud enough to distinguish the words, unfortunately. It did have some use, though. In the twenty-four-hour light we lived in it served to differentiate night from day.

The immigration hearing was quick and straightforward. When he heard I only wanted to go home the judge stood me down and I was returned to the jail. I can't recall if I got a conviction but I did hear the magical words that I'd be returned to New Zealand as soon as the authorities could sort out a passport and conventional ride home for me. That was all I needed to hear. Perhaps I'd get to see Dr Hook in concert back in Wellington. What more could a girl ask for?

I was allowed out of my cell under escort to use the phone. I called Grandma collect a few times. She always accepted my calls. No one in New Zealand was impressed by my exploits but I was too tired to care.

The second time I had a shower in prison I was taken to the shower area, then left alone as the guard retreated beyond the locked door at the end of the passageway. When I was finished I went back to my cell and pulled the door closed. Although my door looked shut I was no longer locked in and spent the next three days running up and down the corridor visiting my fellow inmates. Before this I had only been able to see the woman opposite me. She was thin and pale and told the story of how she'd been hitchhiking in Memphis and had been given a ride by Elvis. (She probably spent part of her teens living with the Osmonds too.) The inmate who made most impact on me was a middle-aged black woman who lay on a mattress on the floor of her cell (she had no bed in her room) looking out through the bars at the empty cell opposite. She didn't speak, unlike the others, and seemed as locked in her own inner world as she was in the Dallas County Jail. I wondered how she'd earned her place there.

My state of pseudo-freedom ended when I asked to use the phone again. I told the surprised guard who released me that my door had been unlocked for days. She was most unimpressed — someone would get in trouble over the possible security problem in the single cellblock. I don't know how they expected me to get beyond the locked door at the end of the corridor; I wasn't that resourceful.

After almost three weeks in prison I was on my way home. Dad had paid my fare, so rather than being deported from the US, I voluntarily departed. My passport had been issued from the New Zealand Consulate in Los Angeles and was valid for one journey only.

Flying from Los Angeles I was treated well by the cabin crew, who had heard about me at home. The pilots wanted to hear about my adventure and invited me onto the flight deck. I gave them a sanitised version. I had decided to tell no one except Tracey about the rape and assault, as I was scared of being told I'd asked for it.

During my time in jail I had gained a few kilos and the jeans that fitted well when I entered prison were now uncomfortably tight. I travelled in them and a long top to cover the bulges that escaped over my waistband. To do the jeans up before leaving jail I'd had to lie down on the cell floor, lift my hips and pull like crazy on the zip. The toilet on an aircraft allowed no space to do this. No matter what I did I couldn't get the zip done up after going to the loo. My top was long enough to cover my waist, but didn't reach all the way down to the bottom of my zip. This called for drastic measures. I took my top off, soaked it in water and pulled it enough to stretch the front of it. It would now cover me sufficiently for decency. It was uncomfortable sitting in a wet top wearing too-tight pants. I was grateful for the rum and Coke the cabin crew kept bringing me.

Just out of Auckland I started to panic. It was time to face consequences. Dad was furious; he'd said on the phone that he'd drive from Wellington to meet me and would tell me off for the ten-hour return trip. I wasn't looking forward to this. But he had paid my fare and I was grateful that this gave me the opportunity to maybe return to the US one day.

When I cleared Customs there were several journalists but no mad Dad waiting for me. I gave a few interviews in a brand-new American accent (even I cringed to hear it on TV that night). Dad turned up about half an hour later, angry. He'd heard me interviewed on Radio New Zealand and "couldn't believe the drivel" I'd spouted or the intonation I'd used. He thrust me a ticket to fly back to Wellington as he was certain he'd run off the road if he were to drive me anywhere.

Dr Hook was in Auckland and the papers were making much of my connection with the band. Word had arrived that I'd travelled with them. This had angered the band

and upset their wives. I called Dennis Locorriere at the Hotel Intercontinental. He wasn't at all happy. I phoned around newspapers that hadn't already interviewed me in an attempt to have the misunderstanding addressed. This made me look even more like a publicity-hungry little tart but I was really was trying to put things right.

Home to Miramar and Grandma and Tracey. No one met me at the airport. I got a ride with a radio journalist who was doing her best not to smirk at the pitiful accent I'd picked up in my four months away.

23

It was wonderful to see Tracey. I'd missed her a lot. She and I had always been close and I'd led her into trouble more than once in my life. We immediately went into competition mode — Tracey was slimmer than I was and her hair was longer. She was winning on those counts but I was famous. That had to be worth something in the vanity stakes. Trace was wearing a long-sleeved blouse in an attempt to hide her homemade tattoos from Grandma. She had 'USA', 'NZ' and a few other words tattooed in blue on her left forearm. She hugged me closely. Although only fifteen, Tracey already had Mum's tobacco smell. It was good to see her — thoughts of Tracey had sustained me through a lot of the pain I felt in the States.

Grandma wasn't as welcoming as my little sister, although it usually takes an awful lot to upset her. She was glad, she said, that she didn't have the same surname as me and that things were probably much worse for my Roche grandparents. I was told Shelley was getting a hard time at school because of me and I should be ashamed. I wasn't.

I heard from Judi, the old Canadian phone pal. I'd called her while I was in California and she'd thought I was lying when I told her about the stowing away. When she'd read the story in the Canadian papers she phoned them up and sold her tale of our friendship. She was the stowaway's phone pal! She had her father try to call me at the Dallas County Jail to see if I needed anything, but he was told I wasn't taking calls. We kept in touch for a couple of months, then drifted apart.

In the weeks following my return to New Zealand a peculiar thing happened. I received a telegram supposedly from the New Zealand Consulate in Los Angeles. The Consul was Ainslee Muldrew, a nice woman I had spoken to a couple of times. The telegram said a man was coming to New Zealand from the US to see me. His name was the Reverend Glendall Asbury Jones III and I was to trust him as he wanted to help me. I wondered why this man was coming to see me but as it was obviously okay with Ainslee it must be important. Maybe it had something to do with the court martials of the men who had assisted me on and off the *Polar Star*.

A couple of days later another telegram arrived, this one signed by the Reverend himself. The second telegram gave an arrival time at Wellington Airport and asked that I meet him there. Curiouser and curiouser. As he was a man of the cloth and therefore to be trusted, Grandma agreed he could stay in the best front bedroom. Tracey and I met him at the airport.

Glendall Asbury Jones III was a tall, slightly gaunt man with dark hair. He seemed charming but said "bloody" a couple of times — not a terribly 'reverend' thing to do, thought Tracey and I. He hired a Mini and drove us to Grandma's place.

"I am here," he said, "to return you to the United States to assist in the trials of your friends over there."

I had wondered if I'd be subpoenaed for the court martials, so wasn't that surprised. He then went on to say he'd like me to remain in the US with him as I had the kind of courage he needed for his missions. He said he smuggled Bibles into communist countries and on reading about my exploits, thought I would be the right person to join him. We all thought he was genuine, until the day he told me he'd have to marry me to get me into the US and not to worry, he had the necessary documentation. He showed me a form from the Department of Births, Deaths and Marriages — the one that seeks parental permission for marriage of a minor. He also took long phone calls from the US during which he'd pull the phone into the little front room and whisper for ages — unusual behaviour, I thought. He left, still single, a week later. I don't think he was a real Reverend, certainly not in the Kiwi sense of the word.

After he left I talked to Ainslee Muldrew. She had never sent a telegram to us and although she had met this man who sought information on my whereabouts, she hadn't given him my address either.

Later that year when the Jonestown tragedy came to light, Grandma convinced herself that the Rev G. A. Jones III had in fact been Jim Jones and she'd let him sleep in her special front room. I'm still intrigued about who or what he was, though — probably some nutter with too much money.

After the Reverend departed our shores I thought about the future. Here I was back with Grandma in Wellington, a situation I always seemed to return to. To break this cycle of departure and return I needed to get some new options. A return to school would be a good start. I approached the headmaster at Wellington High, a good Sally bloke. He refused my re-entry, believing I would be a bad influence on the other students.

I was disappointed. I realised that if Wellington High, the most liberal school in the city, wouldn't have me, no other was likely to either. I didn't think correspondence lessons would suit me. I needed the stimulation and interaction of the classroom.

While at the school I bumped into a former teacher, who invited me to a party at the Aro Valley community hall. It was to be a mask party, held the next night, with no admission to anyone with a bare face. The Aro Valley is a Bohemian area of town favoured by the artistic crowd and the cool kids at school. I'd never been invited to one of their 'dos' before. Tracey and I decided we'd attend together. At the last minute we remembered about the masks. No worries — we cut the legs off a pair of pantyhose and knotted them securely under our chins, bank-robber style. These made fabulous masks which didn't need to be removed in order to drink. It was impossible to eat but never mind, food was full of calories. I drank litres of nasty cheap white wine that tasted like vinegar. So much wine in fact that I soon needed to vomit. I couldn't undo the tightly knotted stocking over my face until after it had strained all the food I'd eaten before the party. It took several frenzied minutes in the loo to pick the particles of food out of my eyelashes. This experience taught me to never tie a stocking under my chin before drinking!

24

I couldn't go back to school and wasn't trained for anything. Time for a re-think. McDonald's had just opened in Courtenay Place, at that time a scruffy, central Wellington area, and one of my regular haunts. I could do that, I thought to myself, and secured a job smiling at the public and dispensing burgers and fries with a cheesy grin.

One of my managers was Wayne, a twenty-year-old with a big smile. I thought he looked just like Prince Andrew, although I now doubt the middle royal son ever resembled Wayne, even on his worst day. I was besotted. We started dating on my seventeenth birthday and celebrated with a quick shag on the carpet at his flat. I was IN LOVE. Soon I was living with him. He introduced me to 'Pinkies,' a small pink pill used to treat the symptoms of Parkinson's disease and a favourite drug at the time. He kept his stock of Pinkies in the McDonald's safe. We worked, lived and slept together. We saw the movie *Tommy* utterly smashed on Pinkies. The movie was far easier to understand when I was stoned — I'd seen it a couple of years earlier and found it fun but impenetrable.

I felt pills weren't real drugs. Pills were medicine. Smoking and injecting substances or taking any chemicals not in pill form was wrong. I was staunch about avoiding these. I wouldn't be a junkie like my Mum, I only took the clean stuff. I'd run out of my contraceptive pill and didn't get a repeat prescription. So much had happened to me in the past year — it wouldn't be fair if I was to become pregnant too. It just wouldn't.

Tortured logic I know, but I was young and silly at the time.

I enjoyed McDonald's until Wayne and I had a fight. I can't remember what it was about, but I probably started it. I was moody and feeling nauseous — the smell of burgers and fries made me want to vomit. Whenever I went to the toilet I checked for my overdue period. It didn't come.

I couldn't tell the 'happy father' so I told all my workmates instead, then handed in my notice in a fit of nausea and despondency. Wayne heard about my pregnancy from a co-worker, as I'd hoped, so wasn't at all surprised when I broke the news.

Wayne's response to the news was to invite me to holiday in Australia with him. At that time (1978) there was no accessible abortion service in New Zealand so women travelled to Australia to have the procedure done there. Practical and financial assistance was provided by a group of women calling themselves SOS — Sisters Overseas Service. Wayne obviously wanted me to avail myself of their services. Although I fully supported a woman's right to have a pregnancy terminated, I couldn't go through with the procedure myself. I turned his offer down. He ditched me.

About this time the results of the court martials of the *Polar Star* crew came through. The sailors involved were all demoted a rank and had their records blackened for having assisted my entry into the States. I felt dreadful and resolved to go on a personal mission to the US to apologise to all of the guys.

I had to get a well-paying job and return to the States.

25

There were few employment opportunities for an infamous, unskilled, pregnant seventeen-year-old. I could go on a Social Welfare benefit and keep living with Grandma, or I could be independent and find a job. Through an old school friend who worked in the business I found work as a fire-eater at the Hole in the Wall strip club. Although I was uncoordinated and couldn't dance to save myself, I learned to eat fire from a man who worked at The Purple Onion strip club on Vivian Street — the heart of Wellington's red-light district. With my big breasts burgeoning in pregnancy, I was a sure bet.

The club was dark and shabby, although many of its faults were invisible when the only light was a sole spot on the stage. There were small tables in the middle of the floor and several booths along one wall, where the clients — almost all men — sat to watch us. One wall was covered with mirrors, reflecting the dancers, the men who ogled us, and the illegally-sold alcohol. Cigarettes winked like fireflies in the gloom, their smoke creating a gauzy cloud that wafted above our heads. I thought the club was glamorous and that the workers there were, by default, gorgeous too.

My act, performed in a G-string and shared most times with a male fire-eater, took a whole six minutes. I also took part in the tableaux enacted by all the staff of the club at twenty-minute intervals — we would freeze to music in the most erotic group poses we could imagine. When I worked at the Hole in the Wall most of the girls performed drunk or stoned, which dulled their creativity somewhat.

The other girls who worked there were an interesting bunch. Candy Heather was eighteen and Scottish. She had a big tattoo of a galleon on one arm and was a peroxide blonde. I thought she was sophisticated. Spooky Dee was dark and exotic and rather strange, but she looked after me. She kept a photo of herself, naked, on the mantelpiece of her flat, where I moved in as it was close to work. She liked to dance to 'Are You Old Enough?' standing on a table gyrating in the face of the oldest man she could spy in the audience. There was a short blonde girl who called herself Babette, who was fond of blue eyeshadow and lashings of blue mascara. When the rest of us were in a mood with her (which seemed to be a daily occurrence), we would call her 'Scabette' or 'Crabette.' Babette was still working in Wellington's red light district a couple of years ago. Maree (who called herself Cherie Leticia Fonteyn) was the baby of the group. She was a petite brunette, only sixteen, with a fragile quality. She felt she had been born to be a stripper and certainly had all the moves. She lied about her age in order to work in the club. Maree was a great favourite with the men who attended our shows nightly. She suffered from depression and another mental disorder which meant she had to take a handful of pills twice daily to maintain an equilibrium. She eventually succumbed to alcohol and intravenous drugs to help her get by. Maree committed suicide a few years later, too delicate to survive beyond her twenties.

Only one man worked at our club (apart from Ross, the fire-eater who accompanied me). His name was 'Dave the Rave' and he was as queer as they come. Dave did his main act to 'Sweet Transvestite,' a number from the *Rocky Horror Show*. Before taking to the stage Dave would brush his pubic hair which he groomed "fifty strokes, five times a day" so it looked glossy for the punters.

The music for my set was 'You Ain't Seen Nothing Yet' by Bachman Turner Overdrive, 'Disco Inferno' by The Trammps and 'Fire Will Burn You.' My stage name was 'Diana Gaynor from Seattle, Washington DC' (never mind that Seattle wasn't in Washington DC!). I was unco-ordinated, yelped when the fire burned me and forgot to always breathe out when the flames were in my mouth. I had huge breasts, though, so was accepted by the punters. I ended up with singed vocal cords, no voice for two weeks and a fear that my baby would be abnormal. I probably provided a few laughs at the casualty department, Wellington Hospital, when I called to ask them if the fumes from white spirits, if inhaled, could harm my baby.

Even during the day I was spending time in the red light district. Not much action then, of course, but still some interesting sights and people. I was living in a flat nearby with Babette, Spooky and occasionally Maree, and would get cravings for the creamed-corn toasted sandwiches from the takeaway bar near the strip clubs. No one else's sammies killed my craving. I'd sometimes see Carmen, the famous transsexual and Wellington icon. Carmen was larger-than-life and always immaculately coiffed and made up. She had a dark brown voice which made me think of the rivers of hot chocolate in *Charlie and the Chocolate Factory* — a book by Roald Dahl. Carmen liked to eat Eskimo Pies, slices of vanilla ice cream covered in milk chocolate — divine. A couple of times she bought me one too and we'd sit and talk as we ate them. There was something seductive about the way her ice cream disappeared between huge, ruby lips. Carmen was famous for her lips. Even today others try to emulate them, with injections of collagen. Carmen had a big heart and was always there for advice and a shoulder to cry on for the young street workers. She was especially good for the young ones with questions about their gender identity or sexual orientation. The streets attracted such kids, as here they could find others to identify with. The streets gave a sense of family to those who felt estranged from their own blood kin. Carmen was Grand Matriarch of this family. She's now in King's Cross, Sydney.

My belly was bulging. I could no longer eat fire in a G-string — it looked absurd. Besides, I didn't want any possibility of harm to my baby.

My last performance was to be at the New Year's Eve party at The Hole in the Wall. I decided to hitchhike there with Zoe, who'd been a friend for a couple of years. While fascinated by the strip scene she felt no compulsion to join it. We got a lift in a car near Kilbirnie with two young guys and a German Shepherd dog. The dog was on the back seat until Zoe and I got in. It was obviously nervous about meeting these two strangers and leapt into the front where it tried to hide under the driver's feet. The dog got one paw flat on the accelerator and the other under the brake. The driver panicked. We flew full speed ahead into the side of a hill. The car was written off. Zoe and I were knocked unconscious and needed skull x-rays. After the x-ray I recovered enough to tell the nurses I was pregnant — they reassured me that things should still be okay. We were discharged that night, too late for my special solo act. Oh well. It was time to move on anyway. I decided to be a prostitute for a while, so I could afford to go the US as soon as I was able. To me the pregnancy was only a temporary interlude in my desire for forgiveness from the sailors that I had wronged. A letter or phone call to them wasn't enough. I had to front up to them.

I began to work as a prostitute on the corner of Vivian and Cuba Streets, Wellington, on a chilly evening. I wore jeans, a T-shirt and a warm jacket. It wasn't the usual apparel for a street worker but it worked anyway. The deliberate loiter, the concentrated eye contact and seductive smirk all showed my intentions. Other girls were freezing in short little dresses and not making much more money than I was. They were the ones who got return business though. Most of my clients were Japanese and Korean fishermen. We could tell the two nationalities apart by their smell. The Japanese had a far cleaner smell than the Koreans — something to do with their diet and the sanitary conditions on their ships. I soon teamed up with another girl and an Australian woman who offered to 'protect' us for thirty percent of our takings. Although I'd been doing okay by myself I agreed as it was a lonely job and could be dangerous. Never mind that my pregnancy would soon make things difficult for me.

We picked the sailors up on Vivian or Cuba Streets and took them to our flat on Oak Park Avenue, a two-minute walk away. The flat was on the ground floor of a compact block. The other girls had nice rooms with decent furniture. I had a mattress on the floor and saw no need for other adornments. I had lived rough in the States and it had become part of my persona to be too tough for home comforts. Our lounge had a stereo but no TV as we slept during the day and were busy at night.

We'd pour the sailors a drink in the lounge, then get them to have a shower, steal from their wallets, and possibly have sex with them. Then we'd kick them out into the night so we could find some of their crewmates. If there was more than one john there we'd play *Scissors, paper, rock* to decide who had to service the dirty ones while their mate was in the shower. Sometimes we'd pick our clients up at places like Carmen's Coffee Lounge, where we broke the rules by rolling them for their wallets, even though Carmen and her workers forbade that.

We'd then split what we'd earned that night and became skilled at calculating the number of Yen per dollar. Many of the taxi drivers around town would change the currency for us, so we didn't have to leave our beds during the day to go to the bank. Working girls seldom rose before nightfall and I only did if I had a craving for toasted sandwiches.

I worked on the street until I was nearing the fifth month of my pregnancy, stopping when my shape no longer supported my current role. I wasn't ready to lie back and do nothing though. The Tourism Board had run a campaign called *'Don't leave town till you've seen the country'* to encourage Kiwis to look around our own land before venturing overseas.

I hadn't seen a lot of New Zealand and worried that I never would, as a single parent. I set off on a hitchhiking tour, my last holiday before motherhood. There would be plenty of time to apologise to my sailors; I had to look after my own interests now. I filled a backpack, borrowed a tent and sleeping bag and headed off. The first night I stayed in a motor camp at Waikanae, north of Wellington. Huddled in my little tent I discovered a hint of the excitement I'd felt on the *Polar Star*. I was Girl Alone, taking on the world. Breakfast was cold baked beans and bread. Discomfort just added to my sense of adventure.

From Waikanae I headed up the west coast of the North Island, travelling through towns I'd never seen before. Every town, no matter how small, had a church and at least one pub. Some nights I slept in my tent, others in the homes of people who gave me rides. I had no problems with getting rides or trouble with the people who picked me up. I was picky about which cars I got into. I had learned from my American experience.

I spent five or six weeks on the road. As I had little money I didn't eat much but tried to make sure what I did eat was nutritious. I loathed mixed vegetables but forced myself to eat a couple of cans of them (cold) as I thought they'd be good for my baby. I also ate the iron tablets my doctor prescribed, and blocks of cheese.

Three times during the trip I had returned to Wellington but couldn't face going back to Grandma's. I would turn around and hitchhike north again.

I visited Cape Reinga, Whangarei, Napier, Rotorua and other beautiful places. Wherever I travelled I couldn't escape the reality that I was seventeen, pregnant and alone. No matter how long or far my road, those facts remained unchanged. Eventually I had to return home.

It was a mid-week evening when I arrived back in Wellington. I went straight to the strip club, now called The Perfumed Garden, watched a few numbers and gossiped with the girls before heading home to Grandma's. I walked from the club to Miramar, enjoying my solitude and breathing deeply the sea air around the waterfront.

I loved Wellington. My lighthouse at Point Jerningham winked at me as I passed and I felt that everything, somehow, was going to be all right.

26

Nothing had changed at Miramar. Grandma wasn't too shocked that I was pregnant and asked me frequently if I still was. She phoned Dad for me to break the news. He seemed disappointed but unsurprised. My feelings vacillated between bliss and terror.

I spent a lot of time in bed, or in the bath if I bothered to get up. I read books, wrote in my diary and thought about what a fine mother I'd make to my daughter. I didn't imagine I'd have a son. There were days when I forgot I was pregnant but these didn't happen often. Because of my youth I was assigned two social workers, one by the hospital, the other by the Department of Social Welfare whose brief seemed to be to make me give up my baby for adoption. No way. I was going to be a wonderful mum. I'd had good training in how not to do it, so I was sure I'd be okay. I felt betrayed by Wayne, who claimed I'd slept with other guys when going out with him. This was untrue — I'd been in love with him and believed that if you were in love you didn't do that sort of stuff.

I spent a lot of time alone and miserable. I cried copiously and was beginning to understand how my mother must have felt. I still spent hours at the strip club and around the red light district but didn't work there. The girls were all interested in my changing shape but I could sense the unspoken "I'm glad it's Lauren, not me." So was I, in a way. Perhaps motherhood would give me a good reason to exist. Perhaps it was all I needed. It seemed I had nothing else worthwhile in my life. I had no qualifications, no boyfriend and no future, apart from the one I carried inside me.

My son Christopher was born at St Helens Hospital on 1 August 1979. He was two weeks overdue. I had an epidural anaesthetic because my blood pressure was high, and managed to rest a lot of the time. Having a son was a surprise. I adored him. So did Grandma, who met him when he was half an hour old. She held him and rocked him. He stilled to her voice and touch. Tracey hugged and kissed him. With this many women fussing over him he didn't need a father. He had enough love here.

Wow, I was a mother! And what a mother I'd be — my baby would never be abused, hurt, or abandoned. I would give him whatever he needed and he would know how treasured he was every minute of his life. I knew I would kill anyone who hurt him and that Grandma and Tracey would too. There was no way that a baby loved so much could go wrong.

We stayed in hospital for a week and bonded closely. The nurses told me what a wonderful mum I was. Chris was picked up and cuddled if he made the smallest sound. I breast-fed him on demand, kissed him, rocked him and talked to him. I loved my boy as much as anyone has ever loved her child.

While we were still in hospital I received an unsupportive letter from Grandma and Grandad Roche. I was initially upset but decided to ignore the letter and maybe make my peace in my own time. Meanwhile I was almost happy to be out of their good books — who needed that sort of 'support'?

When we were discharged Christopher and I returned home to Miramar to live with Grandma and Tracey. Chris was the first member of the fifth generation of our family to live in the run-down house in Miramar. He was a funny-looking infant but adorable nonetheless. I couldn't imagine what my life had been like before him — I had a real purpose now, I was a mother. I missed my own Mum terribly but Grandma supported me more than adequately. Grandma cooked for me, washed nappies (I really wanted to do these things myself, but she insisted I needed my rest), taught me how to knit and smock clothes for my baby. Soon it seemed

I was relinquishing more and more of my motherhood role to Grandma. I was becoming Chris's second mum and that was not the role I'd hoped and planned for. I commented to a couple of friends that it seemed Grandma believed she'd given birth a few weeks earlier. At times this was great — at seventeen I was keen to have a social life, go to concerts and for walks on my own — having an infant in a pram got in the way of these things. It was so handy to have a built-in babysitter too. Other times it was frustrating.

I wanted the best of both worlds and ended up succeeding at neither. I felt I wasn't perhaps a good enough mother despite what the hospital nurses said, and Grandma was showing me this in the politest way she knew. I needed to break away and take my baby boy with me, before I was reduced to an even smaller role in his life. Maybe Grandma and I were headed for a tug-of-love over the baby. She loved to care for kids and had done so all her life.

Rather than face my responsibilities and spend more time with Chris I thought I should earn money for a flat. I began work at Kentucky Fried Chicken in Wellington. I earned enough money to lose half my Social Welfare benefit, but loved the freedom I gained. I missed my baby but knew he was safe in Grandma's expert hands. When I returned home at night Chris was pleased to see me. I felt a love for him that was so fierce it could be frightening. Nothing had prepared me for this — the intensity of the feelings I felt towards my darling boy. I couldn't believe my mother had ever felt this way about me. I'd never leave my boy or send him away — it was hard enough being away from him for the four or five hours of my shift.

How things change. Almost imperceptibly the four or five hours expanded to six or seven. Soon it was five days a week instead of two. Grandma began to seem more like his mother than I was. I had to leave her house while I still had my baby. I still thought the problem was more with

Grandma than with me.

I was on the waiting list for a state house and was eventually allocated one in Strathmore Park. Our new home was in the Rigel Flats, Nuku Street, just around the corner from Taiaroa Street where I'd lived as an infant.

My life was mirroring Mum's quite closely, something I didn't notice at the time.

Tracey, Christopher, Jenny (a former classmate of Trace) and I moved in to our new accommodation when Chris was eight months old. The flat had two bedrooms and a big lounge that overlooked Wellington airport. It was on the third floor, and we rejoiced at the number of stairs, imagining how fit we'd get. We bought furnishings from a Salvation Army store and got Mum's old lounge suite from Grandma's. It felt so grown-up to have a place, a baby and flatmates of my own. I was away from Grandma's help but still spoke to her every day from the call box on the corner, we had no phone initially. We had a bond that seemed unbreakable. I stopped working at KFC and became a full-time mum again. I wanted the best for my baby. I bought him lots of books — I wanted him to enjoy reading as much as I did.

27

Tracey, Jenny and I had the usual adolescent weight hang-ups and started a different diet every couple of weeks. Although we were all slim we ate little and exercised constantly. It was a competition where the winner was the girl who managed to eat fewer than five hundred calories each day and burn even more through exercise. We did leg-lifts and walked for miles. It could have been dangerous, but our love of food eventually won out and we all stabilised. We were all attractive but didn't fully believe it. Tracey had grown prettier as she got older. She'd permed her hair and it hung in golden curls down her back. Her peachy skin, big smile and blue eyes were a lovely combination. She was a talented artist, doing sketches that adorned the floor and walls. Jenny was part-Maori with caramel skin and big green eyes. She looked athletic and fit.

Although we were never satisfied with the way we looked, we realised we had power over the men we met. We thought that most of the blokes we met were idiots and we wouldn't condescend to sleep with them. We liked Americans, especially American sailors. Kiwi blokes just didn't meet our expectations.

While we were all caught up in the struggle for perfection, the nuclear powered warship USS *Truxtun* called in to port. New Zealand is nuclear-free, so the visit of nuclear-armed or powered ships caused a huge storm of protest. The reluctance of the US Government to 'confirm or deny' presence of nuclear arms on ships eventually led to the breakdown of the ANZUS defence agreement between Australia, New Zealand and the United States. As the *Truxtun* was deemed unwelcome in our city, she couldn't berth and had to anchor in the harbour like a leper outside the city gate.

Tracey, Jenny and I decided that now we had our own

place we should bring some sailors back for tea to show them they weren't unwelcome, just their nuclear energy. Such ambassadors for world peace! The other reason we wanted them to visit was hormonal. We were all keen on sex and sailors were so easy. We wheeled Christopher (now a year old) into town and wandered into McDonald's, the place where visiting sailors seemed to congregate. The staff had changed since I worked there so there was no likelihood of bumping into Wayne, Chris's dad. We looked around McDonald's — nobody interesting there. Walking down Courtenay Place we met two sailor boys. Both Americans and sailors have a distinctive look — the combination of the two is unmistakable. These two looked like nice guys. They'd just come from Indonesia and exclaimed over Tracey's and my blue eyes and Jenny's green ones. The guys introduced themselves: Franklyn, who was tall, skinny and kind of geeky; and Floyd, who had a nice smile and good muscles. They went gooey over Christopher, which helped me make up my mind that they were okay. We invited them home to dinner. They taxied home with us and stayed the night. The next day we all went to McDonald's together and met their friend Lonnie, a big, beautiful blond bear, who rounded out the numbers nicely.

The guys slept on the couch and the lounge floor, the rest of us in our own beds. We'd kind of paired up though: Floyd and me, Tracey and Frank, Lonnie and Jenny. There was nothing sexual in our relationships for the first day or two until Floyd and I tumbled into bed together, willing victims of a plot cooked up by Tracey and Jenny, who thought we were well-matched. Floyd and I spent most of our remaining two days together in bed. I'd get up to breast-feed Chris, change, bathe and clothe him and when he had a nap, Floyd and I did too. When the *Truxtun* left I was in love. My existence no longer revolved around just Christopher and myself. There was a male love interest in my life, the first since Chris's conception. Floyd was like the sailors who'd helped me stow away. I felt less guilty about their fate now. I realised that they were adults — all older than me — who had willingly taken part in the venture. I still felt bad but not enough to beat myself up over their fates.

I had a new reason to be obsessed — I had a man. I dieted and exercised with a new fervour to look perfect for Floyd when Chris and I joined him in the US. Tracey watched Chris in the evenings while I went jogging. I hated running but it was a means to an end. My mantra became "Floyd-and-Cal-i-for-ni-a-and-no-more-ug-ly-fat", each syllable another step. I would recite this to myself as I ran kilometre after kilometre around the suburbs. Floyd sent mail — cards and letters proclaiming his undying love. The days I received those I felt more cherished than ever before. He sent flowers too — once a dozen red roses — the first time that had ever happened. We exchanged cards and letters almost daily but this wasn't enough. I sent my phone number — "please call me and reverse the charges." He did. Often. Tracey, Jenny, Floyd, Franklyn, Lonnie and I spent hours on the phone. The bill was in my name. I had to pay all $3500 of it. It took sixteen years to pay, the last instalment was made in 1996, but at the time it seemed well worth it.

Part of the 'body beautiful' plan was to get the best suntan possible — otherwise how would I ever compete with all those California Girls when Chris and I got to the States? I saw an ad on TV for a suntan clinic, the first in the Wellington region, and signed up. There I met the manager, who offered me a job at one of her other businesses. Since I now had a new need for cash, to save to visit the United States, I accepted her offer and became a masseuse at the San Francisco Bathhouse.

28

In the early days there I loved the San Fran. It was a big bathhouse in downtown Wellington and a favourite meeting place of the gay and theatrical communities. It had a big open lounge area on the top floor with a gymnasium, solarium and hairdresser. There were pool tables and a coin-operated Space Invaders game (very cool at the time) at one end of the lounge.

Several massage rooms opened off a dim corridor which led to a shower room. Down a winding wooden staircase were the private sauna, two big public saunas, an extremely hot spa pool and a large icy plunge pool. On the walls around the big pool were murals depicting San Francisco. These were painted with fluorescent paint and looked stunning in the ultraviolet light that illuminated most of the lower level. There was music, usually a cruisey jazz-blues album, although sometimes The Eagles ('Hotel California'), or Boney M played. I felt so sophisticated working there, wandering around in my white sarong and feeling fabulous.

The girls who worked at the San Francisco were paid 30 percent of what we earned from our massages. Our duties were to massage the clients, sometimes to accompany them in the saunas as well, to do outcalls to hotels and private residences and to keep the place clean and tidy. We accepted credit cards; our receipts for these named a deerstalkers association so spouses couldn't tell where the money had been spent. 'Extras' (sexual activity with the clients) were optional. We were to be discreet about extras and could keep all the money we made performing them. I decided I wouldn't do extras. I was in love, so couldn't possibly have sex with anyone else. My sexual needs were well met by the steamy mail arriving from my equally hot sailor in San Diego, the *Truxtun's* home port.

Extras weren't such a big deal in those days. We were all on the pill, so herpes was the worst we could catch. There were seven of us working at the San Fran. All were young and good-looking — some of the girls were stunning — and all of us wiser than our years. Two of the girls were sisters, part-Maori with gorgeous faces and figures. They were at the San Fran to support boyfriends with drug habits. The younger one also sported occasional bruises in the crook of her elbow. I felt so frustrated with them — they could have done so much more with their lives. I couldn't see the same potential in myself.

I told Floyd about my new job. He wasn't thrilled but knew I had to do something to pay the rent and phone bill. He also wanted me to come to the States but couldn't pay for my fare, so accepted something had to give.

I was the only girl at the bathhouse to claim my own room and decorate it. The rooms were spartan. They were small, almost twice as long as they were wide, with cream walls and a beige vinyl-covered massage bed in the middle. There was just enough room to walk around the sides of the massage table and avoid the other pieces of furniture. Each room held a lockable wardrobe and a chair on which to place clothing. I hung posters on my walls, placed an old radio on top of the wardrobe and taped photos of Christopher and Floyd on the wardrobe door. I had scented candles burning constantly in my room, a reference to some Queen lyrics Floyd had sent me: *'Through the shadows of the night, let our candle always burn; Let us never lose the lessons we have learned.'*

The lyrics, copied by Floyd onto a piece of lined paper, were taped next to his photo on the wardrobe door.

Also in my room were books — I was maybe the only parlour girl in the land to have *Einstein's Universe*, *The Dragons of Eden*, *The Body in Question*, *The Art of Sensual Massage* and *The Holy Bible* in her room. The Bible was there was because although I had left my grandparents' faith behind I still found the Scriptures comforting. I read it sporadically, always the Psalms or Song of Solomon as I loved the poetry.

All the time I was working I kept the radio playing to give the clients and me something to listen to. We'd often end up both singing along to it. The Phil Collins' song 'In the Air Tonight' and Ultravox's 'Vienna' still remind me of the San Francisco. It seemed like they were always playing.

29

When I was at work Tracey looked after Chris. I didn't notice it at the time but my relationship with my son was slipping. I was working with the intention of getting a better life for the two of us, but each step I took towards this new life was a step away from him.

Occasionally Chris came to the bathhouse with me but this didn't feel right. I was so tuned into him and his needs that I'd be tense if he was upset, and I couldn't concentrate on my work properly. I also knew it wasn't the right environment for a baby. I was making good money — $50 some days, $100 on others. It certainly paid better than KFC. The girls who did extras were getting over a thousand dollars a week tax-free. They had lovely clothes and make-up. They could pay their bills; I couldn't. After a couple of months of noticing the huge pay disparity I began to calculate how much more money I'd be making if I did do a few extras. If I earned as much as the other girls and saved it all up, Chris and I could get to our new life in California so much faster. Floyd needn't know. I was still in love, but this wasn't about love. Sex for money was different and what Floyd didn't know wouldn't hurt him.

The next day on my way to work I stopped and bought a whole swag of pretty new underwear and two dozen condoms. I was set for my new role.

The prostitution was a means to an end — a better life for my boy and me — so it worried me less than the fact I was deceiving Floyd.

Prostitution has been glamorised as a profession. It's not all Pretty Woman — more like 'Ugly Men,' although this is unfair to some of the guys. There seem to be many ordinary men out there who just need someone to talk to, someone to listen to them. Part of the work of the prostitute is to listen without judging. A lot of the time I worked in the parlour I felt I should have had training in psychology. It seemed sad that these guys needed to remove their clothes before they were able to unburden themselves. It's not as if they were unattractive, they just seemed to lack the confidence or social skills to interact with women on any other level. A few of the men were awful, though. I remember one who had severe body odour. I wouldn't touch him until he'd bathed, so escorted him to the shower room. I stood outside the door until I heard the water running, then returned to my room. When I went back to get him ten minutes later he was sitting outside the cubicle pretending he was in the shower! He hadn't washed himself. He stank badly. The only way I could massage him was to rub Tiger Balm under my nose to neutralise his smell. I did this and tried to hold my breath for as long as was polite, as we weren't allowed to refuse to massage anyone.

Other guys had less straightforward tastes. There was one man, always covered in welts and bruises, who came in to be spanked. I couldn't do this — I looked at his bruised and broken flesh and couldn't inflict any more hurt on him.

The time I was paid to do a golden shower was hopeless too. I'd had a full bladder just prior to the request so had already had a good long pee. All that money down the drain — I had to give it back when I couldn't perform for him.

Other guys remain in my memory in a nicer way. There was the bus driver who paid for a one-hour nude massage each week but really only wanted to talk. He always brought me a gift of a piece of green porcelain. He was a lovely man who I think of with fondness. Another favourite client was the Television New Zealand executive who would pay for a nude massage but take the time to rub me down instead. When he paid for extras it was so he could perform oral sex on me. Another client owned a bookshop and in return for a hand job he gave me four or five paperbacks. I loved books and would happily have been paid this type of paper money by all my clients.

A trick to survival as a prostitute is to see the men — the 'johns' — as the ones who are being degraded. After all, they are the ones who have to pay for it. We had the power to say yes or no to extras — we didn't do anything that we weren't well paid for. As for the fantasy that women who sell their bodies enjoy the sex — it may be true in a minority of cases. All the women I knew who practised prostitution did it for the money, not because they enjoyed it. Drug addiction, big debts and simple greed were reasons for working, not an over-active sex-drive! I didn't like the sex part but soon learned that as long as I didn't kiss the man or have any other oral contact with him, I could imagine myself in another world. At times my pelvis or my hand was at the San Fran earning a living while my mind was miles away. I dreamed of San Diego and Floyd, to whom I'd never reveal my betrayal. I dreamed of a new life for Christopher, who at eighteen months was a bright little boy. I'd read Carl Sagan's Dragons of Eden, so thought of esoteric things like the evolution of human intelligence. I sometimes even pondered the existence of black holes — maybe my head was in one while I earned my living with another! I compiled shopping lists — anything at all to take my mind off the sex. I put on a good act of enjoying the sex for the blokes though — that always helped them come faster — and the faster the better in those circumstances.

Soon the imaginary journeying wasn't enough. I needed more distance between myself and the men whose needs I serviced. I began to drink two or three bottles of cheap bubbly wine each night, and take pills I bought from the other girls. These dulled my senses even more and made time go faster. I was becoming ensnared in the seductive world of chemical abuse. It was a slow entrapment though.

I barely noticed it happening.

I felt physically dirty at times. A lot of the men wouldn't use condoms and their money had become extremely important. I felt I couldn't turn it down. I often had sex with no protection at all, then would douche myself with undiluted disinfectant as soon as the client left.

I massaged quite a few women too and enjoyed their company. I found myself attracted to a couple of them and gave them extra-special erotic massages. Only one asked me for extras and to my surprise I said no. I arranged to meet her in a bar a few days later when I was cleaner and less tired. To my intense disappointment she didn't show up.

At this stage I'd been working at the sauna for over a year. Chris was growing up fast. I'd work all night at the San Fran then head home in the early hours to get a brief sleep before my baby woke up. The daytime was filled with naps, sunbathing, endless boring exercising (had to slim those thighs down), visits to Grandma's and housework. Tracey and Jenny helped out by looking after Chris while I worked. Sometimes they'd look after him during the day too while I slept. I began to rely on them more and see less of my son. He was well cared for but I placed far too much of the responsibility for him on my sister. It seemed like the right thing to do at the time — I was exhausted from the long and irregular hours I was working and was developing a short fuse. I was becoming increasingly despondent.

I was turning into my mother but didn't realise it.

30

The San Francisco Bathhouse was a favourite hunting ground for the single or searching gay population. Dozens of gay men frequented the place and I made a number of close friends. Male homosexuality plus promiscuity didn't ring any alarm bells then — news about the strange virus which was killing young gay men was a couple of years away. We were all ignorant of the risks. One of my closest friends at that time was Peter, who was queeny and preferred to be called Petal. I loved Petal. He was in a relationship with Grant (also known as Gloria), a straight-acting gay with a top civil service job. Petal was promiscuous even by the standards of the time, but this was an understood part of his relationship with Gloria. He delighted in picking up men who claimed to be straight and having sexual encounters with them in the San Fran's private sauna. I'd watch Petal cruise the guys, flirting and flattering them. He'd give me a big wink as he disappeared with them, to emerge a few minutes later, giggling. "Smell my breath, honey," spoken in his deep camp, was his usual greeting after one of these encounters. Sperm breath. Yuk.

Petal and I socialised out of working hours. We'd drop acid together and wander around Wellington in the middle of the night gazing at the buildings with kaleidoscope eyes. The acid was a chemical-soaked square or triangle of blotting paper that was held under the tongue. It had a horrible taste like the smell of old socks. After taking it, colours seemed brighter and noises louder but more melodic. Jokes were funnier by about a million times. I found my visual senses far more alive, to the point that there seemed to be more than three visible dimensions. There were a lot of features to some of our older architecture that didn't show themselves at other times — plaster gargoyles and trimmings, that seemed to retreat into the masonry during daylight, flaunted themselves for our eyes alone. It was an education.

One night we both saw a rabbit in the grounds of the old Government buildings in the middle of the central business district. We were each relieved the other person saw it too. Nobody else ever believed us. It took a few hours for normal, drab perception to return. I looked forward to our next 'girls night out.'

One night Petal and I sat down to rest in Manners Mall in the centre of Wellington City. We'd taken a fair few drugs — all in pill or tablet form, so they didn't count — and sat under a tree, our backs to a new complex being built, and stared up at the starry sky. We bemoaned the fact that the stars were so much less visible in the city, but did think we saw a few more when using hallucinogenic drugs. As we returned our gaze to our earthly surrounds it began to rain. Gentle, warm drops from the cloudless heavens. We looked at one another — yes, I feel it too — then back up at the sky. Not a cloud in sight... The drops fell heavier, more insistently; we were being teemed on. We both stood and turned as quickly as we could to see what was happening above and behind us. We spied a couple of gang members standing high on the scaffolding of the building under construction at our backs — they were urinating on us. They thought it was a huge joke. This put a whole new slant on the expression 'pissing down.'

Early the following morning, still high, we walked home to Gloria. It was too late for me to get back to the flat, everyone'd be asleep. We walked several kilometres through the city and an adjacent hillside suburb. Closed curtains shielded sleeping families from our gaze. There was humour in everything that night. We began to sing. Quietly at first, our volume increasing as we neared the house Petal and Gloria shared. We didn't need to knock on the door to wake

Gloria — he'd heard us coming. We'd woken him and all the neighbours with our rendition of Getcha, getcha getcha getcha feathers away from my nose — a top-ten hit at the time — punctuated with gasps for air and hysterical laughter. Gloria, resplendent in burgundy silk pyjamas, was not amused.

I slept between the boys that night, following a dressing down from Gloria about our noise. I slept safely and well. The following morning Gloria dropped me home. On the way we stopped at the cemetery so I could give Mum a flower. I understood her more now than I ever had before.

George was the manager of a posh men's store in downtown Wellington and had the wickedest grin. He couldn't believe I'd never had my toes sucked (I don't know how this came out in conversation!) so one night at the sauna he set about to showing how pleasurable it could be. He told me it was his prime seduction tactic and that any man whose toes he sucked would allow him to do anything he liked to them. He washed and massaged my feet before taking one toe at a time into his mouth and performing the most sublime foreplay I've ever experienced. Oh... George truly helped my education that night. I've never met with his success using this technique but I think he'd had an awful lot of practice.

My attachment to Chris was now tenuous. I saw him sporadically; sometimes a couple of days would go by without seeing him.

I took him to Grandma's one day, where he raced outside to play in the back yard. There was nowhere safe for him to play at our flat so visits to Grandma were a real treat. Grandma and I were having a cup of tea at the kitchen table when we heard Chris howl with pain and rage. He'd fallen and grazed his knee. He came into her kitchen yelling, tears tracking down his grubby cheeks.

I ran to him and dropped to my knees, arms open to console him. Chris ran straight past me into Grandma's arms. I might have been an apparition. I felt hurt beyond belief. What had I done? I'd failed him and myself. Or had I? I was too upset and confused to analyse things. Besides, he'd probably be better off without a whore for a mother.

I began to spend even less time at home.

The Olympics in Moscow in 1980 were boycotted by the United States and several other Western countries in protest at the Soviet invasion of Afghanistan. New Zealand was one of the many boycotting nations that offered to host alternative games for the disappointed athletes. Hataitai Velodrome in Wellington was the site of the cycling events and hosted teams from Europe, Australia and the Americas. I met the US Olympic cycling team while I was jogging around the waterfront one day on my way to the San Francisco. They stopped me, purportedly to ask directions. One of them wanted my phone number and I gave them the address of the bathhouse. Oh, the bodies — they were hot. Even their manager was cute... cuter than Floyd.

Three of the cyclists met me at the sauna later that night and invited me to watch their races. They were a long way from home and seemed lonely, as well as disappointed that their games had been ruined.

I continued to work at the San Francisco and spent some time with Grandma and Chris, but mostly I stayed at the Airport Hotel with the American team and went out around Wellington with them on lay days. At the opening ceremony at the Velodrome, Christopher ran around bare-bottomed after removing his own nappy. The former Prime Minister Bill Rowling was there and chuckled at the semi-nude baby. Not everyone was so impressed though. We got a few disapproving looks.

I became the unofficial mascot of the US team and

attended all the events with them, even staying in their motel most nights. I also made friends with members of the Mexican and Italian teams and the Kiwis. One of the Kiwi cyclists assumed I was an American who had travelled to New Zealand with the team. I didn't want to embarrass him so started to talk with an American accent. It would have been so much simpler to correct him ... less embarrassing for me in the long run too.

The team was close-knit and a lot of good-natured teasing took place between the individual athletes. One of the guys was called Brent Emery. He was nicknamed 'Burnt Mammary' or 'Bent Memory' by his team-mates, who said he was a prima donna, his bent memory leading him to believe he was the most valuable team member.

There was track racing at the Velodrome, the competition culminating in a road race around the Basin Reserve and central Wellington streets. I bought a bucket of KFC and gave chicken pieces to the guys as they cycled by, my alternative to the oranges and energy drinks other people were handing out. They probably didn't eat the chicken but I got some smiles. They were lovely guys and my time with them gave me some special memories. We took the team van to Plimmerton, 45 minutes north of Wellington and jumped from a road bridge into the sea two metres below, finishing the day with a swim.

I corresponded with a couple of the American cyclists for about a year but we gradually lost touch. They told me that a photo of me taken showering with the sole team member I slept with was on the wall of the van the US cycling team used for training.

31

I needed to keep the California dream alive. After all that was what led to my work at the San Francisco. I still heard regularly from Floyd, Frank and Lonnie in San Diego. They kept promising to sponsor Tracey, Chris and me to visit them in America, but never filled in the requisite forms. It was frustrating and the phone bills were piling up. I was spending my earnings on designer clothes, alcohol, pills and restaurant meals, and saving nothing. I still wanted to travel to the US but it was beginning to look too hard. I felt I needed to reward myself with nice clothes for doing a job that I hated. The pills and booze had become as essential as oxygen. Without them I couldn't have continued.

I approached the American Embassy to see if I could get a visa to visit the US without a sponsor. I was told this would be difficult, in view of the hassles I'd caused by stowing away. Even though Dad had paid my return fare this did not guarantee me right of return to the US should I request it. They suggested I be a good girl, save hard and apply for a visa when I had enough money for a return ticket. I had to remember that I'd need a few thousand dollars to support my child and myself while visiting the States too, otherwise I could be turned back at the border. I began to worry — maybe they'd never let me return to America. I needed Plan B. Fast.

My fantasy remained, that escape to America would improve my life. All I needed was the money and a visa. One morning around 2am, Plan B walked up to me and shook my hand. I was working at the San Francisco in a muddled and somewhat chemically-altered state of mind when one of the other girls introduced me to the future Mr Roche. James David (or was it David James?) Gee was a Canadian looking for a Kiwi wife to help him get a visa for New Zealand, which would assist his 'import business' (it turned out he brought cocaine into the country). He was big, brash and instantly likeable in a 'bad boy' kind of way. He was a great con artist and could make anyone comfortable in his presence within a few moments. I liked him and immediately agreed we should be married. Our marriage would give me easy access to Canada (therefore, I thought, the US) and get him the New Zealand visa he required. He promised to throw in a trip to Fiji for me, a half-share of his Corvette Stingray, and a few thousand dollars in cash. I was rapt, perhaps Chris and I would be in California soon; I was getting more out of this arrangement than the groom-to-be. Marriage plans are meant to take time but Mr Gee and I were married twelve hours later in the registry office in Anvil House, Wellington. He'd found a way to speed the process up. Tracey was our witness — I'd woken her up to come and do the deed for us and she'd leapt out of bed at the prospect of easing our access to the States. I'd promised I'd take her there as soon as I was able to. The only possible snag was Dad. I was under twenty so needed parental permission to wed. Dad had no problem with the marriage. In a way this disappointed me — I wish now he had made some semblance of protest. Perhaps he was sick of bailing me out and was hoping my new husband would take on this role instead.

The night of the nuptials we got a room at the Abel Tasman hotel, a few doors up Willis Street from the San Francisco. The three of us slept together — Tracey in between my husband and me. We all slept well — nothing consummated.

I was now Mrs Gee. I'd known my husband for thirty-six hours when he left me, leaving me no ticket for Fiji, no cash and no forwarding address. I got the consolation prize though — an easy trip to Canada and a story for my grandkids if I ever had any. A few days later there was news of him — The Evening Post carried a story about a

Canadian man who'd conned several thousand dollars out of other tourists staying in a Christchurch backpackers hostel. His full name and description were in the paper. No mistaking it — my first husband was trouble. Oh well, there was always divorce.

One of the other interesting people I met through the San Francisco was Andy, an Adonis and about the only straight one to ever enter our parlour. He and I teamed up. My hair was newly bleached, my tan was dark and I was at the most flattering weight I'd ever been. I was looking good. I was attending a deportment course at 'The Academy of Elegance' and fancied myself as a model. Andy was a model — he would go on to do TV and print ads — and I thought he was sophistication personified. Andy introduced me to a seedy photographer who took photos of me in various stages of undress (and a couple of Andy and me showering together — taken without our permission). With my blonde hair and made-up face I felt soooooo glamorous. I carried my photographs around everywhere with me. One of the other girls at the bathhouse told me I looked just like Marilyn Monroe — a few weeks after her death... Bitch.

Despite looking good I was becoming depressed — there was no mistaking the symptoms. I was lethargic and tearful and my self-esteem was about as low as it had ever been. It seemed there were two of me: the over-confident blonde who strutted around the place, and the tearful mouse that cowered inside her. Few people realised how miserable I was. I felt trapped and although I'd willingly entered this place, it seemed there was no way out. I would lie on the massage table in my room, where I was now working some days as well as most nights, and look out the window at the sky. There were often seagulls flying over the San Fran — I envied them their ability to fly away and would cry as I watched them wheeling against the sky. Why was my life so hard? I was still drinking and popping pills — they helped the day go by faster. The alcohol and drugs fuelled the depression and I needed to take more and more of them to feel I had any clarity of vision at all. I was falling apart. I still couldn't see that I was responsible for my own misery.

One man who spent a lot of time at the bathhouse was Tony. He was tall, well built and blond. He became my confidant and occasional lover. We had sex a couple of times on the massage table or on the floor of my room. I was so good at distancing my emotions from the sexual act that it took a mammoth effort on my part to take pleasure from our romps — it was enjoyable but I think that he seemed like he could become a friend was more important to me. I needed a friend, one that lived in the same country as me. One I could believe in. A year or so later I met Tony again and was amazed that I hadn't seen the obvious at the time. Tony was a cop, working undercover at the San Fran — when I met him again he was in police uniform, buying chicken from me in my second incarnation as a 'KFC chick.' I wonder if I looked as surprised as he did?

Despite my misery I still enjoyed some good parties. The rock band Kiss came to Wellington and the San Francisco girls were invited to a post-concert party to 'liven things up.' Wow, a real live, major league rock band and they wanted us … We'd met a few minor stars in the entertainment world but this was different. Six of us taxied to their hotel, which had a big indoor swimming pool where the party was held. Gene Simmons looked disgustedly at us as we arrived — "I see the children are here." At that stage he was dating Cher so I guess a bunch of girls in their late teens and early twenties did seem very young. We felt old enough though. The other guys were slightly more polite. Jeannie, another San Fran girl, and I sat at the feet of the new drummer Eric Carr, and sang along to the music on the stereo. Eric told us our voices were awful — we told him we didn't care what he thought and kept right on singing. What did he know, he was just a drummer. We met all the band members without their make-up, a privilege because the black-and-white face paint they always wore was a big part of the band's image.

The party moved up a gear. Local music personalities and record company personnel were there, as well as the band, the roadies and us. The San Fran girls began to strip off and swim in the pool. Other people followed suit. None of the band members joined us — they stood on the side of the pool and pissed on the swimmers. One of the roadies crapped into the pool at the deep end. He asked one of the record company guys to pick up the dark object he'd dropped on the bottom of the pool, saying it was his watch. The hapless guy took his glasses off and dived to the bottom to get the 'watch', smearing shit all over the bottom of the pool. Gross. Time to get out and get dressed.

The national tabloid Truth ran an article about the party headlined 'Sex, Debauchery and Destruction.' They were completely over the top, saying that dozens of prostitutes had been hired and that there was a trail of panties from the pool to the hotel bedrooms. I did lose a pair of knickers that night — someone souvenired them when I was swimming. None of the other girls lost theirs and we all got home reasonably early. Jeannie and I befriended one of the roadies who promised that if we got ourselves to the Auckland venue he'd let us backstage and give us free passes to the concert.

We were off again.

32

Christopher stayed with Grandma for a couple of days while Jeannie and I travelled to Auckland. I had no sleep for over forty-eight hours before we left. It was getting busy at the San Francisco and I was exhausted by the time we got to Auckland. We tracked down our friendly roadie at his hotel and uplifted passes that would allow us access to the backstage as well as the usual concert areas. We caught the bus to the Western Springs Stadium several hours before the concert was due to start and were admitted by one of the road crew to the backstage area. We kept out of the way as much as possible. I was far too tired to make mischief anyway. One of the roadies asked for a blowjob. Jeannie and I laughed at him and said we didn't believe in doing things that gave us no pleasure at all. He seemed to think that was fair enough.

While we were talking to him we saw a TV crew pull up at the gates. Dylan Taite was with them, the man who'd upset my former heroes, the Bay City Rollers. He was looking for an interview with Kiss, who were due for a sound check at any time. I told the road manager that Mr Taite had a reputation for stirring up problems, (even though it had been many years since I'd seen him last). The road manager sent him and his camera crew packing. I felt smug about that. Roller fans have long memories...

The Kiss concert was great. Jeannie and I stood right up the front and yelled and cheered, our passes pinned conspicuously to our chests. The party afterwards was at an Auckland nightclub that had been booked out for the event. We travelled in a limo with some of the crew and were looked at enviously by girls who'd arrived at the venue in the hope of seeing the band. I couldn't keep my eyes open though — my head kept falling over onto the table as sheer exhaustion took over. I ended up getting the limo back early with one of the minor management types. I tried to stay awake while he had sex with me — after all he was providing a place for me to stay. But I fell asleep and can only assume he finished the deed. I hadn't even got drunk or anything. The next day we hitchhiked back to Wellington, picking Christopher up on our way through.

Looking back I feel so sorry for Chris. Those days my childish shuffling of him from pillar to post didn't seem wrong. I was repeating the way Mum had parented me; the very thing I'd promised I'd never do. My mind was befuddled by drugs, alcohol and depression, just as Mum's had been. Before I could understand and forgive myself, I had to do the same for her. I wasn't ready for that yet.

One of the good things about having lots of gay friends was the variety of parties and nightclubs I got to attend. The Dorian Society was a club where gay men and a few transvestites met to drink and disco. The club had weekly gatherings in central Wellington, across the road from the San Francisco. I loved going there. There were loads of men, none of them the least bit interested in sleeping with me. (After doing it several times a day for a living it gets unattractive as a recreational act.) The guys were courteous, usually gorgeous and well dressed. They would buy me drinks, we would chat; none of it predatory or with ulterior motives.

Few women were invited to the Dorian. I was because so many of the members knew me and realised I was harmless. It was a great place to socialise. The only other place I've felt so comfortable in 'clubby' surroundings is at lesbian gatherings, where the predatory element is usually absent.

One of the most memorable parties I went to was not a gay one but was put on by the photographer who'd captured the shots of Andy and me in the shower. Andy and I got dressed up and arrived together at the party in his battered old Cortina. We parked down the road so no one would see the state of the vehicle. Andy and I complemented one another well — we made a lovely couple — it's a shame there was no sexual attraction between us. We entered the party together — parakeets among the sparrows. We'd overdone the dress-up. There were probably thirty people there but I only remember Andy, Gina, and me.

The moment I met Gina I couldn't take my eyes off her. She was butch — absolutely unmistakably lesbian — and ugly. She was missing her lower teeth and didn't like to wear a plate. She was dressed in baggy khaki overalls. There was a huge, palpable sexual energy between us. I'd never had full sex with a woman before. I regularly showered at the bathhouse with one of the other girls, accidentally brushing her breasts with my hand and dropping the soap a few times so I could brush my face past her groin, but had never gone further than this. Within twenty minutes of our meeting Gina and I were in bed. The guys wanted to view the momentous occasion, but we refused. We pushed a chest of drawers against the bedroom door and fell on the bed together.

I remember the first sex I had with a woman far more clearly than the fumbling with my first male lover. Perhaps it was the difference in the circumstances and my experience level — but I think it was because it felt so right. The sex was entirely different to what I was accustomed to — I finally knew what the fuss was about. It would be many years before I accepted myself as a lesbian, but this night set the scene.

Sex with a woman is far more sensual than with a man. The heat, aroma, taste of Gina; the weight and softness of her breasts, her erect nipples so much more responsive than a man's; and the way our bodies matched each other's are still vivid. There is also the sense of mutuality — a feeling that the sex is between equals. This was something that always seemed to be missing when I had sex with a man.

We spent hours in bed together, finally emerging when the party was ending. My make-up was a mess, my clothes were crushed, but I felt more beautiful than I had when Andy and I arrived.

Gina and I saw each other for a few weeks, but I became embarrassed by her toothless grin (she'd taken to leaving her top teeth as well as the bottom ones out), the way she dressed, and the way she called me "darling" all the time. I could have handled it if she made an effort with her appearance — I was afraid people would be laughing at me for my choice of mate.

Apart from The Dorian Society and the brief interlude with Gina, my life was turning to shit. I was having my first major encounter with what would be a lifetime companion — depression.

It began with a further loss of self-esteem and motivation. Soon I was tearful and felt worthless. I knew I was an awful mother — and after such a promising start, how did I let things get this way? I felt trapped in my situation, now realising that the chance of being rescued and taken to California was remote. It seemed the San Francisco Bathhouse was as close to California as I'd ever get. Chris was bonded to Grandma and Tracey and would be fine without me. I had lost one of my main reasons to live.

I'd held on as long as I could, drowning my misery with alcohol, drugs and parties, but was sliding inexorably towards suicide. Death seemed my only chance of escape. Maybe then I'd feel as free as the seagulls that flew past my window. Maybe then I could feel unconfined again.

One quiet night at the San Francisco I sat on my massage bed and cut my wrists with my Swiss Army knife. It hurt more than I expected — so much for 'Suicide is Painless' as the song claims. I didn't get much deeper than the skin before thinking there'd have to be an easier way. I put iodine over the cuts and bound them tightly, after letting a few drops of blood seep through the bandages to add to the dramatic effect. I made sure everyone noticed I'd hurt myself. Someone sent me roses with a card telling me to keep my chin up, which made me cry more. There had to be more to life than this.

Money had become the reason for my existence — Chris had been supplanted. The trouble was, the more I earned, the more I needed to earn. There was never enough. I had to work longer hours. Soon I was doing two full-time jobs. During the day I was a kitchenhand and waitress at Rafters restaurant and in the evenings I was a masseuse at the San Fran. I'd try to catch a couple of hours sleep between jobs, then nap at the sauna for three or four hours before starting work again. I jumped at any opportunity to earn more money.

Once I spent a weekend in Masterton with one of my San Fran clients who was sixtyish, overweight and revolting. His best erection was bendy like a carrot that'd been left in the vegetable bin too long. Sex with him was horrible — his sheer bulk made it hard to ignore him and the thought of a whole weekend of it was almost intolerable. He did promise to pay me $500 though, which made me shut up and get on with it. We stayed one night at the Solway Park Hotel and another at a nice little homestay where I read a collection of James K. Baxter poems and tried to ignore Mr Carrot-cock as much as possible. I didn't get the money — he didn't think I seemed interested enough in him to have earned it.

Another potential earner I agreed to take part in was an amateur porn movie, to be shot in Wellington. As I believed I had no future in New Zealand and would never find someone to 'really' marry me there was no problem about being immortalised like this. I thought I was hardly likely to get the chance to regret it. I had a couple of rehearsals in a room at a scruffy little motor lodge at the southern end of The Terrace. The day filming was to begin I received a call at home. It had been called off — the place had been busted and all the equipment confiscated.

A few years later I was told that Tony — the one who turned out to be a cop — had tipped his colleagues off about the filming. Thank you, Tony — thank you, thank you, thank you.

33

The *Polar Star* and *Glacier* returned to town. I went to visit them with Andy and Mitch, the girl I showered with at the bathhouse. I got part-way round each ship before I was recognised and asked to leave. I was told my photograph had been distributed to all US military ships visiting Wellington. The photo would be kept on the quarterdeck of all visiting vessels so I could be denied access and the chance of my making more of a nuisance of myself would be minimised. I put up some token resistance, secretly pleased by the power I seemed to have. It has been reported that I screamed obscenities at the *Glacier* when asked to leave her. I don't recall this and frankly don't want to imagine myself doing it. If I did I am truly embarrassed and sorry. I guess we all did stupid things in our teens. I just made my mistakes more public than they needed to be.

Tracey, Jenny, Chris and I were still living at 11 Rigel Flats. The door was always left unlocked because we had nothing to steal and hoped that Floyd, Frank or Lonnie would come back to New Zealand to visit us. My cousins also knew the address and it came to be a safe place for them to stay when they needed time out. It wasn't unusual for me to get home from work to an unexpected but welcome guest asleep on the couch. I was so flattered they wanted to stay with me. In a way our flat became the equivalent of Mum's little bedroom, a haven for our cousins and a place where they gravitated when in trouble. I was grateful to have inherited some of Mum's good qualities along with the not-so-good ones.

Some of my sauna friends and I were getting bored. We needed something big to liven up our lives — a diversion. One of the downsides of working in the sex industry was the jadedness that quickly set in. Going to the movies was no longer a cure for boredom — it was several degrees of

magnitude short. One of the gay boys suggested an orgy —
a great big mixed one — in the private sauna. That would
surely liven things up! There were about five gay boys keen,
a couple of women and two straight boys. The latter would
only join in if they made all the overtures and would be
allowed to have sex with the women only — straight guys
have no sense of adventure. An orgy sounded like fun. I'd
never had one before. We planned it for a couple of weeks
but then somehow all lost interest. I think the thought
of women finally got to the gay boys, while the straights
were worried about their bent brothers. I was keen but
depressed and didn't have the energy to convince the
others to do it.

I'm glad our orgy didn't happen. We didn't know about
HIV then but five years later two of those who were to
participate in the big event had Aids. Three years after
that my friends Petal and George were both dead. Had
they already contracted the virus? Possibly. None of us
knew about HIV so none of us took precautions. Petal was
promiscuous but so were many of us. I was lucky.

One of the ways my depression manifests itself is in
intense self-hatred. Feeling fat and ugly is one of the first
indications that I'm heading down the darker road. I was
always attempting to alter or optimise my body's shape and
size — this time in my life was no different. I'd always had
oversized breasts — something Grandma had teased me
about repeatedly while I was growing up. Twenty months of
breast-feeding hadn't helped. Rather than reducing in size
my breasts got bigger but hung lower. I decided I needed
cosmetic surgery. I needed a breast reduction and lift. I
bought myself one, paying it off over the next year. I had
my surgery two days before the marriage of Diana to Prince
Charles. I watched the Royal wedding in the big lounge
at the San Francisco Bathhouse, tightly bandaged from
waist to neck but feeling surprisingly comfortable. I lay

on the couch, waited on by the other girls, and cried into my hanky when Charlie wed Di. We drank cheap sparkling wine to toast the couple. The San Fran was quiet that night. All the regular queens — those who weren't at the Palace, that is — were no doubt watching the show at home.

It was time to move back in with Grandma too. With the burgeoning depression I was spending less and less time at the flat. It was filthy. Tracey had had enough of being left with the baby and was spending a lot of time with Chris at Miramar. Jenny didn't want to live alone in a pigsty and thought she'd move back in with her Dad. It was hard saying goodbye to the flat, to independence, to the link with Floyd, Lonnie and Frank, but we had to do it. We'd already sold most of our furniture to raise cash to travel to America so there was little to pack up.

I learned that I had a distant cousin in the police. Paul worked as a sergeant in the drug squad. He was related to me on my father's side, the branch of the family I had little to do with. I set about meeting him — a new rellie, one on the opposite side of the law to myself. I had a good relationship with the police so whenever I bumped into cops I knew I asked them to get my cousin to contact me. I was told he had longish curly hair and looked like a cross between John McEnroe and Bodie, a character in *The Professionals* — a British TV thriller series. He did — I recognised him as soon as he came into the sauna. I guess his reasons for our meeting were similar to mine — it gave us the opportunity to briefly walk on the wilder side. He was nice to me, as was his friend James who came along for moral support. We didn't sort out the exact extent of our blood tie, it seemed too complicated. We had a coffee together and arranged to meet for a drink later. Paul didn't look like a cop, nor did he carry himself like one. His hair was longer than regulations allowed, he had a false front tooth — his police ID photo clearly showed it missing —

and he was a lot more relaxed than the other cops I knew. I thought he was great.

We met for a drink a few days later at the Clyde Quay tavern. Paul was alone this time and seemed more relaxed. We were at a bar he didn't usually drink at — he was uncomfortable at the thought of us being seen together, although he didn't say so at the time. I thought he was a guy who liked to thumb his nose at restrictions and traditions. He thought he was too. He was conventional about some things though — his choice of partner was one area this conservatism showed up.

Still, he wanted to see me again. I wasn't used to the idea of men seeing me as interesting company. Paul didn't even seem to want to sleep with me — I guess we were related but it seemed a distant enough thing not to interfere if we didn't want it to. It added to the attraction I felt for him. The little touch of illicitness was a turn-on for me. I took him to meet Grandma, Tracey and Chris. He was distant with Chris, explaining he had a son a few months younger whom he was estranged from. Poor Paul — this lent him a tragic air and made him seem even more desirable. I'd make him happy again ... He told me his wife was in Australia, but didn't say that it was for a two-week holiday. I assumed she was gone forever.

In time our hugs and kisses became less cousinly and more intimate. There seemed no hurry. We still met occasionally for drinks. I liked him a lot and felt pleased with myself too. I was now somebody, going out with a policeman. I can't have been scum. I was still getting depressed though. The only way I was headed at the time seemed down, down, down.

34

That same week the Springbok tour burst upon New Zealand. It caused division and distress to families and communities all over the country. The New Zealand Rugby Football Union had extended an invitation to the South African Springbok rugby team to tour our country. The South Africans accepted and the tour was under way.

Protesters argued that South Africans were as fanatical about their sport as New Zealanders and Australians. By limiting their opportunities to play sport at an international level the rest of the world could encourage the South Africans to reassess their policy of apartheid. Others firmly believed that sports and politics should not mix.

There was a well-organised anti-sporting-contact protest movement, whose New Zealand membership consisted mostly of left-leaning liberals, often better educated, pro-Maori, and anti-fascist. A few disaffected people, including many patched gang members who were itching for a fight, joined this group. On the other side was the bulk of the rugby public and people who wanted to keep politics out of sport — their 'side' also aided and abetted by those who were just looking for a few heads to crack. It was an ugly and frightening time. Mostly though, the people who went to war on the streets that winter were sincere and deeply committed to what they believed was right.

The first protest meeting I attended was outside the St George Hotel in Willis Street. I came upon it by accident while walking to the San Fran. It was less than a week after my surgery and bandages still tightly bound my chest. I joined the huge mass of people, careful to keep my reduced and lifted assets protected, and listened to the speeches.

I agreed with what I heard — apartheid was abhorrent and by sustaining sporting contact with South Africa we were colluding with a racist regime. It was such a different world then — Nelson Mandela was still in prison and there seemed no prospect for his release. Black and coloured South Africans had a tiny fraction of the power and freedom of the white population. It was so obviously wrong. I was inspired by what I heard. It was time for me to look outside myself again. Here was something important to worry about — something I could do to make the world better for someone else. As a welcome side-effect I made many new friends.

We genuinely believed we could make a difference, all the way down here at the bottom of the world in the southern winter of 1981. I think we did.

Nelson Mandela said, "You made us feel at home in the world" to describe the impact of our protests in bringing reforms to South Africa. He obviously believed we made a difference too.

The tour's second game was called off when protesters invaded the Hamilton rugby field. I was watching this unfold on the television at the San Francisco and was jubilant. I shared the news with all the clients. Their reactions were equally divided between those who thought the protest was a good thing and those who disapproved. No one sat on the fence — it seemed everyone had a strong opinion and few were hesitant to share their view. The protesters rejoiced at their victory, the government refused to call off the tour, and the police promised to tighten up security at the remainder of the matches. New Zealand became unrecognisable. Rugby fields were surrounded with barbed wire fences and big steel rubbish skips blocked access roads outside the games. Hundreds of thousands of people took to the streets. Civil disobedience was rampant and being encouraged from the pulpit and by the most unlikely people — grandparents, post office workers, doctors. It was a bizarre time.

Before the tour got to Wellington there was a big demonstration outside the South African Consul's residence in Wellington. Arrests were made for obstruction and breaching the peace. Those of us who weren't arrested marched on Central Police Station to await the release of our comrades. There were thousands of us, all chanting 'Free Nelson Mandela', 'Amandla Ngawethu,' 'The whole world's watching' and other slogans. There were dozens of police, plainclothes and uniforms, lined up against us. Things were still reasonably good-humoured, although there was the occasional call for violence against the cops. I heard someone yell out that some police had their ID numbers on upside down to make it more difficult for protesters to lodge complaints against them. This became common practice during the tour. Another person scolded a cop good-naturedly for his hair being too long. Our relationship with the police didn't stay this way for long.

The tour came to Wellington with a test match at Athletic Park. The police had formed special units — Red, Blue and Yellow Squads — to cope with the unprecedented number of protesters. These squads were equipped with full riot gear, including the special long baton which became known as the Minto Bar, after John Minto, a protest leader.

The protesters also organised themselves into squads. I was in Brown Squad and Pink Squad at different times that day in Wellington. Protesters on the front line wore crash helmets and carried shields. Men wore cricket boxes for protection and many had steel-capped boots. It had turned deadly serious.

I was barefoot that day, having been at a nightclub until the early hours of the morning. I had a tracksuit to change into but no proper shoes, and bare feet seemed more appropriate than stilettos, given the circumstances. I was on the outskirts of the protest when approached by a well-known Maori activist, who stomped on my feet. He told me to get used to it, it was what the pigs would do if they saw my unshod feet. I moved further back into the body of the crowd. The stomping brought reality to my fears of being injured at the front. It hurt.

We surrounded Athletic Park, 'The home of Wellington Rugby,' and watched the public file in. We chanted "Shame, shame" and "The whole world's watching" as the fans crowded past. I saw Andy, the boy with whom I'd showered on film, entering the park. I called out his name, soon picked up by the other protesters. "Shame, Andy, shame" we chanted at him. He seemed delighted at the attention.

The rugby fans were as hyped as we were. Both groups needed little incentive to ignite to violence. Overall the police did an effective job keeping the sides apart — it would have taken so little for the situation to become uncontrollable. There was focus on the incidents where the cops used excessive force, the news showing protesters battered and bleeding. The cops were the enemy during the tour, yet their ranks must have been divided too. They had to present a united front to ensure order.

That day in Newtown people were barricaded in their homes along the route, looking through curtains at the mayhem on the streets outside. There was barbed wire outside Athletic Park — was this really New Zealand? We rushed the police lines, chanting in unison — "Shame, shame, shame." I passed a cop I knew from the sauna and smiled at him. "Hi Ross, how are you?" — his eyes glazed, unrecognising, facing the enemy. When we reached the Cambridge Hotel after the game (New Zealand lost, increasing the hostility of the rugby fans) I was restrained by other protesters from going over for a drink in defiance of the rugby fans jeering at us from outside. I was hyped and looking for trouble.

Fortunately the people I was with had more sense.

Some of us volunteered to take part in 'sideshows' — little attention-getting acts to ensure the public didn't lose sight of what we were saying. I'd had a special T-shirt made to wear at the sideshows — it was white and *tight*. Written across the front was "Help the Riot Squad — Beat Yourself Up." This is the design I submitted to the printer, anyway. The finished result was misspelled "Help the Riot Sqaud…" I picked the T-shirt up on the way to the first sideshow, so had to brazen it out. Unfortunately a literate journalist noticed the error and printed my picture in a Sunday paper.

I had two sideshow roles. The first was to distract the police during a protest march by climbing onto the verandahs of the shops along the route. Five or six of us had this task, which was kind of fun but scary for someone like me with a fear of heights. I was pulled down off one of the verandahs by an irate policeman and badly sprained my ankle. It hurt a lot that night when I was safely home at Grandma's. During the day though adrenaline made it support me just fine.

Another of the sideshows earned me my only police conviction. Air New Zealand, the national airline and the only one to fly the domestic route at the time, had the task of transporting the Springboks and their touring party. They had to be stopped. The entrance to the Air New Zealand head office in Wellington had double glass doors. Our brief was simple — a group of twenty of us were to storm the building in the middle of the day — a busy time for Air New Zealand. Eighteen were to chain themselves between the glass doors, stopping public access to the commercial area of the building. The other two — Alan and I — were to remain inside the building to ensure the others were able to padlock the doors without hindrance. The protest went off as planned. The police arrived after twenty minutes and cautioned Alan and me. We were given the option of leaving immediately or remaining to face arrest and possible criminal conviction along with the rest of our group. There seemed to be a vast audience — how could we possibly back down? We elected to stay and were arrested and charged with being unlawfully on premises. We were taken in the police van to Central, where a large number of protesters had congregated. They cheered us as we arrived. Wow! I had done something great. I was so glad I hadn't backed down.

While in the cells, where the sexes were segregated, I checked my breasts — the bandages were off and I'd been bumped around in the police van and needed to check if my stitches were still okay. My self-examination prompted one of the other women to ask, "What have the cops done to you?" All the women disapproved of my surgery — they called it self-mutilation, but I was pleased with the result.

They were a great group, all politically aware. Many of them were experienced in this kind of action but few were conversant with my line of work. They were all firmly committed to the beliefs of the protest movement and were politically active in other arenas too. I felt horribly naïve in their presence.

We were all charged with the same offence. Many of the others thought we should appear in court with our faces made up half-black and half-white to hammer home the point we were making about apartheid. I just wanted to get it over with as soon as possible, so disagreed, as did one other. As we didn't all agree we turned up in court as ourselves. Our charges were to be heard together — there were so many cases related to tour protests that the courts couldn't afford to hear them individually.

35

I didn't see much of Paul at this time. Like other police officers his leave had been cancelled and he was compelled to work. I missed him but was occupied myself with the bathhouse, the tour and Chris.

The tour continued despite the mayhem and division it was causing. I paraded around the San Francisco wearing my 'Stop the Tour' badge. The St George Hotel just down the street was where members of the Springbok's touring party were staying. The management of the San Fran were worried. Should I be allowed to wear the badge on the night of the test, when rugby supporters — maybe including South Africans — were likely to visit? They thought not.

While the bosses argued over my badge I went with one of the other girls to the main bar at the St George. We had received a phone call at the sauna saying some South Africans needed company for a few hours. My badge was well hidden of course — I didn't want my politics to get in the way of enterprise — and I wanted to earn a few Rand that night. In the house bar we met several Springbok supporters, who seemed nice enough guys. Older than us, drunk and pleased to tell us how things 'really' were in their Southern African paradise. We had expected to meet the Springboks themselves so were disappointed. One of the men lived in Namibia and promised to pay my airfares to his country so I could see what the political system was really like. He was certain I'd be convinced the South Africans had things the right way round. I politely declined, knowing well what it was like to be stuck in a country thousands of miles from home with no prospect of escape. One experience like that was enough. He wrote to me several times after his return home, offering to pay my return fare to his homeland, always politely insistent. I never went.

Back at the San Fran later that night the management was still undecided on the fate of my badge. Ewan, one of my gay friends, told me The Dorian was meeting that night. We were so busy at the San Fran that they wouldn't allow me the night off, even though they were giving me grief about my badge. This called for drastic action.

Ewan and I sneaked out of the San Fran to a callbox down the road. He rang Radio Windy, then I rang the Television New Zealand newsdesk. We relayed the same message: "I have heard the Springbok rugby team are to visit the San Francisco Bathhouse later tonight — I have planted a bomb there to kill the racist bastards. The bomb will detonate in one-and-a-half hours."

Radio Windy treated the call as a hoax. TVNZ believed me. Ewan and I dropped acid and returned to the bathhouse, waiting for the police to close us down so I could go to The Dorian. We sat on the couch and waited. The drugs kicked in at about the same time as a horde of uniformed police marched up the stairs. Ewan and I sat mesmerised on the couch, counting the coppers. One, two, three.... fourteen. We were stunned. It was more force than we had expected. We were thrilled — we'd get to The Dorian on time.

We'd made a mistake by giving the police too much lead-time — they had an hour before the alleged device would go off. It was all the time they needed to search our premises. I was given the honour of showing the officers around. I tried to arrange my face into a semblance of shock and total sobriety as I showed the stony-faced policemen through the bathhouse. I had to open cupboards (including my own — they pretended not to notice the $20 notes and the boxes of condoms that fell to the floor) and report anything that seemed out of the ordinary.

It took less than twenty minutes for the police to search our premises and declare us free from threat and fit to operate. I had to stay and work. Ewan went to The Dorian without me. I was severely pissed off.

As the night wore on, the management's demands for me to remove my anti-tour badge escalated. After midnight I was dismissed for refusing to remove it. By then The Dorian had closed.

I'd lost on both fronts, but I was *free*.

I had felt unable to leave the San Fran myself, yet the relief at my dismissal was huge. Never mind the money, it had done me no good anyway. It was time for a rest, and for some time with my boy. Time for a break from the pills and booze, I couldn't afford them now anyway. I'd miss my friends, especially Petal, but there was no reason I couldn't continue to see them.

For the first few days my relief and joy at having escaped the sex industry was boundless. I spent hours snuggled up to Christopher, learning the feel of his little embrace again. I slept well at night, not missing the drugs or alcohol that had been constant companions. I missed my friends though. Life at Grandma's had a serene monotony which began to grate on my nerves. Tracey, freed from her unpaid role as Chris's nanny, began to go out more often. I envied her freedom, yet felt relieved to have a second chance at being a perfect mother.

I applied for another Social Welfare benefit and was mortified when I cried all over the clerk at the welfare office. The tears were unexpected and seemed to be caused by a mixture of exhaustion and shame. They were soon never far away.

I began to see more of Paul. The Springbok tour was over and I was no longer a working girl — perhaps our relationship could become less covert. Six weeks had passed since our first drink together. I'd never been out with anyone for that long before. We still hadn't slept together but had done a bit socially and had met together in small, dark bars

— surely this constituted 'going out together.'

Finally Paul invited me to spend the night with him. Grandma was pleased I'd found a boyfriend and was happy to look after Chris for the night. I always asked now if she'd mind him, no longer assuming my right to just leave him with her.

Paul picked me up in his horrible little car and drove us towards the Hutt. I knew he lived in the Western Hills — at last I was to see Chez Paul. He must be serious about me. Next I'd be meeting his mother.

I spent ages preparing — legs shaved till they were smooth and shiny, eyelashes mascara'd to thrice their normal thickness, skin buffed and perfumed. As we drove I hoped he'd notice the effort I'd made. The anticipation was delicious, my imagination in overdrive — I could smell his body, very male. His hands were big and strong. I could imagine them kneading my body, stroking my hair, parting my thighs. I touched his leg through his jeans. I was trembling. I wouldn't need any foreplay at this rate.

We pulled up outside a motel in Lower Hutt — my assumption about seeing his place had been wrong. Oh well, perhaps there were too many memories of his dead marriage there? Maybe we'd be better off away from the former marital home. On the other hand, maybe there still was a Mrs Paul... I didn't ask, it might spoil the moment.

Paul was a superb lover — considerate, gentle and rough in the right proportions. He took his time with me and urged me back to my body when my mind began to wander off. He helped me to relax, stay in the present and enjoy his lovemaking. This was sex with no time limits — we had the whole night, there was no one waiting to rent me for the next half-hour. There was no contract — it was priceless. Paul showed me I could enjoy my body and trust that it knew what it liked. After several energetic hours I excused myself to go to the loo. I glanced in the bathroom mirror.

Rather than being flushed with bliss my cheeks were black with mascara! All six coats of it had abandoned my lashes and melted down my cheeks. So attractive... I washed my face until it shone as much from the scrubbing as from embarrassment. The light was off when I returned to bed. I lay in Paul's arms and we started again. That night was sublime.

I wrote to Floyd and broke off our relationship. I told him he'd really like my new man. He didn't reply.

•

Paul and I were headed for a turbulent relationship which lasted many years. There was fault on both sides. He eventually became stressed and unwell and this manifested as anger against the world.

He has now been well for many years and is happy, loving and generous again. I love him deeply. He is now one of my best friends and in no way the angry man portrayed later in this story.

•

It was time to look for more work. I was qualified for nothing, but keen to work as I thought a job might help me to feel better about myself. I'd had enough of working in fast food joints. I did have a certificate from the Academy of Elegance, gained while I worked at the San Fran. This proved I could paint faces — which might be helpful in the job market.

I read the papers daily looking for work. An ad for an embalmer — all training provided — seemed interesting. I could put make-up on the faces of the deceased before their families saw them. This would put my one certificated skill to use.

At the interview I was asked about my previous work history. I answered honestly. The funeral director next asked me why I wanted this job. I laughed and tossed my hair, unable to resist the chance for a little joke. "It'll be a change for me, but really it's just swapping one kind of stiff for another."

I didn't get the job.

36

Depression was beginning to settle on my shoulders like a leaden cloak. Apart from the time I spent with Paul I was tired, irritable, snappy and cried easily. I felt the need to get away from Wellington and asked Paul if I could borrow a tent and backpack from him. I thought a couple of weeks alone camping on a remote beach and swimming each day would lift my mood. He didn't understand — he'd never felt this bad — so refused.

I went to see my GP, who diagnosed depression and prescribed Tryptanol. This was one of the drugs that Maree, the youngest girl at the strip club, had been on. It seemed to help her so was worth a try. After two weeks I was feeling better and had more energy. I cried less and liked myself again. This was more like the Lauren people were used to.

I got out of bed during the day and acted like a normal person again. One dark spot in paradise was Paul's refusal to allow me to see any of my friends from the old days. The way he put it, it sounded reasonable — a policeman could not be seen to be in a relationship with a practising whore. If one of Paul's colleagues saw me entering the San Fran or drinking with any of the girls it would be assumed I was still working with them.

I wasn't to see my gay friends either. In those days Paul hated 'poofters.' It didn't matter to me that he seemed so full of hatred. He loved me, which was all that mattered at the time.

Paul wasn't pleased I was taking medication. He kept telling me I'd become addicted. I had him; what was there to be miserable about? Although I'd felt better in the last month than I had for years, he persuaded me to stop taking the 'happy pills.' He would look after me — what more did I need? He also finally managed to tell me that although his marriage wasn't happy it was still intact.

About a month after I took my last Tryptanol the depression was back. Paul called me at Grandma's. He was aggressive and sarcastic. "I hope you're happy — I've left my wife." No, I wasn't happy — about that or anything else. I'd had enough. I was tired and miserable and felt very alone. I went to bed, cuddled up to Christopher and cried myself to sleep.

The next morning things were no better. I wanted to pull the blankets over my head and never get up. Paul hadn't called back. He was probably sleeping off a hangover somewhere. I needed to do something to sort myself out. Maybe I'd go back on the Tryptanol. I went to see my GP and got another prescription. I had lots of Tryptanol now, lots and lots of it. With this much medication I could end my misery. I'd be better off dead. Chris would be better off too — he wouldn't have Grandma and me fighting over him any more.

I sat on my bed, hands trembling with fear and exhilaration. I'd take things a step at a time to be certain I was doing the right thing. I pressed the pills from their foil compartments. There were 143 of them, counting the ones I'd saved and those from the new prescription. I piled them on the bedspread — little yellow promises of eternal happiness. I made up my mind to take them. I had nothing left to live for. Chris didn't need me and it seemed I had more than enough experiences for one lifetime — what was left?

I had to die — it was all I had left. I went to the kitchen for some yoghurt, thinking it would help the handfuls of pills go down. Grandma was there and Aunty Jenny, who was staying the week with us. I was polite to them, telling them I was sorry for being moody but the pills I got that morning would make it all right. I hugged them goodbye saying I needed a sleep and went back to bed. It took ten handfuls to get the pills down, each followed with a spoonful of peach yoghurt.

I had a delicious sense of anticipation — almost like Christmas Eve as a child — something big and exciting was going to happen.

As I lay down to sleep Christopher climbed into bed with me, wanting a nap. I snuggled up to my clean little boy, his blonde curls smelling of baby shampoo, his trusting little body moulding to mine. He'd get up and go to Grandma as soon as his sleep was over — he didn't need me.

There were no tears of self-pity — I knew what I was doing was right for myself and for everybody else. I wondered if this was how Mum's last sleep felt...

•

I am so sleepy — I wake to hands shaking me roughly. It's dark but I went to bed in the middle of the day. It's Paul, grumpy and harassed. "I came to apologise, you stupid bitch. Ring me when you've got over this drug thing. I don't need this in my life."

As he storms out of the darkened bedroom I grab his hand. "I'm just having a good sleep — so tired — took all my pills — be okay in the morning."

I smile to myself as he leaves — I can still tell a good lie while dying.

•

Terrible tightness on my upper arm, repeated several times. Each time becoming more aware of my surroundings. Groan aloud as my blood pressure taken again. Told by the nurse at my side that things will be all right — I'm out of danger. I wake fully several hours later. I'm in the Intensive Care Unit connected to machines and being carefully monitored for further problems with my cardiac rhythm.

I've been here since last night, brought in by ambulance after Paul called them from Grandma's. After leaving me in a huff, Paul drove back to the Police College in Porirua where he was doing a course. As he cooled off he began to worry and called a doctor friend, who told him I was probably already dead. He jumped back into his car and raced to Grandma's, where, unable to rouse me at all, he called the ambulance.

Paul, Grandma and Aunty Jenny came to visit me in ICU that day. Paul had to say he was a relative to see me. Our embraces probably didn't look cousinly but he was allowed to stay. I was required to see a psychiatric social worker before I could leave and was later transferred from ICU to the Psych unit at Wellington Hospital.

I was still alive. The sense of disappointment and desolation was huge. I'd failed my son and myself.

37

The first few days in the Psych unit were awful. I was in the 'acutes' area where both medical and psychiatric observations occurred regularly. My head was fuzzy and my sense of defeat and shame immense. The day nurse was a complete bitch. She obviously didn't approve of bleached blonde suicide failures. Apart from the night nurse, the rest of the staff were unmemorable.

I placed a sign by my bed requesting euthanasia. 'Nurse Ratched' removed it with a scowl.

Sister Garlick was the night nurse. Each night she would sit on my bed and give me a hug. She seemed to know the turmoil behind the sometimes-distant face I wore. She was a brilliant nurse — her daytime colleague could have learned a lot from her.

An earnest psychiatric house surgeon took my history. He asked if I'd ever had any ambitions — what did I want from life? I told him I'd once wanted to be a doctor, but had long abandoned the idea. I mentioned my interest in embalming and said that was perhaps as close as I could get to the medical profession. He wrote quickly in his notes, trying to keep up with me. He said he couldn't see any connection between being an embalmer and a doctor and closed his file to leave.

He said it was good to have goals, but perhaps I could come up with some realistic ones during my stay in the unit.

Many years later when I was a medical student I read his report. He wrote that I had no grip on reality when it came to plans for the future. Me — train to be a doctor? How stupid and unrealistic was that?

I hope he reads this one day and remembers. Not all big dreams are impossible.

Each day we had group therapy. There were about thirty

patients, over half of us depressed. I was the only depressive who gained weight when I was unwell and I felt like an elephant among gazelles. The others were in varying states of wellness, from the hollow-cheeked woman who rarely spoke and only after great trembling of limbs and stammering, to the young man with the big-mouth grandiose ideas of the unmedicated manic.

I spent my twentieth birthday in hospital learning how to cope with the condition that brought me here.

Winston Churchill was a depressive and described his condition as a black dog that forever snapped at his heels. My beast is altogether more vicious. It's a huge mangy brown-black bear — twice my weight — which wrestles me to the ground, leaving me immobile. Its pulse thumps in my ear, dulling all pleasant sound, while one massive paw rests across my throat choking breath and energy away.

It whispers hatred in my ear and I believe it when it tells me I am worthless, ugly and would be better off dead.

This beast called depression brings death to joy, light and motivation. It is doom to hope, dreams and love. It plays with me like an animal with its prey. Misery, not death seems to be its object. *Yes* it seems to say to me, *death would be too easy, let me have my fun with you first.*

It waits for me always, able to conceal itself in the smallest shred of shadow. In the dark clouds that enshroud all silver linings, it waits. I am given medication to banish it, but still it lurks. *Depression* is too benign a name.

I remained a month at the Psych unit. During my time there I realised my life was headed nowhere and I needed to become organised if I was to have an existence of any worth. I decided to return to high school as an adult student and gain qualifications to equip me for the workforce. I was unemployable, but this no longer spelled freedom for me — it was a prison.

Education was the key — my only way out. Paul said

I was wasting my time — what was the point of me doing any training? He still didn't believe I had a brain in my head.

I enrolled for fifth form English, maths, science, economics and accounting. I would be in a class with fifteen-year-old students but felt happy about this. I had a future. Grandma said she'd look after Chris during the day so I could attend classes.

After my month as an in-patient was over I spent a further month as a day patient of the unit attending courses and counselling at the hospital for six hours each week day. The combination of the therapy, exercise and medication lifted my spirits enormously. I was getting much better.

The psych patients put on a Christmas play for staff and relatives. I was Goldilocks in a blue crepe paper dress which tore while we were on stage. I didn't notice the huge rip in the garment until Mama Bear hissed in my ear. I was a red-cheeked Goldilocks holding my torn dress together firmly for the rest of the production.

In early January Paul was called into his Senior Sergeant's office and told he would have to end his relationship with me or leave the police. Due to a gross breach of confidentiality at the Psych unit, senior police officers were aware one of their number was dating a former prostitute.

Furious, I left the unit and planned to take legal action against the leak. It was a professor at the nearby university who'd been acting as an advisor to the unit staff. A lawyer friend told me not to take legal action as it would be costly and would expose me to more scrutiny than I wanted. Who would be most believable — the eminent professor or an uneducated mental case who used to be a hooker?

•

The trial over the Springbok tour charges took place at the Wellington District Court. We all appeared without counsel. My brainwave was to plead insanity. I didn't realise that wasn't an option when a minor charge was being heard. Just as well I didn't want to become a lawyer — future opposition counsel would have a great time with that. We were all convicted and ordered to pay a fine of around $100. My plea of insanity wasn't accepted.

To celebrate the end of the court case Paul took me out for a drink. It was late in the evening and dark. We planned to go to the St George Hotel but were turned away by the doorman who thought my jeans were too scruffy. Paul had decided we were going to drink at the St George, so drink there we must. Rather than take me home to change he beckoned me to follow him up the fire escape at the back of the building. Once up there we tried the windows of all the rooms that opened onto the escape. When he found one that opened easily he rapped on it with his knuckles. Receiving no answer he climbed through the window. I followed him. We successfully navigated our way through the dark and thankfully empty room, then down the internal stairs to the bar. We had a good night and an extra big smile for the doorman when we left.

It was soon time for school to start. I was starting high school again, the girl with no education who once boasted of having no goals. I had never been more excited. It seemed there was a whole world of learning in the schoolroom. All of it now accessible to me.

Although I'd done okay at a Mensa intelligence test and read a lot of scientific books and other weighty tomes, I still had no idea of myself as an intelligent person. I knew I could — and would — work long and hard to earn myself an education. I wasn't lacking in motivation. Although I still had no firm long-term goal there was tons of time to develop one. First I had to taste education and try all sorts of different courses to find what I liked and was good at.

38

Hell, school was good. The more I studied, the greater was my enthusiasm for life and learning. I was there by my own choosing, a powerful incentive to achievement. I was rediscovering the Lauren who once had promise, who once embraced life.

My relationship with Paul was continuing pretty much unchanged. I was extremely flattered that he wanted to spend time with me and he was attentive and caring while we were together, but still hesitant to be seen in public with me. He was pleased I was enjoying my return to school.

Chris was thriving and seemed to love being back at Grandma's. I moved to the sleepout in the back yard so I could have quiet for my homework. Chris slept in the main house but woke me in the mornings climbing into my bed.

I had started the school year in the fifth form but discovered to my amazement that the work was too easy for me. I'd spent years envying people with their School Certificate and here I was smart enough to have passed it myself. What else was I about to discover?

The other adult students were a mixed bunch. Some had finished high school in their youth but needed a refresher course prior to going to university. Some simply wanted to pursue a new interest. Others were like me — people whose education had met an untimely end the first time around — needing a boost to their CVs and employment prospects.

We were all keen, not one of us underestimating the value of education. We knew why we were there and were able to share our insights and experiences with the younger students. I was now doing sixth form economics, accounting, maths, and English and School Certificate science. That first year I excelled at my studies.

Paul and I should have ended our relationship. Some time in the middle of the year he made a couple of nocturnal visits to his estranged wife and she was now pregnant again. I felt incredibly betrayed. He obviously didn't love me. Somehow we weathered his infidelity to me, but our relationship changed a lot.

The USS *Truxtun* returned to New Zealand for two days. Franklyn and Lonnie came to Grandma's for a visit. I guiltily avoided Floyd, especially when he sent me a big bunch of roses and an invitation to dinner. I now had a new love, though I never did lose the feelings I had for Floyd. He was the first person I'd loved as an adult and that was special. I idealised our relationship for many years.

At the end of the school year I had my sixth form exams accredited and didn't have to sit them. I'd earned my entrance to university, to a new and amazing world. My year had prepared me for commerce, which I wasn't interested in pursuing. Science had given me an appetite for biology and I planned to return to school for a second year. It seemed I could become anyone and anything I wanted by the simple expedient of study. It was thrilling.

During the summer holidays I worked as a waitress, hotel maid and fast food server. The textbooks for my course were expensive and I liked to own as many as possible to supplement the ones the school loaned me.

Although Paul and I were having a relationship of sorts we did not live together so I was eligible to continue receiving a Social Welfare benefit. This helped with study costs but was not enough to pay the whole lot, hence the four part-time jobs I was working.

The hours of study and work meant I was back to seeing little of Chris. Tracey and Grandma were doing the bulk of his care. He seemed happy and content. He was a bright little boy and better looking than we'd thought he'd be when he was born. He was blond with hazel eyes and skin that tanned easily. When he laughed he threw his head back.

He was mischievous and adventurous. He once got an electric shock from playing with a frayed vacuum-cleaner cord. The shock was enough to throw him across the room. For months after he would torment us up by saying, "I think I'll play with electricity today."

My estrangement from him was supposed to be temporary. My studies would get me a job I could be proud of, where I earned enough money to care for him well. A job he could tell his friends about without fear of ridicule.

My baby, the boy I'd promised so much to, was missing out. I was too busy finding myself at the time to be aware of his needs.

39

My second year as an adult student began badly. Paul's son was born — an event that caused a huge rift in our relationship. Guilt made him shitty and upset and he took it out on me.

My depression took this opportunity to flourish. Although I was taking subjects I enjoyed — chemistry, physics, biology, English, maths — I began to cut classes. Halfway through the year I realised I'd missed too much work to pass the final exams, so I left school. Before leaving I formed a new goal — I would become a scientist or a doctor. Not a bad ambition for a woman who'd been a whore just two years earlier. I was determined. I would work hard enough to achieve everything I wanted.

Although Paul and I were being more open about our relationship, he still took me to few parties where senior policemen were likely to be. Paul was a detective sergeant in the Drug Squad now and I knew most of the young guys he worked with. My past was never alluded to but I knew they were aware of it. Their knowledge was an almost palpable presence at times. The guys were interested in what I was doing at school and some couldn't believe it when I told them I wanted to go to university, maybe even med school. One cop laughed in my face. I was told he'd said "Once a whore, always a whore" after I'd left the room.

Grandma tried to be supportive of the new plan but her response was tempered by her wish for me not to be too disappointed when I failed in my ambition, as she believed I inevitably would.

Other family members were politely supportive too. Paul thought I was silly. He didn't want to admit I was at least as smart as he was; that might disturb the delicate balance of our relationship. Perhaps I wouldn't like him as much if I didn't need to look up to him. He needed me

209

to adore him.

Whatever anyone else thought, once the idea of a tertiary education was planted it grew and grew.

Some of my best support that tumultuous year came from teachers from Wellington High. Len Wilson was my English teacher. He and his wife Aina, the school librarian, were always available for a chat, advice and a cup of coffee. Jane Henson, a guidance counsellor and dean of the adult students, also mopped up a few of my tears. These three had an unwavering confidence in me and gave me the strength to keep trying and to ignore my detractors. They were my mainstays. Jane was working on her PhD. When I told her of my ambition she decided we'd have a race to see who would become a 'doctor' first. Without the help and confidence of these three, I don't think I would have persisted.

Around this time, Aids was hitting the headlines. I thought back over all the unprotected sex I'd had over the previous three years. Some had been with people who could have contracted the virus and passed it on to me — guys who did IV drugs or who swung both ways. I had had literally thousands of episodes of sex, generally without condoms. I was too frightened to get a blood test when it was revealed that some New Zealanders — including women — had tested HIV positive.

So far, everyone I knew was well. I hadn't seen any of my gay friends for a long time and resolved to look out for them, although I knew Paul would disapprove.

I soon caught up with Petal. Paul and a friend had tickets to a rugby test at Athletic Park. The All Blacks were playing the British Lions. Paul — to my surprise and delight — took me with him. Before the game we stopped at the St George for a few drinks. The restaurant and bar areas were packed. Petal was the barman. It was so good to see him! He hugged me and wanted to know how I was getting on. I started to tell him about school when Paul elbowed me in the back and told me to sit down at our table — he'd get the drinks.

I said a hasty goodbye to Petal whose look and wink showed me he understood what was going on. Paul got our drinks back to the table without making a scene, then slammed mine down in front of me before saying, "I told you I don't like you talking to those fucking faggots!" I drank quietly, knowing that Paul was capable of making a bigger fuss if he wanted to.

We had a few drinks before leaving for the Park. I looked for Petal but he was busy. Paul saw my intention and called across the room in his best 'policeman voice': "Does everybody know that's a ho-mo-sex-shu-al behind the bar?" It was so humiliating — I wanted to apologise to Petal and to strike out at Paul, but did neither.

We slunk up the hill to Athletic Park and watched the game. I'd learned my lesson about talking to my gay friends in front of Paul. I'd never do it again — it would invite too many hassles for them.

Other times, Paul was fun to be with. I loved him intensely and felt extremely lucky he wanted to go out with me. I believed ours was a unique love — more fierce that any that had ever been experienced before. Perhaps Edward and Mrs Simpson had come close, but I doubted it.

Paul and I redecorated the sleepout. We painted the walls bright yellow and placed Mum's old double bed (the one she'd died in) up there. Paul stayed every few nights. If he stayed on a Friday or Saturday night I could lie in bed for a few hours after he left. I'd try to keep the heat from his body alive under the bedclothes so I could still feel close to him. It became a charm against losing him — while my bed was warm from his body, he wouldn't leave me. I was besotted and gullible, unable to defend myself. I put up with Paul's insults and rudeness in return for sex and companionship. It could be good, but it could be hell too.

40

The favourite drinking place of the drug squad was the Southern Cross. Many of Mum and Dad's old friends drank there in the public bar. The cops preferred the more sedate and dressy lounge bar. One evening after school I met Paul and other drug squad cops at The Cross for a beer. There were about ten cops there in varying states of drunkenness. A few of the other adult students had come down with me and I had a drink with them before approaching the police table. Sitting near Paul was an attractive blonde policewoman I'd never met. I asked one of Paul's workmates who she was. My voice must have carried because Paul heard me. He pointed at me and shouted: "Don't worry about her — she's just a fat little mental." The woman cop smirked, some of the guys looked embarrassed and Paul seemed pleased with himself. He'd showed me.

I never did find out who the woman cop was. I slunk over to the table where the adult students were drinking, had a couple for the road then walked the five kilometres home. My indignation didn't last long though — I loved Paul and still felt privileged he wanted to go out with me. The stigma of my sex work still made me feel unworthy of him.

.

The drug squad and their wives or partners had an annual Christmas party. This year it was at Toad Hall, a small restaurant on two levels in central Wellington. I wore a red backless dress to show off my tan and newly-acquired muscles — I was going to a gym and solarium and looking good. Since being called a fat little mental I'd resolved to look happy and try my hardest to be slim enough for Paul.

Several tables at Toad Hall had been pushed together for us. There were over twenty of us on the restaurant's upper level, which was accessed by a steep, narrow staircase. There was another large group upstairs and several smaller tables seating two to four diners. There was about to be an unscheduled floorshow.

The other large group was already rowdy when we arrived — they'd obviously been drinking for a while. They were all well dressed and there was a preponderance of men — unlike our table where none of the women wanted to turn down their one-and-only opportunity to socialise with their husbands and colleagues.

Our table actually had a spare woman. The female drug squad detective was single. Even if she hadn't been she would have realised any man she brought to a gathering such as this would probably have been ritually humiliated by her male colleagues. She knew it was wiser for her to attend on her own. Policemen were competitive and territorial and found it difficult to tolerate any new male presence in their arena.

What started as a good evening soon deteriorated. The other table was full of lawyers and the drunker ones were soon oinking at the 'pigs' at our table. I got up to go to the loo, passing the lawyers' table to get there. One of them said something smart to me; I ignored it.

When I came out of the loo the offending lawyer was being pinned against the restaurant wall by Paul, who wanted him to apologise. If he refused, his punishment was to be beaten.

He said he was sorry.

When that was sorted and we'd sat down again the oinking escalated, along with other rude remarks about policemen. Food and paper napkins were thrown by the lawyers and returned with vigour by the police. The other diners in the room, sensing trouble, began to leave their tables. Now curses and epithets were bouncing between the two remaining groups.

There was a scuffle between a cop and a lawyer. Then it was all on. One of the police wives picked up a heavy glass ashtray and was about to bring it down on the head of the noisiest lawyer when her husband restrained her.

Lawyers were pushed down the narrow staircase. The girlfriend of one of them yelled, "Call the police!" to a chorus of guffaws and "We are the police" from our side.

No one was injured. The bills were paid and, apart from some food on the walls and carpet, no property damage was done. A complaint was made to the police the following day by the solicitor who had faced concussion by ashtray.

There was an internal inquiry. All the drug squad members were questioned. No one was punished. It was accepted that there had been provocation — although I suspect that the story the cops gave differed somewhat from other witnesses' accounts.

I was enjoying my time at the gym, working out, losing weight and gaining energy. I did weights and aerobic classes and spent between two and four hours a day there. I bought a ten-speed bike and cycled for hours to get trim for my man. I didn't think I was obsessed. I lost several kilos — the same several I'd spent years losing then regaining. My poor skin had seen me through so many shapes that it seemed to be losing its elasticity. If I lay on my side a big apron of skin would fall onto the bed beside me. I had stretch marks from carrying Chris — the ones on my breasts had disappeared with the breast reduction — maybe I needed a tummy tuck as well. While I was at it, how about a butt tuck?

I had my surgery less than a month later. For several thousand dollars I had my saggy baggy bits removed and the rest tightened. This time it took two years to pay the surgeon off. Paul was embarrassed and insisted I wasn't to tell anyone. Poor Paul...

Poor me too — thinking I had to go through with a major operation so someone would like me more.

The skin on my tummy was now so tight I couldn't stand up properly and wandered around bunched over until the wounds healed and I could put tension back on them. I was back at the gym ten days after the operation — hundreds of stitches holding me together. I only did a light aerobic workout. I wasn't totally crazy.

Those days I used an intrauterine contraceptive device (IUCD) as I thought the oral and injectable contraceptives might be contributing to my depression and weight fluctuations. The IUCD gave me awful cramps. I wasn't happy using it. Paul wouldn't use condoms and no-one would sterilise me. I'd seen a couple of gynaecologists to request a tubal ligation — they all but laughed at me. It seemed I was stuck with the method I was using.

One evening Paul and I had a fight. I was beginning to argue back. At the height of the argument I realised I had finally had enough. I dropped my trousers and underwear, reached inside myself and yanked out the IUCD by its string. I then threw it in his face. He was speechless. I dressed, grabbed my bag and walked from his flat in Island Bay to Miramar, a two-hour journey around the water's edge. I still felt triumphant when I got to Grandma's.

A couple of days later we were friends again. I went back to Family Planning to have a new IUCD inserted. I told the doctor and nurses what had happened to the last one — they laughed. The doctor who placed the new device advised me to go out and buy something heavy and expensive to throw at my boyfriend next time.

The cramping from the contraceptive was much worse this time. I couldn't bear it so went looking for an alternative. A nurse told me about Natural Family Planning, staffed by Catholic nuns, and I decided to try them. Paul came with me. As a good Catholic boy he knew all about nuns and how to handle them. The woman we saw was gentle, wore mufti — "Obviously an undercover nun," whispered Paul as we entered her office — and nice. If she disapproved of premarital sex she didn't let it show.

Paul sat in on our interview. We got to the bit where I had to discuss my menstrual and contraceptive history. I went through my usual litany of complaints about contraceptives and their side effects. Paul had heard this all before and switched off until one of the nun's questions jolted him awake.

"Have you been cycling regularly?"

Paul's face lit up — "Yes, of course... your new ten-speed. That must be what's causing you the pain." He was full of admiration for the nun who had discovered the problem just like that. I tried not to laugh as I interpreted her question for him. "She's talking about menstrual cycles, Paul. Periods, not ten-speeds." He was quiet again after that.

The new method was complicated — three different indices of fertility, each to be checked every day. It took a lot of effort but seemed worth it.

Using this contraceptive method I conceived Paul, my second son and Paul's third.

My pregnancy was not a cause for celebration. I was near the end of my seventh form year and had been excelling. I had already decided to take the medical intermediate course at Victoria University the following year.

My life was feeling planned.

Paul was dreadfully upset. He did not want another child. The only time he was loving and supportive was when I toyed with the idea of abortion. Otherwise he was distant and told me the conception was a deliberate ploy to trap him. He didn't stop to think that I stood to lose more than he did.

In an attempt to get enough space to sort out my options,

216

I fled to Christchurch to stay with my Uncle Dave. Grandma and Tracey were the only ones who knew where I was going. They swore not to tell Paul. After a fortnight down south I returned determined I would continue the pregnancy and manage on my own, if being alone was to be the only option.

My university plans would go on hold briefly, but I'd not abandon them. I'd come too far to give up now.

41

I spent most of the next few months in tears. Would I ever know the joy of a wanted pregnancy? I rarely saw Paul. I got a flat of my own a couple of blocks from Grandma's, and Christopher lived with me. I finished the year at Wellington High gaining an A Bursary and prizes for the school's top marks in English and biology. I was proud of my success, but what was the point when I would spend the next couple of years up to my elbows in nappies?

I rang the drug squad to let Paul know my exam results. He said he was happy for me.

I loved having my own flat and being my own boss. Chris visited Grandma and Tracey on his way to and from school each day. Tracey had a steady boyfriend so she wouldn't be living with Grandma much longer. She would be lonely — just as well we were not too far away.

Chris had some great toys, his own room and friends who came to play after school. I felt like a real mum again — the first time I'd felt this way in years. I was giving my son things I'd yearned for at his age.

It was brilliant to have my big boy back. Chris wasn't so sure, though. I cooked vegetables and expected him to eat them. I made meals with herbs, garlic and other yucky things. Grandma knew what he liked to eat and fed him only the right stuff. There were tears and tantrums at least two or three times a week, after which Chris would run down the hill to Grandma's.

Initially I fought to get him back, but I was pregnant and it was summer — not good conditions for hauling a struggling six-year-old up the steep hill. Grandma loved Chris and didn't want to lose her boy. I had wondered at Grandma's reluctance to give me many of Chris's things she kept at her house. Now I realised it meant she could look after him when he regularly turned up at her place.

Late one night when I couldn't get Chris to sleep I sat on his bed to see what the trouble was. He reached up to hug me.

"I don't want to be here after you have the baby, Mum."

"Why, sweetheart?"

"Grandma says that babies cry in the night and wake you up at midnight, and that's the witching hour. I'm too scared to be awake at midnight."

I tried to reassure Chris as much as I could, but felt uneasy. Kissing his forehead, I tucked him in and said I'd think of a way to keep his room quiet so the baby wouldn't wake him. I think I realised even then that this was a battle I was unlikely to win.

Chris began to spend more and more time at Grandma's. When I protested, she told me it was my own fault. He didn't know me the way he knew her. It was natural that he'd prefer her company to mine. I tried to be strong, but Chris and Grandma thwarted any efforts I made. I had to relent. Although he wasn't obeying my wishes, Chris was still receiving loving care from a member of his family. My childhood made me aware of the need for stability and Grandma was a stable influence.

I decided to ease up.

Some of Paul's things remained in my flat until near the end of the pregnancy. He phoned to ask me to leave them outside the front door and picked them up in the middle of the night. I heard him arrive but stayed quietly in my bed as he gathered his things. I was only a little sad he was acting so cowardly.

In the final fortnight of my pregnancy Paul appeared on the scene again. He offered me moral support. He said he could see my life was stressful and asked if I had thought about adoption. There were couples who would love to have this baby and it would mean I could finish my studies. I laughed at him. I had not got all this way through my pregnancy just to relinquish my baby at the end of it.

We began to see each other again intermittently. This time I was not so besotted. Paul promised to be at the baby's birth but reiterated that he would not provide any support once it was born.

●

Tracey was married to her long-time boyfriend David suddenly one day. They decided not to do the full service they'd been planning. Instead they wed in the registry office with a couple of friends as witnesses. They were looking for a flat. The one below me was vacant and after seeing it they decided they'd rent there. Now Chris had an alternative place to bolt to. Although he spent most of his time at Grandma's and Tracey's he was still supposed to be living with me. Tracey wasn't quite so accommodating of him now though. Her husband thought they should start on their own family, not worry about mine.

A week before my due date the baby's movements slowed right down. I rang the obstetrician in a panic, having felt no movements for several hours. He reassured me and said he didn't need to see or monitor the baby or me. I still felt there was something wrong. I told Paul I was afraid, but he wasn't alarmed. I worried; I had grown attached to this little one, despite the shaky start.

The lack of movement continued, until a week later I went into labour on the due date, 18 May 1985. I phoned Paul at 6am, spoiling his plans to go duck shooting. Paul James Roche was born at 2.40pm at Wellington Women's Hospital. It was a straightforward labour and birth and he was active and breathed spontaneously.

He was beautiful, weighing 3520g (about 7lb 13oz). There were no obvious problems with him. His birth was a cause for celebration — a new beginning, even if he and I had to live apart from his father. I chose his Christian names in a deliberate attempt to bond his father to him.

Paulie was an awful baby. He cried twice each hour wanting to be fed and was wakeful and active from the moment of his birth. The only time he managed to get to sleep in the first few days, hospital doctors woke him to check his hips or take his blood.

He was so different to Christopher, who was placid and slept more often than he was awake. Paulie was restless, and as he matured a lot slower to learn things than Chris had been. Chris had been advanced for his age, though, so I tried not to compare the two of them.

As Paulie grew he became cuddlier and slept more. He became my laughing boy, with a sunny nature and ready smile. He was an angel.

He was always active. People told me this was a good sign of intelligence. They were wrong. Paulie didn't make the advances expected at the right times. He was slow to sit, to pull himself up, and to stand. I took him to my GP, worried about him, and was reassured that all was well. He said there is a wide range of 'normal' and Paulie was in it. He was wrong too.

•

When Paulie was eight months old I started the medical intermediate course at Victoria. On the first and many subsequent days my eyes would fill with tears and my heart would thump. Here I was at university. I couldn't believe it. Other students, young intelligent people, surrounded me. How would I survive? How long before they realised I was an imposter in their midst?

I resolved to study hard, to achieve the best I could and make the most of this opportunity. That way I hoped to feel that I really belonged there.

42

The course was gruelling. It would have been easier had I not taken a year off my studies for the pregnancy. I had a full timetable and hours of prep needed for laboratories and assignments in addition to the lecture programme. Paulie attended the university creche most days, although if Paul had time off he would look after him.

Paul had turned into a far less benign person. He was edgy, short-tempered and quick to lash out. His foul mood didn't lessen until he'd taken several weeks off work. He was breaking down.

Still in the drug squad, he was having problems with his health, had constant nightmares and dreaded going to work. A psychiatrist diagnosed post-traumatic stress disorder (PTSD) related to his occupation. He had hundreds of hours of overtime due to him and elected to have time off to see if his mental state improved. It seemed to. He became calmer and more motivated.

The rest from work gave him time to seek therapy. It was something he'd always shied from as he felt it made him appear weak to need psychological assistance. The psychiatrist put him on anti-depressant and other medication and advised he seek early retirement on psychological grounds. Paul, who was now second-in-charge of the Wellington Drug Squad, was not impressed. He was tough enough to cope. He tried to be more helpful to Paulie and me.

I came off the benefit for a while, left my flat in Miramar and moved into Paul's in Island Bay. Chris had long since opted to live with Grandma. He seemed to enjoy the idea of having a baby brother but was reluctant to spend time with us.

Paul looked after Paulie while I studied, and always had

a meal waiting for me when I returned from university. There were sausages and roast potatoes most nights; plates piled high. A welcome treat at the end of a long day.

Domestic bliss didn't last long. Paul tired of the domesticity and Paulie and I moved to a bedsit in Newtown. We only saw Paul when it suited him.

Paul returned to work and Paulie to the university creche. The creche workers were excellent and monitored each child's development closely. They were worried about Paulie. His progress was too slow; they were certain something was wrong. I took him back to my GP, who declared him to be fine.

Things were not fine — they never would be with Paulie. At last the creche, in despair at my denial and my GP's inability to see what was happening, had Paulie assessed by a developmental nurse. The results were sobering.

My darling son — seventeen months old — had only reached the developmental milestones of a ten-month baby. I was stunned. Still not wanting to believe the piece of paper presented to me by the creche, I took the test results to the person I thought was most likely to be able to interpret them, the professor who had precipitated my early departure from the psych unit. The one who told the police that Paul was dating a drug-taking ex-whore. It shamed me that I had to turn to this man for help but there was no one who could better advise me.

He recognised me immediately. Not surprising. I imagine he lost a few nights' sleep after our first interaction. The eminent professor smiled at me kindly and motioned for me to sit beside him. He read the damning document and sighed, pushed his white hair back and said, "You'll have to face it. He's retarded." With the second sentence he removed his hand from his hair and patted me on the knee.

There was no more to say. I picked up the paper and left

his room. I hated him even more than I had previously.

I knew then that if I were to ever be in the position of delivering news of such emotional impact to anyone — no matter what I thought of them — I'd do it better. The professor's insensitivity was to become a potent driving force in my desire to be a doctor who could communicate caringly with people.

Paulie's disability had been confirmed. Now it was possible to begin special investigations and therapies to ensure he had the best chance to make the most of the abilities he did have.

The first few weeks after his diagnosis were awful. There were so many things my baby couldn't do — suddenly his problems were glaringly obvious. How could I have not seen the evidence?

I phoned Paul, his mum and my family to tell them the news. Chris thought it would be nice to have a brother who could go in the Special Olympics.

Now I acknowledged there was a problem, lots of people admitted to their concerns about his slow development. Still, I had a beautiful, chubby, laughing baby and the will to help him succeed. It was still hard to believe though; a part of me refused to accept that Paulie was less than perfect.

The worst thing about the timing of Paulie's diagnosis was that it came shortly before final exams for medical intermediate. He had a CT scan of his brain scheduled two days before one of the finals. I panicked. I was certain he'd need urgent neurosurgery right in the middle of the exam period and I'd fail the papers and never get my chance to be a doctor.

The tests were fine. Paulie had a normal brain, a normal chromosome and blood screen and EEG. It seemed that somewhere along the way the connections in Paulie's normal-looking brain had become scrambled.

Paul and I were united in our worry about our son, all previous animosities suspended.

We were reassured that our blood relationship had nothing to do with our son's disability — we weren't closely-enough related.

We were not to blame.

We would never know why Paulie's development was so slow. The lack of a clear diagnosis had its frustrations — how could we plan with no idea of what was going to happen to him?

The creche was brilliant. We had quick contact with the early intervention team and were given strategies to help Paulie develop the skills he lacked.

Meanwhile I sat my exams and passed all of them with good grades, despite the fact I had little support from anyone other than the creche during this period.

Next stop, med school.

I employed several tricks to help keep my motivation through the seemingly endless hours of study. A plastic 'Doctor Smurf' toy lived in my pencil-case or pocket. With his stethoscope and white coat he was a constant visual reminder of my ambition. Any time my energy or confidence flagged, I only needed to look at him, or touch his blue head to bring me back to my goal. The seat I chose at the University Library had to have a view of Wellington Hospital. Each time I looked up from my texts to rest my eyes, I'd see the place I was aiming for.

I wanted to be a doctor, as it seemed to me the highest goal I could aim for. I loved people and was good at science – these were other reasons. My main motivation was that I wanted to do something so worthwhile, so GOOD, that all the silly stuff I'd done in the past would be negated. I thought of doctors as honourable people who spent their lives in the service of humanity. These views would one day be severely shaken, but in my year of preparation for Med

225

School they kept me going. One day I'd be conspicuously good. All I had to do to get there was study, so study I did. When friends went to the movies or beach I sat at the desk in my bed sit and swotted.

The University Library stocked some books on the Med School experience. "Boys In White" was the inspirational title of one of them. I read these in my spare time, filling any spaces in my tired brain with visions of me as a medical student, as a doctor. I could see the desired outcome of my studies so clearly that there seemed to be no chance of failure. Each exam pass reinforced my belief in myself; each tutorial and laboratory attended was another step towards my dream. Although terribly tired with study, a restless baby and my deteriorating relationship with Paul, I remember the medical intermediate year as one of hope, of intense satisfaction, and ultimately of a dream realised.

I had no doubt I'd be accepted despite the fact I hadn't achieved straight A's. It just seemed right that I would gain entry to Otago Medical School. I started getting books about Dunedin out of the library to show Christopher — now seven and doing well at school himself — where we'd live. I wanted our family to be complete again and felt Dunedin, several hundred kilometres south, would be a good place to try this.

Chris refused to go — saying he wanted to stay in Miramar with his friends and continue school there. He was certain Dunedin was far too cold. Besides, Grandma needed him. He was her man-about-the-house. There was no way he would leave.

Reluctantly I agreed I would take only Paulie with me. Despite Chris's wish to live with Grandma, he later told me and others that he felt I'd abandoned him.

I set about finding a place to live in Dunedin and preparing for my new life. I tracked down a flat and was about to fly down to sign a contract for it when I received the news — I'd missed out on selection to med school. My grades weren't good enough.

My arrogance in assuming I'd get a place had been misplaced. I was bereft.

I couldn't believe it.

I was meant to be a doctor.

Still — plans had been made — there was no way I'd back out now. I'd move to Dunedin anyway, do a Bachelor of Science degree and apply for graduate entry to medical school after I'd finished.

Meanwhile I'd appeal the selectors' decision. I deserved to go to med school. I'd be a damn good doctor. They *had* to let me in.

43

Paulie and I moved south. We were in a part of the country I'd never seen and we knew no one there. I found a flat in Brownville Crescent, Maori Hill, which was expensive but nice. We could just afford it on the Social Welfare benefit and the A bursary I'd earned at high school. The house in Brownville Crescent, although on a hill, was within walking distance of the university — an ideal place to live. I was extremely disappointed to miss out on med school but I kept the dream alive. I was not yet ready to walk right past the school where young doctors were trained, but I did wander on the banks of the Leith which flowed through the university campus. Otago looked like a real university, one with a long tradition, its stone buildings old and dignified. I could imagine strolling along the river banks with Paulie feeding the ducks after classes were over. I would enjoy my two years here while awaiting admission to the medical course as a graduate student. I had to — I was committed to it now.

Paulie settled in well. I found a place for him at the university creche and set about meeting some Dunedinites.

Paul was stressed again and was phoning me at all hours of the night to check that Paulie and I were alone. The phone in my flat was wired into the wall and couldn't be disconnected. When I left it off the hook to get some peace he'd have Telecom send a squeal down the wire to make me answer his call. I put up with it.

After two weeks in Dunedin I was beginning to feel I fitted in. The city was smaller and friendlier than Wellington. People smiled and chatted to one another in the street. Our new city also seemed more gentrified and surprisingly lacking in young adults. As a university city I expected Dunedin to teem with youth. Instead it seemed the Pied Piper had called, abducting all those in their teens and early adulthood. The students came back at term time and left Dunedin quiet and thinly populated during the holiday breaks.

Our new neighbours were elderly, helpful and caring. Paulie seemed to enjoy his new surroundings. We walked a lot and had picnics in a nearby park. We were alone and making the most of it. Paul seemed far away.

One morning I received a letter from the University of Otago Medical School. I didn't open it immediately, leaving the slim white envelope until I'd readied Paulie for a walk into town. I tore the envelope open, tossing it to the floor, and read the letter unbelievingly. It began "Congratulations …"

I had been accepted into the medical course. Some of those who'd been allocated places in the first selection had changed their minds. Oh my God! — I was in — I was a medical student! Somehow the thought of being a med student had always appealed more to me than the idea of being a doctor. There was something mysterious about being a med student. The initiation into a life of medicine seemed so mystical — so important somehow — even more significant than the end result.

I cried and read the letter again and again. It didn't look like a hoax.

I spent the day on the phone — vindicated. I'd known there was a place for me and I was right. Paul, his mum, my Grandma all got calls that day. I'd been accepted into med school. I must be okay. Only good people became doctors, didn't they? Only good people, respectable ones. Whatever I'd done in the past would now be forgotten. I was going to be a doctor.

I wish I could have called Petal or George, but there was no way to contact them. Paul had hinted that it was easy for him to trace anyone I called — no matter where from. His attitude was controlling and made a difference to my behaviour. I only phoned people Paul would approve of and only associated with people Paul would like. The thought of him hassling anyone I was selfish enough to become involved with — even in an innocent fashion — was too much.

Meanwhile Paulie and I waited for school to begin. He started creche a week before the beginning of term to get used to it before my classes began.

The eye department at the hospital saw him about his squint, diagnosed severe long-sightedness and prescribed coke-bottle glasses. Although I despaired of him keeping them on — initially he hid them in the garden — Paulie came to realise they helped, and kept them on. I hoped he would make major advances — eventually becoming as able as Christopher — now that his vision was corrected. The eye problem was only a symptom of Paulie's brain dysfunction, however, not the cause of it. If there ever was a cure it would not be that easy.

Paulie started creche with his new glasses. I said as little as I could about his disability; I didn't want them accepting him with preconceived ideas. I wanted him to stand on his own and achieve as much as possible. But it took the new creche less than two days to realise it wasn't just Paulie's eyesight that was imperfect.

The neighbours too told me they thought my little man was 'different.' As much as I wanted to believe otherwise it was being confirmed from many quarters — my boy had big problems. It is difficult to describe how it felt to learn Paulie was disabled. I alternated between a sense of loss for the things he may never do and a denial that there was anything wrong.

I kept hoping. Surely my son — my happy smiling boy — surely my baby would be okay.

44

The day I learned I was to train to be a doctor I walked past the School of Medicine for the first time. I paused outside the Scott Building, an imposing stone structure with 'Medical School' picked out in large letters above its entrance, and imagined how it would feel to enter those halls for the first time.

As it turned out the Scott Building was no longer the main entranceway to the school of medicine, which was accessed through an anonymous door in another building. I wanted to remember forever the moment of my arrival in the new world — the respectable world of medicine — but it was not to be. I do recall the sense of space in the entrance to the building, the drab colours and an overwhelming feeling of awe. Doctors had trained here. I was going to be a doctor.

The first day was hectic. We sat in the large lecture theatre that was our base for the year and were greeted by a succession of lecturers and professors. Awe was quickly tempered with cynicism. The first speaker, a physiologist, told us in a deep, thoughtful monotone that we were 'The Chosen' and were to disport ourselves with the dignity appropriate to our station. The Chosen? They obviously didn't want us to get inflated ideas of ourselves! I thought a further injection of self-importance wasn't needed; looking at him it seemed there was already more than enough of that in the profession.

Alongside my cynicism was a deep fear that my classmates would find I wasn't as smart as they were and would hound me out. The sense of not quite belonging was so strong that I had a series of dreams where the dean of the school came to me to tell me I'd been admitted to the course accidentally and would have to withdraw. Each time I dreamed this I meekly agreed with the dean —

of course he was right — there was no place here for the likes of me.

We all lined up to have our photos taken — a permanent reminder to us of how enthusiastic we were on the first day of our training. I looked back over those photos frequently in the years to come. The tired, pale hospital doctors we later became had once been clear-skinned, tanned, rested. Who would have believed the damage our training would do; the skills and joys we would lose along the way? Sure, we learned a great deal, more than any of us could have imagined. There were sacrifices required — the singers had less time to sing, the musicians less time to play. The dancers were too tired to dance.

The photos also give a reminder of those who didn't complete the course for one reason or another. Here is the young man who left after two or three weeks because he wanted "a life." There is Duncan who died in a car accident just a few months short of graduation. Nothing about their photos stood out — they were not marked as different from the outset. Their fates could as easily have been mine.

We did not look as though we envisaged any problems in the years ahead.

In time we would find that the difficulty with our chosen course was not the level of work required — by virtue of our intermediate grades we were all smart enough to fly through. It was the sheer volume of material to learn, to fully understand. The quantity made it difficult for all but the most brilliant to get by without hard work.

We were encouraged, that first day, to continue with our hobbies and sports — "they will make you more rounded doctors" — but were not given any idea how to find the time for them.

I had no hobbies to give up. There was Paulie and me in my life. The two of us and my medical training took all my stamina. There were times when I used more than my allotted energy in a week and wanted to take to my bed and sleep — perhaps for weeks.

In the first few days we learned to do basic doctorly things — pulse taking, listening to heart sounds and a few other skills we wouldn't need for some time. We had a physiology lab where we were taught about electrocardiograph tracing. This involved placing electrodes on the bare chests of volunteers who then had their heart rhythms monitored and analysed. The smarmy physiology professor — he who'd called us The Chosen — was back.

"Of course," he pontificated, "only the male medical students will want to volunteer for this." Oh yes? I didn't want to volunteer but couldn't believe his presumption. I took my shirt off when the time came and volunteered to be guinea pig for a group of women students. I was self-conscious and embarrassed at the ordeal but did it to make a point. I draped my shirt as modestly as I could to avoid too many red faces.

Despite being different to most students I worked hard, was elected class rep on the medical students association and did sundry chores for the class to claim my place among them. I'm sure none of them realised how estranged I felt from them all. Compounding this was my physical isolation from the campus. Most students lived in town; those who didn't had cars, or parents with transport. None of the other students had kids in their care.

My relationship with Paul was another constant presence despite the fact that he lived in Wellington.

He began arriving on my doorstep unannounced as if to see if he could catch me in a compromising situation. A couple of times he wandered through the medical school looking for me, to later arrive at my home, shouting and yelling that he knew I was skipping class and screwing around. I began to dread he'd turn up to a lecture and harangue me in front of my new friends. I lived in fear.

This, coupled with my need to rise at 4am to ensure I had time to study, was wearing me down. Life as the single parent of a handicapped, hyperactive child, coping with the demands of medical school seemed too much at times.

Both Paulie and his father seemed to sleep between four and seven in the morning. There would be no wakeful toddler or abusive phone calls then, so it became the best time for me to study. This added to my estrangement from others in my class — I was exhausted by eight in the evening so even if I could socialise, I didn't have the energy to. Occasionally I had other med students over to watch videos or have a meal. If the phone rang while my guests were there they all had to be quiet so Paul would think I was alone — otherwise the invective from him would ruin the whole evening. I was silly to collude with Paul like this but had a strong streak of self-preservation. Paul seemed mad at times, an extremely frightening man. I didn't want to come to any physical harm and fully believed he was capable of inflicting it. It was hard to imagine him ever being normal, gentle and loving again.

Living on the hill above the university had its compensations. Each morning Paulie and I would trek down the hill to the creche before my classes began. In the cold, clear air Dunedin looked stunning. If there had been a frost or snow we would slip and slide down the steep streets — Paulie in his pushchair, me pulled along behind him. If the snow lay deeply in the park we passed I'd pull him out of his chair in his snowsuit and pelt him with snowballs. On snowy or wet days it was no fun walking back up the hill after school. Often other parents from the creche would feel sorry for us and give us a ride home.

On a Monday morning we would sometimes pass the evidence of weekend student parties — piles of vomit on the footpath and broken glass in the streets. There was a period where all the marauding students seemed to have eaten Asian takeaways before drinking themselves sick — we would pass sparrows squabbling over heaps of undigested noodles lying on the footpaths. I guess to the birds they looked like long, thin, pallid worms.

The drinking was a part of student life I felt too old for. I'd been there, done that an awful lot of years earlier. Besides, these days I felt I needed all of my brain cells.

Paul retired from the police on psychological grounds. There had at last been some recognition of his fragile mental state and I hoped the break from work would give him a chance to rest and get better. There was no immediate benefit though. He had become paranoid and was scary one minute, loving and needy the next. I felt both too sorry for him and too afraid of him to quit, so our destructive relationship continued. He did some extremely helpful things for Paulie and me — a house came up for sale across the road from the flat I was renting and he helped me negotiate to buy it. I ended up paying about half as much on the mortgage as I had on rent and had an asset to call my own.

My own home! Never mind that the lawn was waist-high in grass and weeds, the plumbing wasn't working properly and the kitchen ceiling was grey and greasy with fly dirt. These things were easily and cheaply fixed. I had my own little piece of the Kiwi dream. Paul promised to help with renovations and maintenance. Despite the occasional helping hand, though, he was not yet through his difficulties.

Anthony was an older student in my class and the first to realise how sick my partner was. He had initially trained for the priesthood and came to med school part-way through his seminary training.

He was a lovely, gentle man who wanted to help me out in some way. The med school revue — *Humerus* — was running and I couldn't attend as I had no childcare.

Anthony volunteered to look after Paulie and refused to take no for an answer. Part of the reason I was hesitant to go was the anticipation of Paul's reaction if he realised I had a man in my house. I attended the revue with Mandy, my closest friend in the class. As we left the house I called back to Anthony: "If the phone rings don't answer it."

He misheard me and took a call from Paul, who was furious that an unknown man answered my phone. He shouted at Anthony and threatened to get even with him. That was the last time Anthony, or any of the other guys at med school, offered to babysit for me. It was also the last time I went out without permission.

I did enjoy *Humerus* but not enough to make up for the furore my attendance caused.

45

As my studies continued I found, to my relief, that I was as bright as some of the others. I had a profusion of life experience not available to my classmates. I became a confidante and adviser to a couple of them. I needed to feel I was contributing something to my classmates and tried hard to be helpful to them. I organised a roster of students to watch post-mortems; signed up most of the class as organ donors; and became their supplier of stethoscopes, ophthalmoscopes and other medical equipment.

As class rep I also organised class parties and outings. Our second year 'Jungle Party' was a great success and one Paul allowed me to attend — in fact he travelled from Wellington to babysit Paulie so I could go. I realised this was a way of ensuring I came home alone and on time, but was still grateful to him. It was bizarre — I had never felt less like sex but here I was being accused constantly of hunting for it. I was heartily sick of Paul's fixations.

The police hadn't finished with Paul. A drug case came up where he had been the arresting officer and he had to appear in court, never mind that he was in no fit state to give evidence. The night before the case his grandmother died and Paul spent the night by her bedside. After no sleep he arrived at the court in a highly anxious state. After the judge and jury had taken their seats and before any evidence was heard the defendant directed "a look" at Paul. This was too much provocation. He leapt towards the defendant and grabbed him by the throat, attempting to strangle him in full view of the court. Bailiffs removed him from the courtroom and the case was stood down — the defence lawyer, Peter Williams, describing Paul as a "psychopathological killer." The TV network news that night mentioned a "frenzied attack" in a Wellington courtroom but gave no details. Paul did not face any charges as the Police Department was aware of the extraordinary stresses he was under when they asked him to appear. He was never again asked to appear in court — much to the relief of Paul and all who knew him. It would have caused his former police bosses further embarrassment if he'd performed like that again so I'm sure they happily agreed to his release from further duties.

Following this episode he spent a couple of days with me in Dunedin. He was stressed, dejected and unusually demanding. After an argument late the first evening he told me he was going down into the basement of my house to kill himself. I couldn't cope any more and told him to do what he wanted. I was tired and went to bed. I could hear him in the basement moving around. The sound of items being dragged and shifted and of hammering reached me. I almost wished he would harm himself — at least that way Paulie and I could get on with our lives which were being disrupted most nights. Paul desperately needed my love and support but I was past the stage where I could give it to him. Things were just too hard. I put my ear to the floor so I could hear him better. There was a pulling noise then a crash, the ping of a rope going taut and the creaking of a beam. Then silence.

It was all over.

I couldn't go downstairs in the dark to deal with his remains. In the morning I'd get the police to go downstairs to cut him down from the beam on which he must be hanging. My inaction wasn't due to a lack of love or of appreciation for the good things that Paul had done — it was extreme weariness and an utter inability to cope. I fell asleep to the silence from the basement below.

I woke shortly after 3am. Paul was trying to slip into my single bed beside me. He was subdued and seemed embarrassed. He had slung a rope over a beam in the basement and had swung on it to frighten me. Disappointed at my lack of response, he drove around Dunedin to sit on a high bridge and contemplate jumping. After several cold and boring hours he decided to return home. My lack of action over his 'suicide' had confused and sobered him. The next day he returned to Wellington. The nasty calls stopped for a while and loving letters took their place. I threw myself back into my studies. Things were getting better.

Christopher and Grandma kept in touch. Chris sent me a letter offering to give me $40 pocket money he'd saved, as Grandma had told him I was broke. I had promised to bring him to Dunedin in the school holidays but I spent all my breaks in Wellington with Paulie so Paul could see his son. I still saw Chris in the holidays though and spoke to him on the phone when I could afford to. It was good to hear he was doing okay at school. I missed him but was reassured that he was happy and well.

Despite my fears and anxieties about being at medical school I loved it. The work was stimulating and was taught in a way that made even the esoteric seem relevant. It was everything I'd hoped it would be. I kept up with my classmates and was not told to leave. It was exhilarating to be learning so much, and a privilege to be entrusted with the knowledge that I would one day use to help others. I attended operations and post mortems as often as I could, hoping that exposure to the innermost recesses of the human body would assist me in the years to come. I felt so honoured to be where I was — nothing in my life before my return to high school had prepared me for this. I was surprised each day to find myself studying medicine. It was many years before I could take my new position for granted. No wonder I felt estranged from the students who felt that a medical training was their right — who had been raised to be where they were now. I was certainly not the only student who had worked hard to be here — just the only one who'd taken such a circuitous and unconventional route.

The second year exams came too soon. Exam time was always heralded in Dunedin by the spring growth on the trees outside the medical and dental schools. Spring meant it was time for the lump in the throat — the weight in the pit of the stomach — the exhilaration of being tested and the fear of failure. There had already been some mid-year exams and I had done well in them.

I entered the end-of-year exams thinking I'd do okay. Even after the exams were over I was certain I had passed them. It was a shock when results came out to discover I had failed biochemistry and had to sit a pass/fail oral exam. This was an additional test offered to students who had narrowly failed their written paper.

Oral exams — called vivas — are cruel and intimidating, one of the most fearful parts of medical training. Two examiners, who can prompt or snort with derision at the answers given, question the student. If it is possible to keep cool and answer quickly the exam need not be too much more traumatic than a written one. If the first question is difficult and the student becomes tongue-tied or confused they can find it extremely difficult to redeem themselves with good answers to the remaining questions.

The biochemistry orals were awful. Fifteen students were required to sit them. We were kept waiting in a corridor for three-quarters of an hour past the time set down and were all tense and miserable by the time our names were called. There were four women in my group. My examiners included an Australian professor — the external examiner — who (according to student lore) was always present when the most marginal students were quizzed. I blushed and stammered and fought back tears for the forty minutes of my exam. I fumbled over words, abandoned by my memory and hours of study. Eventually I wept all over the two biochemists, an act even more humiliating than my poor academic performance. All four women in my group were in tears by the time we were released from the room. We all passed, but it was an extremely unpleasant experience. I refined my studying techniques for the following year, vowing to never need to sit a pass/fail viva again.

I spent the Christmas holidays quietly delighted a whole year had passed and I was still a med student. I spent time with Paul and with Christopher and reacquainted myself with Wellington. Chris and Paulie enjoyed each other's company and played together well.

Paul insisted on escorting me everywhere. He still didn't like the idea of me having any freedom. A walk to the shops by myself caused him to hyperventilate and imagine passionate affairs in the half-hour it took me to buy milk or bread. It was tedious but I loved him and I could endure the way he was.

Third year at med school was more interesting. My scrape-through in biochemistry had frightened me so I sought extra tutoring from Dr Peter Schwartz, a slight, unassuming American. He coached me in his spare time and helped me see the value and significance of biochemistry in medical practice. He was the best teacher I have ever encountered and made me want to learn to teach so that one day I might assist others in the way he had helped me.

At the end of the third year, students from the Otago Medical School had to elect which of three clinical schools they would attend to continue their training. These schools are hospital-based in Wellington, Christchurch and Dunedin. It is important because of funding and resource allocation for the split to be even between the three schools. Our year, this did not happen. Few students wanted to move to Wellington — most were happy to stay in Dunedin. We were lobbied by the administration to choose Wellington and a few reluctantly changed their vote. There was still a serious mismatch with an excess of students choosi᠁ Dunedin and too few wishing to transfer to Welling᠁

ballot was required to see who'd be redirected. As class rep I had to pull the names of the unfortunate students out of a hat to decide their clinical placement. There was a great deal of gloom about the place as people awaited the posting of the list that would officially spell out who was being sent where. The situation needed an injection of levity. I got together with five of my classmates: Mandy, Lynn, Steve, Kirsty and Arran. We regularly hung out at a café around the corner from the med school and the staff there gave us the leftovers at the end of the day. Over a pot of coffee and plate of biscuits we hatched our heinous plan.

Later that night the list of who was to attend which clinical school was due to be placed on the notice board outside the lecture theatres. We planned to steal this before anyone read it, take it to my place where I had an electric typewriter — a recent gift from Paul — and alter it. That night we played God — an exhilarating task — and posted some students to the clinical school we thought they'd least like to attend. We were careful not to reverse any of the official redirections but split up some couples who thought they'd be going to the same school and separated other students from their indulgent families. The sense of power was immense. Of course we redirected a couple of our own group too, so that suspicion wouldn't fall on us.

We replaced the list on the notice board and waited for the reaction. The next morning there was commotion in the lobby outside the lecture theatres. Our classmates had discovered the errors. Surprisingly few realised the list was a fake. Two students reported to the dean to demand an explanation. While they were gone the real list was discovered d our doctored one and further panic was averted. I it was a wonderful practical joke but others didn't. l administration staff now felt they needed to post portance, including exam results, inside a locked re documents would be tampered with.

46

Aids had become a local plague, not just an overseas one. Its characteristics and mode of transmission were well-documented and the medical school was doing its best to educate doctors and the public about the best ways to avoid infection. We had a series of superb lectures attended by students, academics, the public and media. Jenna, one of the other mature students and the mother of twin boys who lived in Christchurch with their father, was a friend of the man who then headed the Aids Foundation. He came to speak to us and his mannerisms reminded me of the friendships I'd enjoyed with Petal and George, among others. I told a few of my friends about Petal and my desire to see him again. It seemed unrealistic though, as I knew Paul would be furious. I didn't want to expose Petal or myself to his anger.

The desire to see my friend wouldn't go away though. It niggled at the back of my mind. Was Petal well? Was he still in New Zealand? Many gay guys spent time in Australia where the scene and its opportunities were bigger. Perhaps he was there. I hoped to find out one day. Once I thought I saw him get out of an elevator in the hospital and I followed him, only to realise it was not him at all. I missed my friend. Petal had always seemed like the older brother I would never have and I knew I must find him one day.

•

It was soon time to return to Wellington for the clinical (patient-contact) years of the medical course. While in Dunedin we had been tutored using the new method of problem-based learning, which seemed to the six involved in the altered class list to be a vastly superior method to the traditional teaching we'd been used to. We set about getting problem-based learning established at the Wellington Clinical School. We had a series of meetings with the dean of the Wellington School and offered ourselves as a trial group to use the new method. Our offer was accepted and we became the first Wellington group to receive all our teaching in this fashion. We constituted a minor irritant to some of the other students, who learned whichever way they were taught and didn't find it necessary to ask for change.

At the end of third year I had my first major gynaecological operation. I'd been getting symptoms from my weak pelvic floor muscles — probably caused by the assault with the bottle in the US — which meant I couldn't control my bladder well. This was causing me severe embarrassment. I dreaded the day I'd inevitably wet my pants at med school or in the hospital. So far all accidents had occurred at home. I elected to have my tubes tied at the time of the operation as I wanted no further kids. The fear of producing another child like Paulie was a strong motivator. Much as I loved him I wouldn't voluntarily have another handicapped child. The surgery was performed a week after the results of final exams came out. I spent ten days in hospital recuperating before heading home and packing up my things.

Paul came down from Wellington to help us move north. He worked on the house, bringing it to a state where I could make some money on its sale. He was more stable, as he'd finally realised it was important to see a psychiatrist regularly and to take the medicine she prescribed.

I was looking forward to getting home, to live with my older boy again and to be closer to my family. Although I wasn't close to my Dad, the lack of a blood relation in Dunedin was unsettling. There was no one there to help me if things went wrong. I also thought things might be easier between Paul and me if we lived in the same city — easier to tolerate or simpler to break off. Whatever the outcome it had to be better than what we'd had when so far apart.

Paul had built a house with the severance money he received from the police. He lived about half-an-hour north of Wellington in a secluded rural block. Paulie and I got a flat in Newtown across the road from the medical school and furnished it from the local Salvation Army store. Mandy and the others in our problem-based learning group had been allocated a flat at the back of the Parkview abortion clinic just up the road from me, but were shifted from there by the med school when anti-abortion activists threatened to bomb or burn the clinic.

I saw a lot of Chris and tried to get him to move in with me. He agreed with Grandma that it wouldn't be fair to move him from his school. He spent weekends with Paulie and me though. I was not going to find it easy to win this tug-of-love. Did I need to fight it anyway? Chris was happy and Grandma was fit and well enough to care for him.

I needed to get on with the battles I could win.

47

Paulie enjoyed the hospital creche and had further assessments by paediatricians in Wellington. He was allocated government-funded hours with a speech therapist and occupational therapist, and received special kindergarten visits to help him prepare for school. He was bespectacled, sturdy and alternately serious and beaming with joy. His glasses were always smeary and rode low on his nose and fat little cheeks. He was almost four, had few recognisable words or phrases and still messed his pants. He was impulsive, fearless and obsessed by water and electrical sockets. He had asthma — diagnosed by a Dunedin GP when he was two — poor eyesight and his intellectual disability. Through his new therapists I learned to focus on the things Paulie was able to do rather than those he couldn't. As he was so inquisitive and fearless he needed to be watched constantly. He could move extremely quickly and cover a great deal of ground in a couple of minutes. Time with Paulie was always spent on full alert.

The creche workers were marvellous. I never worried about him when he was in their care. He had a special carer provided by IHC (formerly the Intellectually Handicapped Children's Society) who looked after him occasionally after creche — there were times when I needed to stay later at the hospital to complete an assignment or class. The time he was with her caused me the most worry. She was a lovely woman but seemed easily distracted, and Paulie could outsmart her. Once she took him to Kilbirnie, a couple of miles away, to visit the library. When she stopped to speak to a friend Paulie took off. She searched for a few minutes, then, realising he was lost, phoned the police who began to search for him.

He was found, coincidentally, by one of his creche workers a few hundred metres from her house, a thirty-minute walk from the library. Miranda had heard traffic noise — tooting and braking — coming from the intersection just down the road from her house. When she went out to investigate she found Paulie in the middle of the street chasing a tyre he'd found and was rolling in and out of the lanes of traffic. No one had tried to restrain him. Drivers were yelling at him in what must have seemed to him a foreign language — at that stage he still looked to me to 'translate' the speech of others. She grabbed him and took him to my flat where she met the weeping IHC worker and a policeman. This was the first of Paulie's major encounters with his guardian angel, who was kept extremely busy for the next three or four years.

The clinical years of the medical course were both more demanding and more enjoyable than the earlier years. Our training was done on hospital wards and we saw patients every day. This was what it would feel like to be a real doctor; this was what all the work was for. I loved patient contact and found that the communication skills that some of the others struggled with came naturally to me.

I was surprised and embarrassed when the past caught up with me on the wards. The first time it happened I was doing a round with two consultants, three junior doctors, a nurse and another medical student — quite a circus. We stopped outside the door of a middle-aged female patient while the consultant lowered his voice and talked about the scourge of drug use. We solemnly filed into the patient's room, prepared to examine this piece of human misery whose addictions had caused multiple health woes and were costing the taxpayer dearly.

She sat up in bed peering at my face, then my name badge.

"Mmm — Lauren Roche, eh? Pam's daughter — good to see you darling. Can't wait till you've gotcha name hanging on ya door and a big fat prescription pad." She chuckled,

I blushed and the consultants cleared their throats and shuffled their papers. The patient was one of the old whores and junkies from the Southern Cross pub. She had known my parents and also knew a great deal more about me than she was letting on — for the time being anyway. We listened to her heart and lungs and left her room, not before she boomed "Don't let the old farts get ya down love" to my retreating white-coated back. I guessed she meant my consultants; from the looks they gave me after we'd left the room I think that was their impression too. I didn't offer any explanation for what she'd said. I didn't know what to say.

Some months later while doing a round in the psychiatric unit my old friend Maree, who'd worked in the strip club with me, hugged me in front of the Professor of Psychiatry. Maree was an in-patient — there to rest her battered psyche and get onto a medication regime that she couldn't abuse too easily.

"Lauren — Oh my God, they're going to let you be a doctor. After all the things you've done! Jesus wept!" Professor Mellsop tried to hide his smirk, but was too late. Here I was trying to be a clean-cut, intelligent medical student and I was still being accosted by visions from the past. It was scary. How long before someone saw through my disguise? At least it was too late for them to throw me out — there were only a couple of years until graduation.

Paulie was progressing — slowly, slowly. He would bolt for freedom any time he could, but no longer ran away from the woman from the IHC. When I asked how she managed to contain him she told me she had to tie him to the washing line with a short leash if she went outside. This obviously wasn't satisfactory. I had to sort something out that would work well for both Paulie and me.

We spent some time with Paul and Chris, mostly visiting Paul's mother in Upper Hutt. Chris decided he wanted Paul for a Dad but still didn't want us all to live together as a family. He desired the predictability of Grandma's house with the alternative of a 'real family' to bolt to if the wish arose. I couldn't play family just to keep him happy.

Paul began to slip again. He'd realised he did love me and adored Paulie. He didn't want to lose us but was so unsure of himself he felt certain he would. His actions were pushing us further apart.

Paul still insisted he was going to commit suicide "any time now" and as he had a number of guns of varying calibres it seemed he might well someday shoot himself. His property was five kilometres from the motorway on an unsealed rural road. There were no close neighbours, and rabbits and goats ran wild on surrounding properties. Once while I was on the phone to him he fired a shotgun out of his window, then sat silently so I'd think he'd shot himself. After a few seconds of stillness I knew he'd have dropped the phone receiver if he was dead, so I kept talking to him. He then shouted, "I got it!" and told me he'd been shooting at seagulls.

He added a frightening new twist to his threats. If he didn't have me, no one could. He would kill the two of us together. There were times I didn't doubt this. We were tied to one another even though it had been some time since our relationship had been healthy for either of us.

He came to visit one evening, just on dusk. He pulled me into his arms, asking if Paulie was asleep. He was, in my bed. Paul held my hands, placing them on his buttocks. He was wearing jeans in the back pockets of which I could feel shotgun ammunition — two cartridges — one for each of us. He had my full attention.

"I'm sick. I'm gonna do it. I can't live any more," he mumbled. "I love you. Always have. Always will. Gonna just shoot myself."

Darkness had fallen outside. We were in my cold little

kitchen. The light was off. We could see the Newtown shops out the window. It was all so domestic. No one out there knew there was any drama at my house. I pulled away from Paul. I had heard this story many times before and here he was — still alive and hurting both of us. I told him to leave — that if he was in so much pain maybe he needed to see a friend about it. I was no help. I was hurting too. He needed someone strong. I ushered him to the door, relieved when it closed behind him. I went to my bedroom, checked on Paulie and wiped a sweaty curl from his cheek. Would he have a daddy in the morning?

There was another knock on the front door. Paul. "I just want to say goodbye before I die — I want you to know how much I've always loved you. Let me in."

I peeped past the edge of the blind in my bedroom. He was at the front door, a shotgun leaning by him.

This was it.

Maybe Paulie would be fatherless when he woke. There was a glass panel alongside the front door. Aware of this and fearful Paul would shoot me through it, I gently pushed my bedroom door closed, lifted my sleeping boy to the floor, and reached for the phone. The best thing would have been to call 111 and get the police to rescue us but I didn't want Paul in any more trouble. I phoned a friend of his and begged him to come round and disarm him. He told me to let Paul into the house, then put him on the phone.

I couldn't — "What if he shoots me?" Mike promised he'd get there as soon as possible.

We were alone again. Paulie slept on.

Paul knocked again and on receiving no answer took his gun and drove away. Before Mike arrived Paul phoned me twice, from different phone boxes in Newtown. In one call he spoke strangely, telling me he had the gun in his mouth. Mike drove around Newtown looking for him and brought him back an hour later — calm and disarmed. He took Paul home to stay with him.

•

Many years later Paul told me that he was suicidal that night, but not homicidal. He really regrets what he did.

•

I shivered in my bed after they had gone, the hot little boy next to me not enough to remove the chill of fear.

48

The next morning, to make up for the night before, Paul took me shopping. I put a thousand dollars worth of clothes on his credit card and tried to tell myself I wasn't being mercenary. This felt like a well-earned payback. I once thought that I could work things out with Paul but had finally reached the point where to continue a relationship with him was more scary than ending it, whatever he threatened to do if I left. I broke it off — an extremely difficult severance.

I felt terribly guilty at not standing by Paul while he was obviously seriously mentally unwell but I had enough stuff in my own life to deal with. I was doing well in my course but finding it exhausting trying to live the double life: the woman with the neurotic boyfriend/the serious, responsible medical student and mother. Chris was upset that we'd parted. He thought of Paul as the father figure he so desperately wanted and was angry I'd ended things with him.

•

There was now no impediment to my trying to find Petal, my dear old friend. I wanted someone from 'back then' to be proud of me, to know that I was doing the impossible. I didn't know if he was in New Zealand, even if he was alive or dead. During one lunch break I called the menswear store where George worked. It didn't take much reminding for him to know who I was or whom I wanted to track down. He was busy, he told me, but if I gave him half an hour he'd get me the information I wanted. Petal was living in Auckland and he was sick. He had Aids.

I made myself a coffee and paced around the house waiting for the phone to ring. When it did, George had the number for me. We chatted briefly about what I was up to but I was only half-listening. I wanted — no, needed — to talk to Petal.

The voice, when he answered the phone, was unmistakably Petal's. Although weak, there was still a trace of the deep camp, mixed with mischief and irony. He was sick, he told me. Dying, he hoped. He'd been ill for so long his resolve and energy for the task of living had left him. His plan was to starve himself to death to hasten the end. He'd love to see me though — when could I make the trip north?

I'd found him, my old friend, the big brother I'd wanted and missed for years, and he was dying. I had to get to Auckland immediately. There wasn't time to wait. I went first to Mandy, my closest friend at med school and the only one who seemed willing or able to look after Paulie. She promised that if I could get permission from the dean to take some time off she'd care for Paulie for me.

Permission from the dean was not easy to get. Even when I explained that my friend was dying and I needed to go to him, he seemed unmoved. On seeing I was on a surgical run he told me that if I could get permission from the Head of Surgery for a week away from my classes he'd let me go. This was a good ploy. Professor Isbister of the School of Surgery was a scary man. I was petrified of him but could never say why. He had a fierce reputation and that was enough for me to fear and avoid him. I gained an audience with him and sipped nervously on a polystyrene cup of coffee while I waited outside his office for him to call me. Rather than hearing Prof's voice booming out through his half-closed door, I was surprised to be greeted by the man himself. He was an imposing figure in a beautiful suit and well-shined shoes and he was heading right towards me.

"Miss ah — Roche is it?" He held out a giant hand for me

to shake. I stood trembling before him and went to shake his hand before remembering the coffee I was holding. The polystyrene cup slipped in slow motion from my fingers. Open-mouthed I watched it arc towards the floor before bouncing on the immaculate shoes and casually dumping its contents — lukewarm but plentiful — down the trousered legs of the great professor.

"Fuck!" I couldn't hold the word in, "I'm sorry, I'm so sorry." As I blushed and flustered impotently on the spot, a passing man in a white coat got to his knees and wiped the mess up, dabbing at the shoes and suit pants before wiping the floor.

"Come into my office, young lady." Was that a smirk on the Prof's face?

Our meeting was brief and congenial and forever cured me of my fear of him. He agreed to let me have some time off and asked me to let him know how I got on. I was free and what's more seemed to have a new ally. He never again mentioned the coffee to me.

I borrowed money from the bank to take a bus to Auckland to see Petal — the airfare was just too expensive. I stayed with my sister Shelley and her husband, who dropped me off the next day at the house Petal rented with his boyfriend. Nothing had prepared me for the way he looked. He was painfully thin — his body no longer recognisable. His face was much older and thinner and lacked the impish expression it wore when we wandered through Wellington tripping in the old days. He remembered those days well. I wanted to hug him, bury my face in his shoulder, smell him again. Mostly I wanted to hide my face from his scrutiny in case I had failed to shroud my shock from him. He must have been used to it though. Aids makes its hosts look so skeletal, old and frail.

He groaned aloud as I hugged him, the pressure from my arms too much for him to bear. There was no doubt in my mind that he was dying and I hoped for his sake that it would be soon. He asked his lover to bring us a photo album he treasured — the photos from which would one day soon be strewn over his body in its coffin. One of them was a large coloured photo of me taken by those sleazy photographers I met when I was a whore. He'd thought of me often through the years, he said, and confessed that he'd wanted to marry me, have children and settle down. He knew I would allow him to continue to have male lovers, that I'd never expect him to go straight. He had thought about it often but had never found the courage to ask me. Oh, Petal. I was touched, then chilled. Had we had children those kids and I could also be lying in this emaciated state. I cried. I loved Petal, then and now, and would certainly have had children with him had he asked me to.

I spent four days with Petal and his lover. They were days of tears and memories, laughter and gossip. At night he had two television programmes he "couldn't live without" — an Aussie soap and a Kiwi game show. He'd huddle in blankets in front of the TV, chain smoking and stroking his Siamese cat. It wasn't the way I'd choose to spend my last days on earth, but who knows how that will feel? It was what Petal wanted and this was his life.

True to his word, he'd stopped eating in the hope that this would hasten his death. He drank though — sips of water to ease the burn of thrush in his mouth. He also ate ice-blocks to keep his fluids up. He clung on the edge of life. His existence was miserable but his body wouldn't give up.

I had to return to school but promised to come back to Auckland as soon as I could. Before I left, his lover and I took Petal to the supermarket. I pushed his wheelchair through the crowds of people, who openly stared at him. I pushed him defiantly though the aisles. He told me to stop rushing — he wanted some slowness, some time to enjoy his remaining life. It was slipping away quickly enough without me adding to the illusion. I slowed down, and ever since when pushing a wheelchair have done it as slowly as I can, so as not to make a display of my able body and the rush of the rest of the world.

I spent two weeks in Wellington, then returned to Auckland in a holiday break. Petal and I spoke on the phone most of the intervening days. He was weakening but still felt no closer to death. His sister was visiting from Australia and he wanted me to meet her. He hoped we could continue to be friends when he'd gone.

Little and a lot had changed. Petal was thinner, less even-tempered. This long wait was wearing him down. We went out once — to an orchard where Petal wanted to be wheeled so he could see the apples growing. I told him of my desire as a child to eat an apple still on the tree. He said we could both make our dreams come true then. I wheeled him under a huge tree laden with ripening apples. The air was dense with their scent and I watched Petal lean back in his wheelchair, eyes closed, the sun on his face — living. His lover and I walked between the laden trees, never venturing far from our friend. The sun flaunted its energy and the trees and birds displayed their vitality in such contrast to the man who sat in his wheelchair, stranded halfway between life and death. I spent so much time watching Petal that I didn't get to eat my still-growing apple and know that I never will. The time for that has passed. Although the big expedition had tired him Petal seemed more at peace when we took him home.

His sister Cheryl was patiently awaiting the end. She planned to stay with him until his death and organise the funeral before returning home. She would take his cat back to Australia with her as a living memory of her beloved brother. Cheryl had recently had another close tragedy — one of her children had been killed in a car accident near where she lived. Every day she had to drive past the spot where her little one had died and this trip was supposed to help exorcise that memory. She was a remarkably strong woman, full of love and comfort for Petal. There was no avoidance of talk about death. It was discussed matter-of-factly. Except of course, when *Sale of the Century* or *Neighbours* was on the telly. Then we all had to be silent. This was the time Petal held court. He could answer all of the questions on *Sale* — usually before the real contestants did.

Petal didn't die that week or the next. The end came a month later when I was back in Wellington. I had phoned the night before — after a gap of three weeks — to be told he was in the bath and my message would be passed on to him. The next morning I got a call from Ewan with whom I'd made the hoax bomb-threat, to tell me Petal had just died. I didn't go to the funeral — I couldn't afford the fare and doubted I'd get more time off. I loved Petal and wanted to be there for him but was sure he understood. I will always be grateful that I met him again before the end though, and was able to close my relationship with him in a loving way.

49

Newtown, site of the med school, hospital and my flat, is cosmo-politan. People of many races, colours, incomes and faiths live there, which makes walking to the shops a sensory spectacle. Once or twice in the street I'd seen Maree, the youngest girl at the strip club and the one who embraced me at the psych unit.

She was a terrible mess. Barely coherent, usually unkempt, she shuffled round the streets looking for drugs. She always recognised me and asked for money.

The beautiful Maree — the fifteen-year-old with deep brown eyes and tiny features, who laughed loud and often at the world — was gone. In her place was a pitiful creature, far older, with eyes that were shiny. Her pupils were either hugely dilated or shrunk to a pinprick. Maree, who'd had a lot of style and once obsessed over her appearance, was walking around in dirty clothes far too big for her. She had shrunk in every way a person can.

Each time I saw her I felt ashamed that I didn't want her in my flat or in my life. We'd been friends but now she was an embarrassment to me and a painful reminder of where I might have ended up. I exchanged phone numbers with her and promised to call and check on her. I hoped she'd lose my number and she must have because she never rang.

Despite my guilt I never did phone Maree or visit her flat, which was only a few blocks from mine. Our relationship never reached any sort of closure. It ended when I read her death notice in *The Evening Post* one night after school had finished. I was alone in the flat when I read she had "died in her sleep" — as pleasant a euphemism for suicide as any. She was 27 years old.

I attended her funeral accompanied by my classmates Lynn and Mandy. She was buried on the Kapiti Coast near her father. The small chapel was full with the family members obvious in their ordinariness. Mandy, Lynn and I looked as though we should have been seated with them. The majority of the mourners were sex workers — straight, gay and transgender. A lot of them recognised me. I reintroduced myself to those who didn't. We all choked on our tears when Maree's mum threw herself weeping onto the coffin.

The time to be ashamed of my past had ended. I would be proud of my achievements and not ignore the path I taken to reach them. It was a major turning point for me and not one I could have reached if Paul and I had still been together.

I became more open with my classmates and took a petition around the hospital and medical school seeking continued police support for sex workers. This raised a few eyebrows but only one person was unwilling to sign. On the infrequent nights I could get a babysitter for Paulie I spent time at the Evergreen coffee bar in Vivian Street, a place frequented by working boys and girls where I could mix with the sex workers I'd known all those years ago. Babette was still working; Marion Street her haunt now. We conferred — never great friends the first time around, it wasn't surprising we didn't hit it off this time either.

Returning to Vivian Street was important to me as I needed to assimilate the parts of my life that I'd ignored to this point. I felt extremely lucky to have left the streets but a part of me still belonged there. Being in medical school still seemed improbable, I felt ill-prepared for it. I also wanted to help the people who were still in the sex industry and thought about gaining special qualifications in sexual health so I could use my skills to assist them.

Sometimes I took classmates with me to introduce them to people they'd been sheltered from. I like to think it was good for all of us. It certainly helped me.

My studies were going well. I was working in a ward

with patients with chronic medical conditions and Aids. I knew many of the guys on the ward though none of the affected women were familiar.

I struck up a friendship with a nineteen-year-old boy with Aids. He was gay and had contracted HIV from his only sexual partner — an older man with whom he'd had sex twice. Still we heard on TV religious zealots calling Aids 'God's judgement.' No one could say this young man's predicament was fair.

Dean seemed young for nineteen and extremely vulnerable. He'd been brought up in a religious family who had abandoned him when his diagnosis was made. They never made their peace with him.

He and I ate pizza and drank wine one night sitting together on his hospital bed. The sheet squeaked on the plastic mattress cover and the bed was too narrow for the two of us but we put up with the discomfort. Dean needed physical contact. He was lonely and frightened and felt abandoned by his parents. His illness itself was a betrayal of love — he didn't need any more of that. Six months later he was dead.

I was surprised to see George in one of the Aids beds. I hadn't known he was sick and was shocked. The tell-tale gauntness was there, as was the unmistakably rapid ageing. He was matter-of-fact about his illness and said he expected to be around for years yet.

He lasted another eighteen months.

My friends from the past were dying — I had to keep them alive in me.

Chris was spending the weekends with Paulie and me. We would sometimes go out for a walk or to the hospital cafeteria for lunch, but mostly stayed at home as Paulie was still running away and time out with him was diabolical.

Paul was improving. He had more patience, more time to spend with Paulie and me in a non-threatening way.

Paulie loved his Dad and seemed to flourish when he saw more of him. Sometimes all four of us would have a meal together over the weekend.

I was beginning to look for sexual companionship. It was hard going at the med school. All the men there seemed to think that sex with me would entail a lifelong commitment to my kids. Casual sex would have been wonderful but didn't seem to be on offer. I had a close relationship with Loretta, a lesbian classmate but I wasn't yet ready to marginalise myself further by coming out. I was already on the wrong side of most of the statistics for doctors and didn't need to join another minority group just yet. There was time for that. I went to dinners and other gatherings with my lesbian friends, only stopping when one of them — with the best of intentions — told me that I couldn't keep hanging around with them unless I came out. I knew I'd do it one day but in my own time.

It was time to get a divorce too. I wanted to cut some of the ties to the past and assert a new independence. My one-day marriage to Mr Gee had remained official for seven years. I advertised in *Truth* newspaper for him or anyone knowing his whereabouts to contact me. My uncontested divorce hearing took place one in the middle of one afternoon. When required to give my husband's name to the court clerk I got the order of his Christian names back to front. I'm still not sure whether his name is David James or James David Gee. The clerk accepted my explanation that he preferred the middle name to the first one.

The courtroom was brown and empty apart from the Judge, the clerk and me. The late afternoon light entering the room looked muted as it highlighted columns of dust motes. I was nervous and dreaded having to explain the full circumstances of my marriage. I told the judge that the marriage had lasted less than a day. When he then asked why it had taken me so long to apply for a divorce I said

I'd been in a situation where it was easier for me to plead inability to marry rather than unwillingness to. He granted the divorce and wished me all the best for the future, noting I was a young lady who didn't appear to be good at picking boyfriends and husbands.

I was still on the New Zealand Medical Students Association, a job that entailed occasional travel around the country. The student reps met three times a year, in Dunedin, Christchurch, Wellington or Auckland. At one of the meetings I met Clayton, a medical student from Christchurch who was a year ahead of me in his studies. We hit it off well and were lovers by the end of the weekend. He was sensitive and sweet with a small edge of arrogance which he wore well. He was a sportsman as well as a med student. He'd found the magical balance others had unsuccessfully striven for. Sexually we seemed well-matched. We wrote to one another daily and phoned when the toll rates were cheap. It was nice to have an outlet for my sexual feelings again and to feel that someone new desired me — in an uncomplicated way.

Paul met Clayton when he came to take Paulie for the day. Clay opened the front door wearing only a towel. Paul wasn't impressed and thereafter referred to my hirsute new boyfriend as 'The Monkey.'

50

Despite the various dramas in my life I seemed to be doing okay at med school. Each different ward taught further skills and knowledge and fired up new passions. When working a surgical run I knew I had to become a surgeon — similarly, listening to people's hearts made me see my true vocation was to be a cardiologist. The most important part of the work was the patients. I had a natural talent for communication and derived great pleasure from the time that I spent with the sick.

Aggie was an eighty-year-old with pneumonia who was admitted to our medical ward. She had lived alone for years and was estranged from her family. Gradually she had lost the skills of caring for herself and was bony and unkempt. Her hair was long and matted in parts, her clothes musty, and she smelled of urine. Aggie longed to be touched and offered herself for daily physical examination. Aggie would complain of an ache or pain so someone would touch her to see where it hurt. She taught me that the symptoms a patient complains about are often not the thing they are most worried about. Aggie's greatest fear was that she'd be put in a home and never be allowed to live alone again. She told me this after several days of examining her. She needed to know I cared enough about her to truly listen to her worries before she could voice them. As a student I was unable to do much but listen and pass her fears on to the social workers. They couldn't reassure her either. Her future placement depended on how well she became during her stay with us. Meanwhile I spent hours at her bedside as she taught me new skills.

Aggie died in hospital and never saw her home again.

The overwhelming feeling I had about being a med student was one of privilege and of gratitude to those who taught me — the patients like Aggie and the physicians.

Despite their fears and pain few patients refuse to be seen by students. This generosity is often unnoticed.

In my fifth year of training a new man came into my life: Bernard, a tall British boy who was in New Zealand to play rugby. He was literate, sensitive, smart and could even do housework. Before we consummated our relationship he was deported for a visa infringement. This seemed to spoil things, but was only a temporary halt. We became lovers and flatmates a few months later on his return from the UK.

Paulie loved Bernard, but Chris felt Paul was the only dad he wanted and made sure Bernard and I realised that.

Chris still spent the weekends with us and refused to spend any more time than this. Grandma's was where his heart was and nothing would change this for him.

Soon after Bernard moved in with me I realised I had gained another dependant. He had a sore throat and was tired a lot. His GP diagnosed glandular fever and told Bernard he'd need to spend a few weeks in bed. He was not to get up to read or watch television — he needed the strictest kind of bed rest, especially as he was an athlete.

When this news was broken to me I cried. Not only were final exams looming, I'd just learned I needed further gynae surgery — the third operation in four years. A little help around the house would have been welcome. The advice Bernard had been given by his GP was outdated. He was a fit, healthy young man who would have derived no benefit whatever from prolonged rest. Added to this was the fact his doctor was a known quack. I begged Bernard to get a second opinion and tried to persuade him he could continue life as usual. No way — the thought of being waited on for a few weeks was too tempting for my Romeo. Rather than kicking him out, I tried to continue my life around him.

Paul was at university himself now. He was happier and more stable than he'd been for years. Paulie and Chris spent occasional weekends at his house. I no longer feared him and began to love and respect him again. Too much had happened between us to resume our relationship, though.

Finals were less than a month away. Bernard was "too sick" to look after Paulie while I studied. I had developed a serious post-operative infection and Paulie kept absconding from school. Paulie was five and attended the special needs unit of a school in the city. He was taxied there in the mornings. Despite their claim to provide a safe environment for disabled children they lost Paulie several times. I was called off the wards to search Wellington for him. Luckily some of the other med students helped in these searches, as did police and taxi drivers, and he was always found safe and well — albeit four or five kilometres from school. The school's response to his wandering was to suspend him.

It was all too much. I approached the administration of the medical school about deferring my exams and graduating late. I was advised through my tears to hang in and sit anyway. The Professor of Obstetrics and Gynaecology arranged some respite care for Paulie so I could study, so study I did.

Bernard was still recuperating so I stayed a few days at Paekakariki at the home of Len and Aina Wilson — my former English teacher and his librarian wife. They gave me a room, all the coffee I could drink and the peace I needed to prepare for the exams. Walks on the beach broke long periods with my texts, as did wonderful meals and discussions about books. Len and Aina have a comprehensive library and loved to introduce me to new authors.

Exams came in late October. Exhilarating, frightening, elating and depressing. The world changed incredibly in the wait for results. The day I learned I'd passed with a B grade overall, the Berlin Wall fell. It seemed anything could happen. Bernard rose, Lazarus-like from bed and declared himself almost fit again. It was truly a time for miracles.

The graduation ceremony with gowns and mortarboards was to be held in Dunedin in December. Visualising the moment I'd be capped had helped me through rough patches in my studies. I couldn't wait. First though the Wellington clinical school had a local graduation ceremony in early November. All of us who'd passed the exams received a picture scroll with the fourth year class ID photos on it and a handshake from the Governor-General and the dean. The lecture theatre was packed with teachers, physicians, invited family and friends. Grandma, Paul, Dad, Len, Aina and Jane from Wellington High School, and Rosa the DJ from the strip club I'd worked in all sat at the back and cheered me on.

It was quite an occasion. I felt triumphant but also fed up with tradition by this time and planned my own little protest at the system.

Earlier in the year I'd had my left shoulder blade tattooed — a large colourful dragon which I named Roger after the tattooist who'd done him. For the ceremony where graduation gowns weren't worn, I donned a red backless dress — the same one worn at the Toad Hall fracas — which displayed Roger beautifully. I wore a jacket to meet the Governor-General, then, berating myself for that cowardice, removed it for the rest of the ceremony and the subsequent drinks. We assembled in the med school cafeteria to meet the dignitaries and other special guests. I mingled well, making certain my back was displayed to the room. No point in having Roger if I didn't exhibit him.

One of my favourite teachers was Professor Kevin Pringle, a paediatric surgeon. He has told me and other people how proud he was that day. He knew how hard I'd found medical school and silently applauded my cheek.

Many years later the new dean of the school told me with a twinkle in her eye that she remembered the red dress and the graduation day well. It seems I had more allies than I realised at the time.

At last I had arrived. The journey from sex worker to doctor had been difficult, but utterly worth it. People took me seriously and I'd succeeded academically.

I'd made it!

After I became a doctor, life continued to be challenging and not as serene as I'd hoped. But … that's another story.

o

AUTHOR'S NOTE

The memories of others — family and friends — have helped me tell the story of my childhood. I have found that I didn't know the full story behind events recalled; children seldom know why things happen the way they do, and interpret things differently to adults. Wherever possible I have corroborated my memories with others. If stories were too conflicting, I have tried to record more than one interpretation.

Some names have been changed to protect the guilty. I have no wish to inflict harm on anybody — most of us do the best we can, and making a few mistakes on the way doesn't invalidate anybody.

•

ACKNOWLEDGEMENTS

Many thanks to Lynn Peck, Roger Whelan, Helen Lehndorf, Graeme Collins and all the others for their work; Alan and Helen Tristram of Green House Books, Paraparaumu Beach for their foresight, excellent coffee and support; Roger Ingerton of Roger's Tatooart for my tattoos; Friends on the Kapiti Coast, especially the 2XX crew and Sunshine Taxi drivers for reading and commenting on the work in progress; Luglenda and the team at New_Writers@onelist.com for advice and encouragement; My sisters Tracey and Shelley for their belief in this project and ongoing support.